Lore of the Dog

ALSO BY PATRICIA DALE-GREEN

Cult of the Cat

Dog-headed St. Christopher

PATRICIA DALE-GREEN

Lore of
the
Dog

ILLUSTRATED
WITH PHOTOGRAPHS

BOSTON
HOUGHTON MIFFLIN COMPANY
1967

First printing R

First American Edition 1967
Copyright © 1966 by Patricia Dale-Green
All rights reserved including the right to
reproduce this book or parts thereof in any form
Library of Congress Catalog Card Number: 66-11225
Printed in the United States of America

I fled Him, down the nights and down the days;
I fled Him, down the arches of the years;
I fled Him, down the labyrinthine ways
Of my own mind . . .

FRANCIS THOMPSON, *The Hound of Heaven*

Acknowledgements

I would like to express my gratitude to Miss Theo Brown, the folk-lorist, who is the authority on dog-ghosts, and has so generously given me references and advice in the course of our correspondence throughout the writing of this book.

I am also most indebted to Mr Patric O'Keeffe for the photograph of the icon of the dog-headed St Christopher, and the research he has done on this; and to Madame Martin-Chesneau for allowing me to study her collection of early postcards depicting the 'Mass of the Dogs' and the ritual staghunt—one of which has been reproduced.

In addition, thanks are due to Dr Ralph Twentyman for his advice on the cult of Asklepios; to Baroness von der Heydt for her advice on alchemy; and to Miss Collett, Miss Elam and the Hon. Mrs Bailey for material on chow chows, Tibetan spaniels and Tibetan apsos respectively.

The quotation on pages 154f. is taken from Dr Margaret Murray's book *My First Hundred Years*, and is reproduced by kind permission of William Kimber and Co. Ltd.

The photographs for plates 1a, 2a, 3a, b, c, d, f, 4c, d, e, 5a, d, e, 6a are the work of John R. Freeman, London.

Contents

Illustrations
and their Sources

St Christopher, Byzantine icon. Reproduced by courtesy of
the Curators, Byzantine Museum, Athens   *frontispiece*

4d   Anubis guiding souls through the Underworld, from the papyrus of Pa-Neb-En-Kemet-Nakht, twenty-first dynasty Cairo Museum. By courtesy of the Department of Antiquities, United Arab Republic Ministry of Culture and National Guidance

4e   'St Margaret of Cortona', *Caracteristiques des Saints dans l'art populaire*, Paris 1867. British Museum

4f   St Roch. Sixteenth-century. Spanish-Painted wood. Victoria and Albert Museum

Between pages 84 and 85

5a   Anubis with priest kneeling in worship. Bronze. Saite period. British Museum

5b   Hermanubis. Bronze. Roman period. British Museum

5c   Bhairava. Stone. Shiva temple in Pattisvaram. Twelfth to thirteenth century. Reproduced by courtesy of the Department of Archaeology, Government of India

5d   'Parsis on Guebre agonisant, dont l'âme est reçus par un chien', from *The Ceremonies and Religious Customs of the Several Nations of the Known World*, B. Picart. British Museum

5e   'Lazarus at the rich man's gate', from fourteenth-century MS. Bibliotheque de l'Arsenal. Reproduced by courtesy of the Bibliotheque Nationale, Paris

5f   Chinese lion-dogs. Chin Ching period. Royal Pavilion, Brighton. By permission of Brighton Corporation

5g   Imperial Palace Dogs. Ch'ien Lung period. British Museum

Between pages 116 and 117

5h   'Mass of the Dogs', in church at Sillé-le-Guillaume, Sarthe, Maine, France. Reproduced by courtesy of Madame Martin-Chesneau

5i   Congolese divining dog. Wood. Modern. British Museum

5j   'The Mass of St Hubert', the Master of the Life of the Virgin. *c.* 1485. Reproduced by courtesy of the National Gallery, London

5k   Chinese tomb dog. Pottery. Han dynasty. British Museum

5l   'Cave canem'. Pompeian mosaic. Naples Museum. Mansell-Alinari

5m   Mandrake, from fifteenth-century herbal. Reproduced by

Introduction

The word 'dog' does not mean the same to everyone for dog-nature has many facets. To some people it means a graceful, loping greyhound, or a fierce and stalwart bull-mastiff; to others, an adoring spaniel or a gay featherweight chihuahua. It may mean an animal with the courage, skill and endurance of a wolf, or with the filthy habits and cowardly nature of a jackal; or it may mean the legendary animal which, when faced, at the time of the Creation, with a gulf ever-widening between Adam and the beasts, leapt across and took its place by the side of man.

The relationship between dog and man is unique, for of all animals the dog alone treats man as a friend and behaves protectively towards him. Many people are dependent on the services they receive from dogs, and dogs need and relish the rewards they earn from human beings. This relationship has existed for thousands of years, and the *rapport* between dog and man can be so close that they seem almost to have become part of one another. We often think we recognize human traits in dogs, and there are scientists who maintain that it is to canine traits in us that dogs respond.

So, what *is* dog?

What part have dogs played in peoples' lives in the past? And what does dog mean to us today?

By what precisely are we guarded, guided, rescued and faithfully served?

By what do we so often feel 'hounded'?

The way to find answers to these questions is to embark on a voyage of discovery. It is not, however, like other journeys, for it takes place on various different planes. The dog is itself 'hounded' back through time, and in its divergent forms it is tracked across space. Since it also exists in depth—out of space and time—it is necessary to 'dig' the dog, allowing oneself to be drawn into the depths of dog-nature. Although exploration starts in the outer world, it ends in the inner, for dogs have their place both in the working and sporting lives of men, and in the hearts and minds of human beings.

The quintessential dog is first to be discovered amongst its ancestors: among wolves from whom it learnt its leg-lifting habits (for the systematic marking of posts and trees formed a highly-developed means of communication in the lupine pack); among the corpse-devouring jackals, and the scavenging pariah dogs of Eastern streets.

Dog is to be found here and now—split up into innumerable shapes, colours and sizes and spread out over the globe—hunting and working with man, and providing him with entertainment and companionship. The intelligent team-work of a pack of beagles; the self-control of well-trained gun dogs; the beauty of a courser; the skill of a ratting terrier—are particularly impressive. The courage of dogs that save the lives of lost, frozen and drowning human beings, and the sensitivity of those that enrich the lives of the blind, are most inspiring. It is easy to be fascinated by the behaviour patterns discernible in the work of herding dogs, of haulage teams and of canine sleuths. It is amusing to discover that hounds suffer from 'nasal fatigue' and after too much sniffing have to indulge their noses in rest periods; and to learn the significance attached to the wrinkles on a pug's forehead.

When the daylight sphere of solid dogs has been thoroughly investigated, attention is turned to dogs of two dimensions that only operate in twilight. Here one is confronted by dog-ghosts that give forewarning of death, or return to protect their owners from danger; by black retriever phantoms with fiery eyes and unearthly howls that track the steps of lonely travellers; by demonic poodles that jump on peoples' shoulders and weigh them down till they sink to the ground. In the twilight world, packs of dogs fly through the air on stormy nights hounding the souls of unbaptized children; and the Devil himself may be discovered in canine form celebrating black mass and receiving homage from witches with their dog-familiars.

From deeper levels still emerge the images of mythical dogs and the dogs that appear in legend, folk-lore and fairy-tale. These include Anubis, the dog-god worshipped by ancient Egyptians; Cerberus, the Greek three-headed Hound of Hell, and the bitch that suckled the infant god of healing; the hunting dogs of Celtic heroes, said to have been 'swifter than eagles, larger than wild oxen' and to have caught every wild beast they saw; fairy dogs that produced unlimited money and jewels; and dogs so faithful that they continued to serve their masters after their heads had been chopped off.

Returning to the surface to examine the many beliefs people have held about dogs and their resultant behaviour towards them, one discovers divine dogs receiving elaborate funeral rites; sacred dogs bred with white blazes on their foreheads in imitation of Buddha, or trained in monasteries to turn prayer wheels; dogs bred in Imperial courts and suckled by ladies-in-waiting; dogs trained by doctors and priests to heal the sick; dogs in French churches receiving benediction; dogs decorated with ribbons and ritually sacrificed with messages tied to feathers round their necks; dogs buried with their masters to guide them through the Underworld.

Thorough exploration of the whole field of dog-man relationship involves not only investigating the relationship between solid dogs and men, but also between men and 'psychic' dogs; men and dogs believed to be gods or devils; solid and psychic dogs; and between ordinary dogs and those considered to be sacred or divine. It also means examining the phenomenon I have referred to as 'dogmanity', a sphere in which dogs are to be discovered that have taken human form, and men who (like the St Christopher of the Eastern Orthodox Church) have grown heads of dogs.

The search terminates in the depths of peoples' psyches where the form and activity of 'the Hound in human nature' is examined; for only by following its paw-prints through the sunlight and the dusk, then, like a terrier, digging down to the Underworld, can we discover all that dog has meant, and means, to man.

Dog Nature and its Ancestry

Full exploration of the phenomenon of dog nature entails journeying back through time and examining the lives of those wild animals from which the dog is descended and whose characteristics are still recognizable in dogs today.

No one knows exactly when dog started. It is thought that it emerged some time during the Ice Age, approximately a million years ago. Cave drawings by people of the Old Stone Age depict hunting animals that appear to be dogs, and there is archeological evidence that dogs existed around 6000 B.C. in certain settlements of northern Europe. By 2000 B.C. the dog was fully domesticated, for it hunted with men of the New Stone Age, shared their food and fires and guarded their caves.

THE CANIDAE

The ancestry of dog is a subject of speculation and contention. *Canis* is the Latin name for dog, and the *Canidae* (dog family) includes wolf (*Canis lupus*), jackal (*Canis aureus*), fox (*Canis vulpes*), and various wild dogs such as the Australian dingo.

1) *Dog's progenitor* Some people believe dogs are directly descended from wolves. Anatomically they certainly have much in common, including skull formation and dentition. One particularly interesting theory is that the wolf is the most completely developed type of dog, and the skull of a fully grown mastiff corresponds to an earlier stage of wolf.

The naturalist, Konrad Lorenz, maintains dogs are descended directly from jackals, and crossed with wolves only after domestication. This theory is based on the results of his research into dog behaviour. Other scientists argue that dog could not have derived from jackal, because the two animals differ widely in dental structure. Similarly, although some dogs are superficially like foxes, since the shape of a fox's skull is unique it is unlikely that much fox blood flows through the veins of dog.

Then there are those who believe wild dogs have played the most important part in the genealogy of domestic dog. The Australian dingo is one of the earliest known wild dogs. It was brought to Australia by the aborigines, and it is closely related to the pariah dogs of south and west Asia. Both breed true to type and have preserved their primitive characters. One difficulty in accepting lupine ancestry is that all primitive breeds of dog are, in size, intermediate between wolf and jackal. It is possible, therefore, that domestic dogs are descended from the Australian dingo, or from an unknown extinct canid of which dingoes and pariah dogs are descendants.

The most commonly accepted theory is that the Eurasiatic wolf is dog's main progenitor, but that crossings with other wild canids have contributed to the strain.

(Although some dogs of primitive breeds, such as dingoes and pariahs, are domesticated, they are scarcely distinguishable from small wolves and jackals, for they lack the physical features that usually indicate domestication. These include erect tails, outward turned elbows, short legs, short straight backs, part of the head raised above the nose bridge, shortened and broadened—or lengthened—facial structure, lop ears, smaller teeth and round eyes.)

The possibility that dogs may derive from an unknown extinct animal arises also from the problem of the short-faced breeds. The numerous breeds of domestic dogs show the greatest possible diversity in shape, size and colour. Much of this can be accounted for in terms of breeding, climate, food, and the work to which they have adapted themselves. Nevertheless, whereas long-headed dogs such as Alsatians, Newfoundlands and corgis may be argued to look more like wolves or jackals, short-faced dogs such as pugs, pekes and bulldogs can hardly be claimed to resemble either of them. Many people maintain that if these dogs are not descended from an unknown extinct canid, they must come from a breed whose jaw development changed at a very early stage of canine development. (Some zoologists believe this change in jaw structure was due to disease. A congenital disease of the bones called *achondroplasia* prevents growth and often results in the shortening and deformity of certain bones. Bulldogs, pekinese and pugs are considered to be *achondroplasic* dogs, the defects of which have become exaggerated as a result of selective breeding. It is suggested that hundreds of years ago, when the Chinese noticed the *achondroplasic* head and legs of pekes, they liked this peculiarity and, finding it to be constant and to breed true, took advantage of it by selection.)

2) *Shared features* There are various features common to most wild members of the dog family. These include keen and highly intelligent hunting: they are very fast runners, hunt usually by scent and often indulge in wanton killing. They bury bones or surplus food, returning to it when in need. They cover excreta by scratching up the earth with their front feet and pushing it back with their hind legs, and they turn round in circles before lying down to sleep. All canids howl, and most of them roll on carrion and other filth, rubbing their necks and backs on it. They indulge in a peculiar method of copulation: after ejaculation the male's sexual organ becomes engorged with blood and held in the female by a bulbous gland. Fixation after mating, or 'tying' as it is called, lasts anything from a few minutes to an hour. Canids have a well-developed social sense and are exceptionally adaptable to changing conditions and environment. Many will band together and hunt in packs: the standard of loyalty and co-operation among pack members is very high, and when the hunt is over they share their spoils. Leg-lifting is a trait common to all canids, and one which is in keeping with the gregariousness and sociability of most of them, for it will be seen how the marking of trees and posts with urine mixed with secretion from preputial glands affords a highly developed means of communication. This habit also has territorial significance, and the glandular secretion plays its part in sexual attraction. All canids are subject to rabies, a fatal infectious disease of the central nervous system caused by a virus excreted in the saliva. The first symptoms of the disease are irritability and viciousness, and these are followed by throat contractions, usually ending in total paralysis.

3) *Diversity in behaviour* Although wild members of the *Canidae* have a considerable amount in common, their individual behaviour patterns show great diversity and have much to contribute to our understanding of the nature of domestic dog.

wolves   The wolf is the largest, most savage and in many ways the most interesting member of the dog family, for it displays extraordinary intelligence, courage and endurance. Wolves are indigenous to arctic, temperate and desert areas over the whole northern hemisphere, and they frequent both open plains and timbered areas. They are fundamentally nomadic, for, as great hunters whose source of food is liable to fluctuate or migrate, they often travel many hundreds of miles. They usually have extensive hunting circuits or runways, the high points of which are used as look-outs. If the area is well stocked with game or cattle, the diameter of the circle may only be about twenty miles, while if food is scarce it may be nearer a hundred miles.

Scent posts—trees and rocks against which wolves have lifted their legs—are scattered over the hunting circuits, forming a network. The urine of individual wolves has a strong identifying odour, and as they travel the runways they periodically stop at what are virtually 'bulletin boards'. By sniffing them they can tell which other wolves have passed during the previous few days, whether they were old or young, male or female, sick or fit, hunted or unworried. This practice constitutes a highly developed method of communication, for news of danger can thus be spread rapidly throughout the entire wolf community.

The hunting technique of wolves is based on exhaustion of their prey, for they are first-class runners and have phenomenal powers of endurance. They can keep up their effortless loping gait all night if necessary and they also know how to conserve their energies. Wolves usually hunt in packs. They are loyal and obedient to the pack leader, who tends to be tyrannical until he starts, for any reason, to fail in strength. When this happens he is soon deposed and, more often than not, dispatched. Other members of the pack stick to each other through thick and thin and their team-work is quite remarkable. They will hunt in relays, mapping out the course over which their quarry is to be pursued. When they have started up a deer they will chase it till it shows signs of fatigue, then one wolf keeps it at full speed while the others watch. Since it is always pursued by a fresh wolf, the deer soon collapses with exhaustion.

Sometimes the wolf pack will split up, some members of it keeping to the windward of a herd of deer and driving them through paths where they will fall prey to the rest of the pack waiting in ambush. Wolves will run howling round a herd of caribou in the knowledge that this so terrifies them that they can be driven exactly where the wolves want them (Plate 1a).

In North America wolf packs follow herds of buffalo. When the pack leader has selected a bull from the flanks, it gives the signal for attack. Rushing forward, the pack cuts the buffalo off from the herd, and wolves chase it in turn until it is fatigued. They then mobilize for the final onslaught, some making for the bull's head, others for its hind-quarters till they succeed in hamstringing it. As the tortured animal falls, it is immediately devoured. Wolves can be seen sitting in a circle round a buffalo, for their system of relief makes their hunting a leisurely affair. As individuals tire from their assaults on a buffalo, they withdraw a short distance where, with lolling tongues, they sit on their haunches and watch the work of the others until sufficiently rested to return to their grisly sport. When the buffalo is completely exhausted the wolves all join in, springing like darts from a circle, to fasten on its head and flanks until it is felled.

Wolves often indulge in wanton killing: their mass slaughter of sheep and cattle appears to result from sheer physical exuberance. They gorge themselves when there is ample food available, but in arctic regions they suffer acutely from famine. Jack London gives a graphic description of the snarling emaciated creatures that surrounded the Alaskan camp every night, and of the famished packs of grey wolf skeletons hunting day and night across the frozen plains.

When wolves are hungry or lonely they sit on their haunches, noses pointing skywards, and emit long, full-throated, wailing howls.

Early in the year the males start to fight over she-wolves and the packs temporarily break up. Wolves fight fiercely and often to the death. They know that the jugular vein, lying beneath the skin of the neck, is one of the most vulnerable parts of the body and they make a dead set at it.

A she-wolf in season can be extremely vicious, snarling and snapping at her 'suitors', and sometimes seriously wounding them. Once, however, she is really ready to mate and the most persistent male has cleared the field of rivals, she settles down and they sniff noses, run, hunt and eat together. He remains with her while they produce and rear a family until their young have grown up. (Wolves that lose their mates seldom either couple again or participate in group hunting. They are the 'lone wolves' that hunt singly and stay very much on their own.)

Wolf dens are usually located near the runways, on high ground affording a good view of the surrounding country. The tunnels are narrow near the entrance, but larger inside, and some run twenty feet back to where the whelps are bedded in a nest lined with moss and hairs from the she-wolf's coat. The male seldom uses the den while the young are being reared: during day-time he acts as a sentinel on a near-by promontory; at night he hunts, often travelling long distances in search of food for the family. He will sometimes swallow large pieces of flesh, then disgorge them in little piles round the entrance to the den. When the wolf cubs are about three weeks old they romp and play all day long. They rapidly develop acute sight, smell and hearing, and when their teeth are well developed their parents teach them to hunt and kill.

Many wolf cubs have been reared in captivity. When properly fed they lose their predatory habits and they are easily taught obedience. Jack London has described how, although the wolf pack is normally self-sufficient and independent of man, hungry wolves will sometimes allow themselves to be tamed in return for food and warmth shared with sledge dogs.

On the whole man and wolf are enemies, for human lives and property have sustained great losses through wolves, and man has done everything he can to exterminate these animals, including shooting, trapping, snaring, lassoing, driving, pitting and poisoning them.

JACKALS Jackals are to be found in more southerly countries, frequenting the Caucasus, Asia Minor, Egypt and India. They are far less gregarious than wolves, and are primarily scavengers and carrion feeders. Jackals skulk about the streets, devouring refuse, offal and filth of every kind and surround camps at night to scavenge garbage. If a dead carcass is left around in the vicinity of jackals, every vestige of its flesh will be devoured, and they haunt burial grounds, disinterring any bodies buried in shallow graves.

In so far as jackals hunt they have a limited territory and assemble in family groups, but there is no sign of the team spirit or loyalty found in wolf packs. Jackals sleep by day concealed in holes, caves or thickets, except when the weather is very hot, when they prefer to lie soaking in water. At night they call to each other with long howls punctuated by occasional barks, and they sally forth visiting towns, villages and farms. They are cunning but cowardly animals, attacking only poultry and small mammals, and finishing off creatures rendered defenceless through sickness or wounds. They are lazy hunters, living on the leavings of other predatory beasts and following men on hunting expeditions, hoping for the offal they leave behind.

The jackal has an offensive smell, and an appalling call. On moonlit nights it sits on its haunches in the open and howls with a wild, wailing, laughing sound.

Jackals breed in burrows. An earth with puppies in it is easily recognizable by the flies gathered around the entrance. Both parents forage for the young, and when they are first weaned the food is regurgitated for them in a half-digested state. The parents are rarely found in the burrows: they are usually watching from a near-by bush. But the puppies have a back door to their holes through which they can escape if hunted by dogs.

Jackals are difficult to catch, but when cornered by dogs display typical cowardice, putting up no resistance at all.

As scavengers they are to a large extent dependent on human beings, and the taming of jackals is a fairly common occurrence.

WILD DOGS AND PARIAHS There is not much to say about wild dogs like the Australian dingo. They live mostly in caves, clefts of rocks and hollow trees, but while some dig burrows and live on their own, others excavate them close together, forming a colony. They hunt singly, in pairs or in small packs, feeding on wallaby, calves, lambs, rabbits, poultry and fish. Pariah dogs live in packs, each having its own lair where it rests during the day. At night they career round cities, scavenging.

It is not known for certain whether the pariahs, so numerous in the Balkans and throughout the East, are wild dogs raised to the status of half-domesticated animals or runaway domestic dogs which have become half wild. They are of medium size and are reddish or yellowish in colour, but in spite of their similarity different types can be recognized among them.

4) *Cross breeding* Most members of the *Canidae* interbreed. Eskimo bitches often cohabit with wolves, and in North America Indians regularly cross their working dogs with wolves to improve their stamina. In the Netherlands the crossing of Alsatians with European wolves has recently produced a popular wolf-dog which is proving both intelligent and trustworthy. Dogs and jackals commonly interbreed, but a cross between a dog and fox is rare. Dogs will ignore a

vixen in season, as will a dog-fox a bitch. It has been suggested that the musky odour of foxes is responsible for the domestic dog's indifference, a theory which is not proven.

DOMESTICATED DOG

1) *Features shared with ancestors*   In addition to the characteristics which domestic dogs share with most wild canids—such as high intelligence, tireless running, leg-lifting, scratching up earth, circling before lying down, and rolling in filth—certain traits and behaviour patterns belonging specifically to wolf life and jackal life are immediately recognizable in the lives of domestic dogs. From the wolf dog has inherited fierceness, powers of endurance and great courage. Dog howls at the moon like a wolf, shares the pack instinct, and is liable, in certain circumstances, to indulge in orgies of 'wanton killing'. From the jackal dog undoubtedly derives its scavenging instinct, and perhaps the cringing, crawling aspect of its character.

An example of an unfortunate aspect of inherited pack instinct can be found among dogs in their reaction to punishment. Typical was the case of a Jack Russell terrier bitch that ran regularly with a pack of foxhounds, ate with them and got on well with them. One day the hounds were being quarrelsome and the kennel-man used his whip. The hounds appeared to accept punishment from him, but suddenly every member of the pack made a simultaneous dive for the terrier and tore her limb from limb. The strength of their social instinct was such that the normal strong taboo on attacking members of the female sex was completely overridden. Among domestic dogs leg-lifting is used mostly to define territorial limits, for, by marking all projections within its territory at nose level, the dog makes clear to its neighbours the extent of its boundaries.

2) *Features peculiar to domestication*   Most people are familiar with the behaviour peculiar to domestic dogs. In addition to the howling and baying of their ancestors, they emit a great variety of sounds, including the piercing yelps, wails, fretful cries and whimperings of puppyhood; the low throaty maternal whines; and the defensive growls and sharp threatening yaps. At the sight of its master dog will bark, bound and career round him in circles, appearing to be beside itself with joy. When calmer its whole body is thrown into flexuous move-

ments, as it frantically wags its tail, draws back its ears, lengthens its eyes and covers him with licks. Its ecstatic behaviour tends, however, to be mixed with submissiveness as it crouches, crawls or throws itself on its back belly upwards. The attentive dog raises its head, pricks its ears and scrutinizes intently the object under observation. Sometimes it will turn its head from side to side, and sit listening with one paw raised as if to be ready to make a stealthy approach. The frightened dog draws its tail between its legs and its ears back. It may tremble and pant, and if threatened by man cringes, cowers and crawls on its belly. When strange dogs meet they approach each other stiff-legged, with tails erect, hair on end, ears pricked forward and staring eyes. If, having sniffed each others' hind quarters (according to folklore the dog's nose is cold because Noah used it to stop a leak in the ark!), their hostility is increased, they snarl, curling upper lips on the side of the enemy and exposing canine teeth, then fall on each other, their deep growls rising to piercing yells. Dog can easily be taught to obey commands and rules of behaviour and it will gladly retrieve objects with very little training. The behaviour of dogs has given rise to such proverbial references as: 'his bark is worse than his bite', 'to lie doggo' and 'to be in the dog-house'. The aversion of dogs and cats is intense—hence people continually snarling and quarrelling are said to lead a 'cat-and-dog life'.

Tamed wolves and jackals have much in common with domestic dogs. When caressed tamed wolves and jackals will jump about with joy, wag their tails, lower their ears, lick their masters' hands, crouch down and even throw themselves on their backs. Although, in their wild state, they only howl, in captivity they soon learn to bark. Tame wolves come when called, obey commands and display loyalty and willingness to serve. Frightened tamed wolves and jackals tuck their tails in between their hind legs, and cringe before man, cowering and crawling on their bellies. In anger they will snarl with curling lips.

It is said that if you scratch the skin of any dog you will find a tractable wolf, and wild canids certainly appear to have a potential capacity for domestication. We shall now see how the various inherited elements in dog nature have combined to render the dog specially suited to live and work with man.

PART II

Dog-Man Partnership

IN PREHISTORIC TIMES

A relationship between dogs and men was undoubtedly established very early on. Prehistoric man was surrounded by canids of one kind or another. The whole of Europe was heavily populated with wolves until comparatively recently, and so were India, Siberia, Japan and North and Central America. Jackals abounded in most Eastern countries and also in south-western Europe.

The association of wild dogs with man probably began on a basis of scavenging. The jackal's highly developed habit of clearing away garbage would have ingratiated it in oriental villages and, since it is not an aggressive animal, it was most likely tolerated in prehistoric camps on account of its usefulness. Scavenging jackals often enter into a loose but regular relationship with men, and their puppies may well have been adopted and reared in the camps and mated when they were fully grown.

Wolf cubs also make attractive and amenable pets. They would, however, have been less easy to acquire, because, although some wolves will scavenge when hard up for food, they usually regard human settlements as hunting grounds.

Both men and wild dogs of prehistoric times were hunters. On the whole men would presumably have kept away from hunting wolves, and wolves would have tried to avoid huntsmen. Nevertheless the hunting expeditions of wolf packs were probably not unlike those of primitive men, and it is considered possible that young wolves growing up near, or in, the camps of hunting tribes regarded men who provided them with food as members of their pack, and, recognizing their superior strength and cunning, transferred to men their natural allegiance to a pack leader. Huntsmen would, no doubt, have been quick to turn such an association to their advantage and thus would have evolved the first hunting expeditions in which men and members of the dog family co-operated.

However the dog-man partnership started, men and dogs have been working together now for at least eight thousand years. Man's relationship with dog is different from that with any other animal, for dog alone treats man as a friend and behaves protectively towards him; and its willingness to co-operate with man distinguishes it from all other beasts. (There is a legend which accurately expresses this phenomenon. It tells how after the Creation a gulf opened between Adam and the beasts that he had named. Among them stood a dog gazing at the ever-widening breach, and when separation was almost complete it leapt across the gulf, taking its place by the side of man.)

Konrad Lorenz maintains there are two different sources of dog's devotion to man: in wolf-derived dogs attachment to the pack leader has been transferred to a human being, while in the jackal-derived dogs it is the puppy's attachment to its mother that is transformed into love for master. The dog was man's first animal servant, and the taming of dog resulted in the subjugation, and guarding, of wild cattle and sheep.

Some types of dog were adapted by selective breeding for special services. Specially fast runners with exceptionally good sight were bred for hunting in the open; slower dogs with highly developed noses were bred for hunting larger game in forests; massive powerful dogs were bred for guard and battle work; while those most intelligent and responsive to discipline were trained for herding and controlling domestic livestock.

TODAY

So, returning from our flight through time—from the past back to the present—we must now orientate towards the next part of the journey in which we are to travel across space. For it is necessary to explore the many different fields of the dog's work in the British Isles and other countries, thoroughly investigating its relationship with man today.

In their partnership with man dogs may be grouped as hunters, workers, entertainers and companions.

1) *Training* Dogs appear to be at their happiest when working in any way. In training the dog man dominates its will, but, unlike his

experience with other animals, he is met half-way by the dog's natural impulses. Whenever possible the dog's instincts are used as a basis for training for the more instinctive an action, the more reliable it is likely to be. The instinct to pursue and seize prey lies, for instance, behind the dog's capacity and willingness to retrieve. The pack instinct, with its loyalties and submissiveness to a leader, lies behind the dog's fidelity and obedience to man. It also accounts for the ease with which the dog is taught 'recall', for life with a human family is a substitute for pack life and immediately the dog is left alone it feels compelled to rejoin the pack. (Sometimes the dog's hunting and pack instincts come into conflict: if in a field with its master it catches sight of a hare, its hunting instinct is aroused and it ignores all whistles and calls until this stimulus subsides. It will then 'voluntarily' return to its master under the compulsion to remain in close association with other members of the pack.) Similarly, the dog's territorial instinct is behind its readiness to be trained as a guard. The versatility of the work done by dogs is due to the combination of training in which certain instinctive behaviour patterns are reinforced, and selective breeding aimed at producing the physique and temperament best suited to specialized work.

In addition to reinforcing the dog's instincts, its training consists in producing certain associations in its mind by means of repetitive habit-forming exercises and the use of reward and compulsion. The point at which training starts is where, from man's point of view, the dog's instinct needs reorientation—diversion, that is, in the direction of human interests. For instance, moving objects are a form of prey to the dog, but although its impulse to chase a ball is inherited there is no inherited mental association between catching a ball and the words 'fetch it', nor does the dog's instinct include presenting its 'prey' to man (it would normally eat it with its pack mates, or drag it to its puppies or to a hiding place). Constant repetition of the words to coincide with the movement of the object will eventually result in the dog's so associating the two that it will seize an object at the words 'fetch it' whether it is moving or not.

Methods of reward and compulsion are used to teach the dog to give up its 'prey' and also to fulfil other orders such as 'sit', 'heel' or 'down'. The dog is unique among animals in the extent to which learning can be induced by intangible rewards such as praise from its handler; and it can be brought closer and closer to the required behaviour pattern by the use of encouraging tones, fondling and tit-bits. Compulsion in training consists of using admonitory words and gestures, of pulls, pressures, use of a choke collar and a switch. In presenting its 'prey' to man, the dog is treating him not as its pack leader but rather as a pack mate.

Working dogs have to be taught to abstain from certain natural activities, and their impulses can be suppressed by the carefully timed infliction of unpleasant experience. For instance, game hunting appears to give the dog great pleasure, but if whenever it kills chickens it is given a few flicks with a switch, an association is formed in the dog's mind between chicken-killing and pain and the change from pleasure to displeasure results in suppression of the impulse. (It is essential that the action and the pain should coincide, for if a dog is not switched till it gets home it is liable to associate the pain with home-coming rather than with the killing of chickens.) Conversely dogs can be trained to perform unnatural actions by the combined use of com-pulsion and reward. If the dog learns that the discomfort inflicted on it ceases immediately it obeys its master's commands, and that the disagreeable actions it has to perform are invariably followed by fondling and praise, it soon develops great zest for them.

Dogs exhibit the greatest delight in any movements that excite the instinct they share with foxes for play, so the more that training can be presented in the form of a game the better. Mimicry also plays its part in training: trainers have been known to go down on their knees holding paper balls in their mouths, and will often sit on their haunches and bark! Where dogs show no special liking or aptitude for the work to which they are introduced and do not willingly co-operate with it, the training usually terminates, because the work of a reluctant, joyless dog is never reliable.

2) Hunting

WITH GUN-DOGS One of the oldest partnerships in existence is undoubtedly the hunting one between gun-dogs and men. Their relationship is an intimate one in which skill, pleasure and fatigue are shared. Dogs specially gifted in the hunting of feathered game are pointers, setters, retrievers and spaniels, and they all hunt primarily by air scent. Each of these breeds has its own particular aptitude and manner of working, and they are trained to use them to best advantage and to work as a team.

Pointers and setters work furthest afield, though they are taught to limit their range to a workable distance. Their job is to 'point' or 'set' the game, but never to flush it. They are excellent for shooting on grouse moors, where it is necessary to walk up the birds. The scenting power of these dogs is extraordinarily good: they detect distant game and are often to be seen winding it with their heads held high and noses exploring the breeze. They 'point' or 'set' at the moment when the bird is preparing to fly. The pointer searches the moor with long strides, moving in a methodical pattern, stiffening as soon as it locates game. Then it points, standing immobile with its head, body and tail in a straight line like an arrow, often with one foreleg raised from the ground. A well-trained pointer will hold a point from a minute to two hours, waiting while the sportsman flushes and shoots the bird and it receives the command to retrieve it. The setter was originally called a 'sitter', because as soon as it scented game it would sit before it. (It has been suggested that this habit was due to a sort of nervous short-circuit—an hypnotic restraint causing it to prolong the moment before it sprang its prey—and that this peculiarity has been put to good use by sportsmen.) Since setters approach game with twisting, weaving movements and their tails beat increasingly fast, the shooter can anticipate with great accuracy when the bird will rise from cover.

Retrievers range close to the gun and their job is primarily to retrieve dead or wounded birds. They have an advantage over pointers and setters in that they are impervious to sharp stones, nettles and thorns, and can nose their way through dense reed beds, swim through clinging weeds and can stand the coldest water and the wildest winter weather. Retrievers are particularly suited to wild-fowling for they will crouch silently under a sea-wall for hours waiting for duck, and happily flounder through deep mud or swim against strong currents carrying game.

Spaniels are specially suitable for rough shooting, for they are adept at working undergrowth and hedgerows. They are used to find, flush and retrieve game for the gun. They quarter the ground just ahead of the shooter, but give no warning when they find game. When a well-trained spaniel has flushed game it sits and does not retrieve until ordered to do so by the sportsman. Spaniels may be 'crouchers' or 'springers': the springers that originally sprang birds to the falcon or greyhound now spring birds to the net or gun.

1a Wolves attacking reindeer (p. 11)

2a Hounds at work (p. 22)

2b Working sheepdog (p. 27)

2c Guiding the blind (p. 34)

3a Black Shuck, the dog-ghost (p. 53)

3b Black dog of
Newgate prison (p. 68)

3c Death of Prince Rupert's supernatural dog (p. 82)

Gun-dogs are usually most enthusiastic workers, and are taught to respond to whistle and hand instructions as well as verbal ones. Man may be in command, but the relationship between a gun-dog and its master is one of interdependence, for the shooter relies heavily on his dogs to sight, point, set, flush and retrieve the game.

WITH HOUNDS Then there is the form of hunting in which man works not with an individual dog but a pack, and virtually takes over the role of pack leader. The character of hounds is different from that of other dogs. The intimate relationship existing between a man and his gun-dog does not obtain with hounds. They do not receive the same intensive training and individual control, and since hounds spend the greater part of their time in kennels, they have not the constant human contact that a gun-dog has, especially when it is given the run of its master's house. Whereas gun-dogs are taught to work with, and for, guns manipulated by sportsmen, hounds hunt and kill by their own efforts.

Hounds specialize in the hunting of small mammals: foxhounds hunt foxes, basset hounds hunt badgers, harriers hunt hares, while beagles hunt hares and rabbits. Hounds have wide, open nostrils, broad muzzles and their scenting power is first-class. They hunt by ground scent, following the trail left by the feet of their quarry, not, as is commonly supposed, by the body scent (except when the quarry is close enough for the hounds to detect direct scent). Foxhounds are trained to stick to fox smell and ignore that of any other animals that may cross their path. The nostrils of a hound point forward and downward, intercepting currents of air rising from the ground. The scent is best when air temperature is below ground temperature, such as in the early morning when cub-hunting takes place. After two minutes' continuous sniffing of a strong scent hounds suffer from nasal fatigue, so when working they give their noses rest periods. During a run some hounds will be working and throwing their tongues, while others merely follow running mute. The whole pack take turns, so there is never a time when all are resting at once.

Packs of foxhounds usually consist of fifteen to twenty couples of either sex, but always of the same sex. The foxhound is chosen for its nose, tongue, drive and stamina. Its nose must be allied to its brain, so that it interprets what it smells in terms of the fox's movements, and can distinguish the scent trail of a fresh fox from that of a hunted one. The foxhound must speak to nothing but fox and it must speak to

every line it owns, for this is the way in which it informs not only the
rest of the pack but the whole field that it has struck a scent. Drive is
an important aspect of the character of a pack. A hard-driving pack
will jump its fences abreast, gallop through a covert full of prickles
and thorns, and when scent is poor it will press on so long as a vestige
remains. As regards stamina, hounds normally cover between thirty
and sixty miles a day twice a week from September to April, in the
course of which they draw for foxes through thick coverts and
negotiate such obstacles as fences, bracken beds, rivers and rocks.

A day's hunting starts with a meet from which the huntsman moves
off with the pack to draw a covert when it is suspected there may be a
fox. The hounds spread themselves and if one of them follows what
seems to be the line of a fox but is not sufficiently certain to speak to
it, it will 'feather'—that is with nose to ground wave its stern vigor-
ously as it whimpers with excitement. (Plate 2a.) When a hound owns
a line and gives tongue the rest of the pack immediately raise their
heads and rush to join it. After a brief chase in and out of bushes the
fox will probably be forced into the open. The hunt begins when it is
viewed speeding across the field to a hedgerow, with the hounds
racing after it, baying in a wild chorus. The huntsman controls the
hounds throughout by his voice and horn, and is assisted by whippers-
in whose job it is to keep them together as a pack.

Hounds show the greatest excitement and joy when they think
they are going on a hunt, and when their blood is up it is obvious that
their instinct is being wholly fulfilled. The relationship between the
huntsman and his pack is a very close one: he usually knows each
hound by its name and if he handles them well they become deeply
attached to him. It is the hounds that hunt, find, kill and eat the fox,
and the huntsman's duty is never to interfere with the hounds, but to
render them such services as they cannot perform for themselves.
Once he has their confidence they turn naturally to him whenever they
need help. It could be said that the followers of a hunt are sort of pack
members, and the huntsman the pack leader, for—almost a hound
himself—he has so impressed the animals by his superiority over
them that to please him they will happily work until they drop.

Much has been written of the beauty and thrill of the baying of
hounds on a scent. In North America farmers have a unique form of
fox-hunting indigenous to their country: a number of them will meet
on a clear night with their individual hounds, which they let loose to

chase a fox, then, repairing to a hill-top, they will sit round a fire in the moonlight listening to hound music.

WITH TERRIERS   Most packs of foxhounds hunt with a brace of terriers. The name 'terrier' means 'earth-dog', for these diggers and burrowers hunt by going to earth. When a fox escapes into an earth or a drain the huntsman sends terriers down to bolt it, and a hunt can end underground with fox and terrier fighting it out. Terriers have a reckless disregard for brambles and thorns and they are often used with beagles, for however thick the cover they can usually force a passage behind a rabbit, pushing it out into the open. They are similarly used in otter-hunting to drive otters out of their halts deep in the roots of trees where hounds cannot penetrate. Terriers have a keen vermin-hunting instinct and are particularly adept at killing rats. Famed for their persistence and readiness to attack, they dispatch rats with one snap at the top of their necks. Farmers sometimes use terriers in combination with ferrets, smoke or gas for bolting vermin. They are invaluable at harvest-time, when they will kill dozens of rats with astonishing rapidity. In addition to fox terriers, Yorkshire, Manchester and bull terriers are all first-class ratters. Sealyhams are used more for badger drawing, as are also German dachshunds (badger dogs). The dachshund will locate a badger underground, then will worry and drive it into its innermost earth, holding it there until it is dug out.

WITH COURSERS   We come now to dogs that hunt larger mammals, and hunt not by scent but by sight. Vision seems to vary inversely with scenting power, and although coursing dogs use their noses at times, their sight is by far their greatest asset. Coursing dogs are descendants of the ancient gaze-hounds. Such dogs were bred for one purpose only—that of sheer speed—for they were not required to track prey but to pursue it by sight over open plains, relying entirely on swiftness to bring it down. Their sight was keener than that of any other breed, and their hunting instincts were aroused by the slightest movement. Streamlined from head to tail, these dogs resembled arrows in flight.

According to a fourteenth-century writer, the greyhound should be 'headed like a snake, footed like a cat, tailed like a rat'. This dog has not altered much during the seven thousand years it has been bred for its speed. King Solomon spoke of greyhounds as animals that 'go well and are comely in going'. They were originally taught to race across the Egyptian desert after game, and would chase jackals, gazelles and hares till they were exhausted, then drag them down. (The huntsman usually followed in a chariot and the rest of the hunt on foot.) The Afghan hound is one of the most ancient breeds in the world (indeed, the Afghans claim it to be directly descended from a dog saved by Noah from the Flood!). The Ghazni Afghan, a hound that specialized in hunting in the highlands of Afghanistan, has a little hollow between its shoulder blades which enables it to keep its foothold when turning quickly to follow game on steep slopes.

Salukis were used throughout the deserts and plains of the Middle East for coursing gazelle, antelope, hares and foxes. The Arabs often used falcons to fly at a far-distant gazelle, hampering it till the salukis appeared with flashing speed for the kill. The borzoi is a Russian courser that hunted wolves. At a wolf hunt each huntsman set out on horseback, holding a leash of three borzoi which were carefully matched in size, colour and speed. When the wolf was beaten out of cover the dogs were slipped and coursed their prey, seizing it by the neck and holding it until the chief huntsman arrived to use his knife. It was considered essential that the borzoi should be well matched, for if one had been faster and had to grapple alone with the wolf it would not have survived. A different technique for dealing with wolves is practised by the Tibetan hunting dog (*sha-kyi*). It is slipped in a place where the wolf can be turned to bay, and in pursuing the wolf it pushes it towards a cliff edge till eventually the quarry turns to bay and tries to butt the dog. The dog holds the wolf's attention by continuous baiting until the huntsman comes up to shoot it at close quarters. (Dogs similarly used by Lapps to keep reindeer at bay are always muzzled.)

There are two main types of coursing employed in this country— 'open', in which any hare is pursued over undetermined territory and without regard to set rules, and 'close', in which the course is marked out by fixed boundaries or is fenced in. In this case a hare is released from custody and, after sufficient time has been allowed for it to get into its stride, the greyhounds or whippets are slipped two at a time. The training of most dogs includes teaching them quietness and restraint, but the enthusiasm of coursing dogs has only to be temporarily stored up, so that when game comes into view they bound forward all the more boisterously.

So much for the dogs with whom men share their instinct to hunt.

This dog-man partnership is one of shared problems, skills, dangers, joy and satisfaction, conducted in an atmosphere of mutual consideration, trust and respect. Man is dependent on the natural gifts of the various breeds of hunting dogs to sight, point, smell out, unearth, run down and retrieve game. By co-operating with man and obeying his instructions, such dogs combine service with fulfilment of their special aptitudes. In destroying vermin and providing men with food they incidentally satisfy one of their strongest instincts.

3) *Working* The category of 'working dogs' is a somewhat ambiguous one, for if the word 'work' means 'purposive effort' no dogs could work harder than the hunting breeds. Dogs probably expend the same amount of energy whether tracking game or criminals, and whether retrieving birds or fishing tackle: in both cases discipline is essential, and since the dog's instinctive drives are indulged in 'sport' and in 'work', both are pleasurable.

WITH GUARDS The instinctive territorial behaviour of dogs is brought into play in the guard work they do for men. As training has produced hunting dogs that are prepared to present their prey to human beings, it has also produced dogs that are prepared to protect the possessions of men and to attack robbers without savaging them.

The build of the mastiff group of dogs has rendered them specially suited for guard work. The name 'mastiff' was originally applied to any massively built dog, such as those employed by the Assyrian kings for hunting lions and capturing wild horses. The early shepherd dogs were short-haired mastiffs which were used to protect their flocks against both animal, and human, robbers. The Romans kept fierce watchdogs chained upon their thresholds. 'A watchdog', they said, 'should be neither too gentle nor too fierce, for if it is too gentle it fawns on everyone including thieves, while if too fierce it will attack members of the household it defends.'

In England the bulldog was used not only for bull-baiting but also to guard herds and flocks against the marauding wolf. It was not until bull-baiting had been made illegal, and all the wolves had been exterminated, that the bulldog's gifts were diverted to the protection of property. Watchdogs of the past were ferocious brutes. Their tempers were ruined by being chained up for long periods and they had no chance to develop intelligence. Among wild dogs defence of territory is one of the strongest incentives for fighting, and the effect of keeping dogs perpetually tied up seems to be greatly to increase their aggressiveness.

Nowadays what is required is not a ferocious animal but an intelligent, dependable and incorruptible dog that has been trained to obey orders and also to act correctly on its own initiative. The natural characteristics of a good guard dog are perpetual alertness, suspiciousness of strangers, courage and fidelity. Most bull mastiffs, boxers and Alsatians are natural watchdogs before they receive any training. During the war Alsatians were used to guard railway sidings, stores, vehicle parks, ammunition dumps and aerodromes, and they are now widely used by the police force and the services.

Wherever possible, guard dogs are allowed to roam within the bounds of the premises to be guarded. The first essential is that they should be able to be relied on to give tongue upon intrusion, and whether chained up or free they are trained both to speak when any attempt is made to touch the object to be guarded and to refrain from molesting people who are not interfering with them. Their capacity to distinguish between friend and foe is based largely on their scenting power, for apparently fear and evil intentions produce a similar smell. Guard dogs are taught to refuse any food offered by strangers. The requirements of those that receive the advanced training given to personal guards are to detect the presence of unauthorized persons, warn their handlers, and stand by to attack if their safety is threatened. At the sight of a raised gun or stick the guard dog will catch hold of the assailant's right arm, and if he runs away will trip him up and hold him, attacking only if he attempts to move.

So the training of a guard dog reinforces and refines its innate territorial impulse, and the handler puts himself in the position of the dog's mate!

WITH HERDERS The sheepdogs that were originally used as guards were of lighter build and swifter pace than watchdogs, for while being strong enough to protect the flock from wolves they were fleet enough to pursue a wolf and make it drop its prey. A Roman writer described how the sheepdog wore a collar broad enough to cover its throat, made of strong leather or iron and set with large spikes to protect it from wild beasts. These dogs were really wolf-dogs, rather than sheepdogs, and gradually, as wolves disappeared, a gentler dog was needed to round up flocks on pastures and drive cattle to market. It was not, however, until the seventeenth century that, with the wolf extinct, herding sheepdogs were generally in use.

The Scottish collie is one of the best sheepdogs in the world. Its name comes from the old title of 'colley dog' given to the dog originally used for herding mountain sheep with black feet and masks called 'colleys'. The gifts of sight, hearing and scent are about equally combined in sheepdogs. Some have the 'wall-eye' which many farmers believe to be an advantage, for they focus on far objects with the light eye and on nearer objects with the darker eye. Much of the sheepdog's capacity for herding and rounding up livestock is inherent, and it shows great eagerness to learn. At a very early age these dogs will stalk and try to herd anything that moves, including lambs, chicks, ducklings, insects and even ripples on a pond. They stare intently at the objects of their interest—behaviour known as 'showing eye', which develops into one of the main techniques used by adult sheepdogs for controlling their flocks. Collie puppies are stimulated by the sight of sheep at ten weeks old, before they have either seen older dogs working or received any training.

Sheepdogs must be capable of great speed and endurance, have active resourceful brains and temperaments, and be calm enough to enable them to work flocks without producing panic. The training of sheepdogs depends on the quality, intelligence and inherited gifts of the individual dog and the patience of the trainer. The work is much easier if the young dog can watch an older experienced one at work. It must learn to round up sheep scattered over wide-stretching moorland, gather them into close order, drive them to fold (Plate 2b), handle them in narrow lanes, and hold them in the corner of a field. It is taught to go out on a wide, silent casting run round the flock, bringing strays back to the mob as unobtrusively as possible, so as to keep them cool, for if it runs straight at them they will panic. (In high country when sheep stampede downhill they have to be headed back to the flock.) The curving outrun drives sheep on the outer fringes to the centre of the circle, and as the bleating woolly mob are bunched the sheepdog sometimes trips across their backs to bring up stragglers before gathering them all into a fold. Where a team of sheepdogs are required to work large flocks there are usually three hunt-aways to one heading dog. Hunt-away dogs are trained to hunt sluggish sheep with much barking, punching and coercing on their way to shearing sheds or along highways. Heading dogs are trained to lead sheep, keeping just ahead of them.

Sheepdogs are taught ten or twelve basic commands, which enable the shepherd to convey his wishes and maintain control. Audible signals are gradually replaced by arm semaphore to prevent disturbance of the flock and to allow the shepherd to direct his dog from greater distances. The dogs are trained to check regularly by looking back towards the shepherd, and will sometimes jump on a boulder to extend their view. Dogs invisible to the shepherd may be directed by a silent whistle. It is said that in training a sheepdog you must get inside its mind, and when you have accomplished this ensure that it gets inside yours.

Border collies have a smooth gliding action, and combine a creeping feline approach to their sheep with an hypnotic eye. Fixed by the eye of a collie, sheep huddle together, mesmerized into obeying its will. Collies are very nimble in mind and body, gentle and patient, and seem to sense the absence of any members of their flocks, however large. In the Scottish Highlands many sheep get lost in drifts of snow, and collies, having the capacity to run lightly across drifts without sinking, are adept at locating buried sheep. They have exceptional powers of endurance, often covering hundreds of miles a day.

No one knows the derivation of the herding instinct of these dogs. The sheepdog seems to display the hunting technique of wolves without their savagery. Wolves will cleverly manoeuvre a herd of buffalo or deer, gathering them, hemming them in, splitting off and isolating individual members. But one sheepdog, with the co-operation of its shepherd, has to do the work of a pack of wolves, and, since it does not kill, the original purpose of the instinct (to control and organize prey) appears to have been lost.

The service rendered to man by sheepdogs is incalculable, for shepherds cannot control many sheep on their own. Collies have been seen driving sheep along lanes alone and herding them to the roadside at the approach of traffic. In Australia a small number of sheepdogs will take complete charge of flocks of several thousand sheep, allowing the stock-breeder to follow on horseback later.

The relationship between the shepherd and his dog is a very harmonious one. On remote hill farms the sheepdog is often the shepherd's only intelligent companion for weeks on end, and it not only provides him with efficient and glad service but also shows him great affection. Collies appear to have an insatiable desire for work and many pine away when too old to carry on.

Other dogs that control livestock include cattle-dogs, swine-herders and goat-droving dogs. South Sea Island dogs herd indigenous pigs, and Russian herding dogs herd reindeer and dromedaries. A descendant of the Celtic droving dog is the Welsh corgi, or 'heeler' as it is often called. Early in the fifteenth century this breed was used for droving herds of black Welsh cattle along roads to English markets. Welsh drovers collected cattle, had them shod for the highway and drove them hundreds of miles over the border to Smithfield and Barnet. Corgis were bred and trained to drive lagging cattle by nipping their heels, and it was their job to ascertain none were lost on the journey. When stage coaches dashed past on narrow highways the dogs lined up the cattle close to the banks to prevent their stampeding; and they usually attacked footpads on sight. It is said that the Swiss mountain dogs known as Appenzells can separate their own cattle from those of other herds, recognizing them by their distinctive scent. The Lapp reindeer dog—a pomeranian—is trained to round up single strays or large herds over extensive grazing areas. It will keep the reindeer together in one place, and when the herd has to be driven the pomeranian controls it.

WITH RESCUERS The rescue work done by dogs is directed not only towards floundering cattle and sheep but also towards men, and many human beings owe their lives to dogs. The two breeds whose aptitudes have been most highly developed in this direction are the Newfoundland and St Bernard.

The Newfoundland is thought to be descended from the Tibetan mastiff, and it is equipped with a powerful frame and, apparently, an instinct for life-saving. It is a first-class ship dog, the usefulness of its work at sea being internationally recognized during the era of sailing ships, when it was customary to take at least one Newfoundland on all voyages. As a powerful swimmer it could often find a footing on rough rocks in heavy seas where men could not survive, and saved many lives by swimming with a line ashore where help was available. Newfoundlands love carrying objects and are natural retrievers. They will haul boats ashore by their painters, carry lifelines to stricken vessels, or retrieve the painter to which a boat is attached. An account has been given of how, in 1919, a coastal steamer was breaking up on rocks off the coast of Nova Scotia, in a blinding snowstorm. The ship was listing heavily and the lifeboats had all been washed away. Rockets were fired and rescue parties came to the shore, but could not launch boats through the pounding surf. One man from the ship drowned in an attempt to swim ashore with a line, so the Newfoundland dog was the last hope for passengers and crew. The captain, placing the end of the line in its mouth, ordered it overboard. It leapt into the water, spun over and over in the swirl among rocks, then steadied, straightened out and headed through the turmoil of foam for the shore. On arrival the line was taken from its mouth, a hawser was drawn from ship to shore, and a boatswain's chair was rigged. As a result of the dog's strength, bravery and training the passengers and crew were all saved.

Typical also is the story of a man fishing off Labrador in a skiff who had left a Newfoundland dog in his schooner anchored a mile away. The dog saw the skiff capsize and its master floundering in the sea. Plunging in, it laboured through the heavy sea, circled above the sinking man, then dived and brought him to the surface. Gripping his shirt, it pushed his lifeless body against the wind and tide to the schooner, where the man was hauled on deck and came round to find the dog licking him and someone pouring rum down his throat. He explained how he had seen the dog swimming, puffing and snorting towards him, but he could not swim, so had started to go down.

The Newfoundland's instinct for life-saving (that is, for retrieve in the element of water) needs little training. This dog is taught to swim round a floundering man in circles, so that if he is still conscious he can grab its neck or tail and allow it to pull him; if the man is unconscious the dog will grab and tow him.

St Bernards also are considered to be descended from the huge Tibetan mastiff, and it is claimed that they have rescued at least two thousand people during the last two hundred and fifty years. These dogs took their name from that member of the Augustine Order, St Bernard, who, in about A.D. 962, founded a monastery more than eight thousand feet up in the Swiss Alps. It was situated on one of the principal roads connecting Switzerland with Italy, which was used by armies of medieval Europe, by merchants, Swiss labourers seeking winter employment in Italy, and by people making the pilgrimage to Rome.

During winter this isolated hospice provided lonely travellers with a refuge from blizzard, avalanche and fog, and the lives of the monks were dedicated to helping the lost, hungry, injured and icebound. It was not until the seventeenth century, however, that dogs were brought to the hospice, and initially they were used as guards. But before long the monks took them out with them on their searches for lost travellers and, discovering that they combined an apparently infallible sense of direction with a natural gift for pathfinding, started to train them as helpers in rescue, and guide, work.

So St Bernards have been bred, raised and trained by the monks for four centuries, and the offspring of good rescue-dogs now need little training. Generations of inbreeding and all-the-year-round work seems to have intensified St Bernards' natural gifts, and in dangerous situations the puppies often act quite spontaneously in the same way as fully trained and experienced adults. Twelve to fifteen dogs are usually kept at the hospice, and their training takes about two years. In addition to the instruction they receive from the monks, they learn a great deal from the example set by the older dogs.

St Bernards appear to have precognition of avalanches, blizzards and storms—a gift put to very good use by the monks. Half an hour before a storm they will suddenly become restless, and there is no peace until they are released to go off on a search. The monks have learnt to trust the dogs' judgement, and follow them if they suddenly leave the path—a sure sign of impending avalanche.

A story is told of Barry, the most famous of all the hospice dogs. Barry was on a routine patrol with a monk and other dogs one day, when suddenly he refused to go any farther and forced them all to stop. A few minutes later a huge avalanche crashed fifty feet down in front of them. When the monk turned towards home with the other dogs, Barry stood still listening and then suddenly broke away and disappeared. This was the first time he had ever been disobedient, showing no response to the monk's whistles and calls. Some hours later monks and dogs went out on a fruitless search for Barry, but they did hear that a woman with a small child had been seen on the pass in the morning near where the avalanche had come down. Just before midnight the prior, hearing familiar sounds above the din of the storm, opened the hospice door to find a whining Barry covered with snow and pressed against the wall. He untied a bundle strapped on the dog's back to find a sleeping-two-year-old child. A patrol led by Barry found the mother lying dead in the snow.

St Bernards also have an extraordinary gift for scenting human beings: in clear weather they can scent a man several miles off, eight hundred feet up or buried seven feet deep in snow. They often go out patrolling on their own, in pairs or packs, wearing brandy flasks round their necks and with bread and blankets strapped on their backs. When they come across an avalanche they examine it for traces of human life, and if they find any they immediately start digging. When the dogs uncover a buried person they do all they can to revive him by licking and by pressure of their warm bodies. If several St Bernards find a collapsed traveller, they try to get him into an upright position. If they fail in their efforts to pull him up, two will lie down beside him to keep him warm while another returns to the hospice and barks until help is forthcoming. When the rescue party arrives the dogs withdraw, without instruction, to the background until the patient has been wrapped up and strapped on the stretcher, then they lead the way back to the hospice.

St Bernards have a remarkable capacity for endurance, often remaining in snowstorms for hours in temperatures twenty degrees below freezing. In 1830 the first long-haired specimens appeared, and it was thought the long hair would give them extra protection against the cold. This was soon proved to be a fallacy, for as soon as the dogs worked in deep snow they became encrusted with ice and were brought to a standstill. So the long-haired St Bernards were sold or given away.

St Bernards show the greatest enthusiasm for their work, and the monks and dogs have a very close 'pack relationship'.

In Austria, Alsatians are trained as avalanche dogs. At a school for training dogs and their owners they are taught to criss-cross an area after a snowstorm like a gun-dog. When they locate a buried human being they start digging and bark until a rescue party arrives. They learn to conserve their energies by running in the ski-tracks of rescue parties, and after a long day's work they are often given a lift home on sled stretchers.

What is now spoken of as the life-saving instinct of these dogs appears to be a combination of their hunting instinct, their instinct to give up prey to their mates or young, and finally, their willingness produced by training, good feeding and praise, to allow their hunting instinct full play in the knowledge that the object does not constitute 'prey' in the ordinary sense at all. Man appears to have an instinct for saving the lives of others as well as his own, and it seems possible that, in the same way as the monks have gradually imbibed something of their dogs' sensitivity to weather and to the presence of buried human beings, Newfoundlands and St Bernards, having worked for generations with men, have come to participate in the human instinct to save the lives of others.

The guide work done by St Bernards is based on their uncanny sense of direction—the instinctive knowledge that they share with tundra-hunting wolves and desert-hunting jackals. The monks seldom leave the hospice without dogs, because the mountain fogs descend so rapidly and, when they are unable to see a foot or so ahead, the dogs easily find their way home. A story is told of how, in 1809, three monks were out on patrol with their dogs, one of which was the famous Barry. Fog descended and when Barry suddenly pulled at his lead he was let off. Following him, the monks found four Italians huddled together under a rock in a state of complete exhaustion. They were bricklayers who were crossing the mountains to Switzerland in search of work, and, although they knew the route well, the thick fog had defeated them, and after wandering about for hours they had collapsed. The monks revived them with the brandy and bread carried by the dogs, and one dog guided a monk back to the hospice to fetch a stretcher party. Nowadays hospice dogs are equipped with fog lamps.

After a heavy snowfall they patrol the mountain passes, leaving tracks for the benefit of travellers (a deliberate form of the service jackals unknowingly render to man in the desert). When St Bernards out on their own locate snowbound travellers they guide them straight back to the hospice. On one occasion a traveller who had been staying at the hospice was, on leaving, overtaken by a sudden fall of snow. A rescue party set out with a dog and, in spite of all tracks having been obliterated by snow, it led the monks to the man, who had fallen down from exhaustion and was covered by a thick blanket of snow.

So a different facet of the dog-man relationship has now emerged. For the drowning, lost, snowbound, frost-bitten victim of the elements finds himself in the position of 'grateful prey' who owes not his death but his life to the hunting dog.

WITH GUIDES In wartime dogs are trained to guide ambulance men to the wounded. While stretcher-bearers move forward over the battlefield, dogs quarter the ground in advance of them from fifty to two hundred yards either side. They are taught to discriminate between the living and the dead, and to ignore the latter. When ambulance dogs find wounded men they return to their handlers to 'report', but must not bark because of the danger of possible lurking enemies.

One of the most interesting and highly developed of dog-man partnerships is that of the blind man and his canine guide. In the Middle Ages blind people were often led about by dogs (Plate 2c), but there is no record of dogs having been trained for the purpose until the eighteenth century, when a hospital in Paris started to keep dogs to guide their blind patients through the streets. After the First World War, Germans trained dogs to guide blinded soldiers, and an international organization, known as 'L'oeil qui voit' ('The Seeing Eye'), was subsequently formed by an American woman.

The breeds usually chosen nowadays for leading the blind are Alsatians, Labrador retrievers and collies. Alsatians are widely used, for they are exceptionally trustworthy and responsive to training. The intelligence, trainability and temperament of retrievers render them specially suited to the work, while collies have the advantage of being exceptionally quick in their reactions to new sensations and experiences, and of having a more-than-average sensitivity to touch. Spayed bitches are usually chosen for the work, as they are less likely to quarrel with other dogs, are more amenable to discipline and produce no leg-lifting problems. Dogs of all these breeds are very intelligent and show a great eagerness for guide work.

Training for the job cannot start before a dog is a year old. It takes about four months in all, including a three-to-four-week period during which the training is shared by the dog's prospective blind owner. At first the dog is a single unit, walked around and instructed by a sighted handler. It is taught to walk on a leash, and later with a harness, in the middle of a footpath; to avoid obstacles, to travel on buses, lifts and staircases, in shops and restaurants. It is also taught curb drill and general obedience, and to pick things up. The idea gradually introduced into the dog's brain is that its handler and itself are a single unit, and it has to act in accordance with the speed, size and height of the inseparable whole. In order to become aware of the difficulties of a human being in meeting obstacles, the dog works for at least a month in a specially constructed cart with a tubular shaft the average height of a man. It learns to stand still as soon as the shaft strikes against lower or higher obstacles and to walk round them.

When the prospective blind owner arrives to join in the latter part of the training the merging of the man-dog entity begins. The bridge between the two is the dog's rigid harness, for it is constructed in such a way that the dog's instinctive movements are felt by its handler and the will of the blind handler is transmitted to the dog. The handler feels every tautness or quiver of the dog's muscles and gradually learns to interpret them. The dog's change in direction, and its increase or decrease in speed are communicated so that its handler knows when to turn right or left, proceed straight ahead or stop. The handler's brain and experience are an essential part of the team-work, and the dog has to become sensitized to the signals and directions it receives thcough the harness. Although the guide dog is taught to obey instructions, it is also trained to exercise discretion, and if a road is not clear it will not cross it however strongly urged to do so.

As the merging of man and dog develop, the senses of both become attuned, and when a deep *rapport* is established it sometimes has the most astonishing results. There are many recorded cases of guide dogs apparently miraculously carrying out instructions to do things that are outside the scope of their training. A dog has, for instance, been taught the significance of the words 'grocer', 'post office' and 'station', but one day its handler suddenly demands for the first time —'find me a phone box', or 'a lavatory'—and the dog leads him straight to one!

Only when there is shared responsibility and mutual trust between the handler and his dog, and a responsive, harmonious and well-balanced unit has been formed, can full use be made of this instrument for combating blindness. When achieved, it brings new confidence, independence and freedom to the blind person, including often, the means of earning a living.

Although the guide dog knows that harness and responsibility are imposed together, since it enjoys work it usually greets the sight of its harness with delight. On the rare occasions when it becomes apparent that a dog is not taking to this work, its training is immediately stopped, for it would be most unsafe for a blind person to be led by a dog that did not enjoy guiding.

It is difficult to see what instinct is brought into play in this particular work, unless it be that of submissiveness. For this reason it represents, perhaps, the peak of the dog's capacity to provide service, since, in supplying man with 'seeing eyes', it is almost wholly identified with the interests of a human being.

WITH TRACKERS The canine sleuth is another form of guide, for it assists the police by scenting and ferreting out people in hiding or running away. The bloodhound is a very gentle dog, its name deriving not from 'bloodthirst' but from 'blooded stock' (thoroughbred). It is directly descended from the old St Hubert hounds, which some say were originally brought over by pilgrims from the Holy Land. These early hounds were named after the patron saint of hunting because their scenting ability was so outstanding. Some of them were black, some pure white and others greyish red, so the bloodhounds of today are probably a blend of all three. The combination of the bloodhound's acute sense of smell, its intelligence and the pertinacity with which it followed up a trail, resulted in its being widely used in olden times for the pursuit of fugitives. Bloodhounds were used by the early Britons against invading Gauls; in Florida and Cuba they were used for hunting down escaping slaves, and in medieval England they were officially recognized as instruments of justice and used to track down thieves, footpads, highwaymen, escaped convicts and lost persons.

Bloodhounds love trailing, and with their highly sensitive noses seem compelled to investigate everything. The longitudinal folds of skin on their faces allow large pockets of air to be held in contact with the olfactory nerves and savoured over a period. This allows a higher degree of scent discrimination than is possible when air is drawn into the nose passages and rapidly expelled, as in the case of foxhounds hunting at speed. Although the bloodhound has a strong power of discrimination, this needs disciplining, and the one thing it has to be taught is not to run the freshest trail, but to stick to the one on which it was started.

During training a tracking harness is used, and the hound soon learns that when wearing this it must concentrate on following a selected trail to the exclusion of all distractions. The lead is later replaced by a long tracking line, and the hound is trained to indicate to its handler any property belonging to the fugitive that it finds on, or adjacent to, the track. The ground scent followed by a hound in tracking is caused by the crushing of grass, leaves and insects, all of which give off a scent and denote a trail. While this scent may remain on soft moist soil for several weeks, on hot dry earth it lasts only a few hours. Bloodhounds are always kept on a leash while tracking, because when patiently working on a trail yard by yard they are completely indifferent to everything else, including traffic. Free-running hounds bay while pursuing their quarry, but bloodhounds are trained to run mute to avoid warning criminals or alarming lost children. Their instinct to tear their victims to bits has been bred away, and nowadays when they have finally tracked down a fugitive they do not attack, but stand guard to prevent his escape.

Alsatians are also used for tracking and, like bloodhounds, they require little training, but have to learn to differentiate one trail from all others. The Alsatian is considered an ideal breed for general police work, which includes teaching it to come, heel, stand, sit, lie down, go, retrieve, jump, scale obstacles, swim, give voice, and tolerate gunfire.

In searching both for persons or lost property, the dog relies entirely on airborne scent—the direct scent of human bodies and clothing. It is trained to search systematically an unknown area of ground, detecting and retrieving objects alien to the surroundings, and to bark if it finds an object which for any reason it cannot retrieve. When searching for persons the police dog is taught to indicate their presence by giving tongue, and it learns to 'chase and attack' an escaping criminal by firmly gripping his arm, and to 'chase and stand off'—that is to circle him—barking, but without touching him, until its handler arrives.

In police dog trials, Alsatians are tested for their tracking ability, discrimination by scent, agility, resolution, initiative and their restraint in tackling men. The hunting instinct of these dogs is invaluable to the police. In searching premises to locate thieves a large number of men would be needed to get the same results as one dog, and not only would they be slower but there would never be the same certainty that the search had been wholly efficient. In built-up areas the Alsatian will swiftly indicate the route by which burglars have escaped; and the speed at which they methodically search a large area for missing persons often results in the saving of human life.

The dog's instinct to trail is given full play in tracking work, and so is its impulse to retrieve—that is to give up 'prey' to its mate or young. The main object of the training of a police dog is to suppress and divert its natural behaviour at the end of a trail, so that instead of tearing to bits and eating (or even biting) its 'prey', it must at best hold it, and more often be content with guarding it, for its handler, or, in the case of inanimate objects, presenting it to him.

Police dogs put at the service of their handlers an instinct far more highly developed than is ever found in human beings, and treat them as both 'pack leaders' and 'mates' in so far as they both obey and give up their 'prey' to them. The relationship of the criminal to the police dog is surely that of the quarry which is not immediately mauled by its relentless pursuer, but is spared only in order to be lacerated by its hunter's pack leader or mate!

WITH HAULERS In addition to all their other services to men, dogs are used for draught and haulage work. They were once commonly used in Great Britain for transportation, hauling bakers', builders' and milkmaids' carts, and tinkers' barrows. Braces of dogs were harnessed to children's carriages, and in London it was customary for costers to take out their womenfolk in dog-drawn carts on Sunday afternoons. In 1837, however, the use of dogs for draught work was prohibited here. In the Low Countries a mastiff type of dog is still used for hauling small dairy and bakery carts, and the Swiss mountain dog draws carts laden with basketwork, milk churns, grocery and logs of wood.

Newfoundlands render very valuable service of this kind. At the beginning of the nineteenth century they were used here to haul fish from Southampton to London. The loads weighed three to four hundredweight and were hauled by teams of four. In Holland they are still used to haul barges, but their main work is carried out in their own country.

In St Johns, in 1824, two thousand dogs were constantly employed. They were worked very hard during the fishing season, helping to pull in the heavy nets and hauling cartloads of fish from harbours to packing sheds and market places. In winter they drew logs of wood from forests for fuel and building purposes. Newfoundlands were used both singly and in teams: three to fifteen dogs, harnessed to a sledge laden with timber or fish, would draw it steadily for miles—often without a driver, when they knew the roads. After delivering their load, they would return to their owner for the reward of dried fish, their staple food. They were also used to transport all kinds of merchandise from one part of the town to another, and a single dog could support its owner by its labour throughout a long winter. Working farther afield, Newfoundlands carried mail between outposts through a chain of settlements, and from outposts to railway junctions. In teams of seven they pulled sledges over frozen marshes, through thick woods and over trails impossible for even the hardiest pony.

During the Second World War, Newfoundlands were used as pack dogs in Alaska and the Aleutian islands. At Fort Robinson they did a three-month basic training in harness, where they often pulled and packed heavy weights through deep snowdrifts and against strong freezing winds. Newfoundlands are very dependable dogs and their heavy coats provided all the protection they needed. When patrols were caught in blinding Aleutian blizzards they were entirely dependent on the dogs to guide them safely back to base. During heavy snowstorms the Newfoundlands lay out in front of their kennels, allowing the snow to cover them completely, and it has been described how anyone looking down a row of kennels in the early morning saw a row of chains leading into the snow and there was not a dog in sight. Newfoundlands do, however, benefit from wearing raw-hide bootees to protect their feet from being cut by the sharp edges of ice. They appear to have lupine powers of endurance: typical is the account given of four dogs that ran twelve hours a day for five days on a three-hundred-mile trip to rescue survivors from a plane crash on the Alaskan mainland.

Newfoundlands obviously have a natural flair for draught work, and they enjoy it. A story is told of how, in 1955, heavy snowfall entirely cut off parts of Cornwall, bringing all road transport to a standstill. A man and his wife, finding themselves short of food, made a light sledge and improvised harness for their two stud Newfoundlands. These dogs had never before worn harness or pulled anything, yet they immediately started hauling and finding tracks where the snow was most firm. They took the sledge to a village a mile away and returned with it laden with groceries. During the following weeks they appeared to enjoy every moment of their draught work, and when the spring came both still became very excited whenever the harness or sledge was handled.

In the arctic belt Newfoundlands sometimes work with huskies. The word 'husky' is a corruption of 'esky' (slang for 'Eskimo'), and it is often used generically to cover various dogs of the spitz group (dogs with rough coats of stand-off hair, and tails with profuse brushes curled over their backs) including keeshonds, elkhounds, samoyeds and malamutes. The true husky is a very tough, courageous and loyal dog.

In Greenland huskies are free for eight months of the year, and as many as three thousand may be found in one village. Each pack has its own territory surrounding the house from which it is occasionally fed, and, although these territories are bounded by imaginary lines on the tundra, the dogs know the exact position of them. These huskies are very wild animals; they are suspicious and dangerous to handle. Teams of them chase up and down the main road, to the greatest possible inconvenience of pedestrians and traffic.

In this wild state they are very quarrelsome and savage, and it is a case of the survival of the fittest. During the husky's life span of five years each day brings the likelihood of its being badly mauled or killed by its pack mates. It has to fight for its food, its bitch, its territory and its status. The struggle for power within the pack causes constant fighting. Each pack has a leader, or king, that rules with tyrannical severity, licking its team into shape and punishing those that do not pull their weight or blunder and shirk in the traces. When a bitch comes into season the king is usually the first to serve her. In a fight between two dogs for leadership, the pack of about sixty will surround them, silently waiting to finish off whichever dog goes down. The potential king has to beat all the others except the reigning leader, and the king dog has continually to defend its position, for if it shows weakness (with loss of authority), through ageing, sickness or any other reason, it is immediately deposed, dispatched and replaced. Sometimes the pack will take a dislike to one particular dog and boycott it. Knowing its days are numbered, it will keep away from the others except when forced to return for food. The pack will then give chase, surround and close in on it, so that it has no chance to escape. No amount of whipping will prevent their killing and devouring this dog, and weaker members of the team are gradually eliminated. On the other hand, huskies often display great loyalty to each other.

There are various methods of running dogs in teams. In Canada, where the teams weave in and out of trees, the tandem method is used. Greenland Eskimos favour the fan trace, while British Antarctic parties use the contra-trace method. In this, four pairs of dogs are attached on either side of a centre trace behind a lead dog that is out on the centre trace in front. Each dog has a harness attached to the centre trace by a two-foot side trace, so that they are allowed plenty of freedom—enough to quarrel with their neighbours or turn on the dog immediately behind.

The team is usually composed of puppies from the same litter. At about eight months old they are introduced to a team, one or two at a time, and learn to pull like the older dogs. Each dog finds its sledging position and learns to keep it. The king and next most powerful dog usually run either side of the bitch, then some show preference for pulling on one flank and some on another. It is essential to have a king, for unless one dog is in a position of supremacy and the others afraid of him, there is ceaseless fighting. If the lead dog is demoted to run as one of the team, their morale goes to pieces and the old leader is scorned. While the driver is allowing the team to get accustomed to their positions he is training them to start, stop and turn at command. Those that never find their positions are killed, and incurable biters of harness have their teeth pulled out. By eighteen months old the sledge dogs are fully fledged, and the older dogs are gradually sifted out and replaced by the young ones until a complete new team is in existence.

Eskimo teams are organized like wolf packs, and the dogs are more dependent on their leader than those of white men's teams ever are. Drivers often speak of the thrill of sledging behind a team of spirited dogs, especially in the moonlight and in the first mad dash early each day. Starting off after several days' inactivity is a tricky business. Even if the team moves away without a fight, unless the driver gains control of it within the first fifty yards the chances are he will be chasing it for the next two hours. The driver gives his commands to the leader of the team and if the king dog responds the team will follow. They will respond only to their own driver.

With good feeding huskies can stand very low temperatures. On dark nights in the Antarctic they are fed on seals chopped up on a sawhorse by the light of storm lanterns. They bark, howl and brawl throughout the preparations, and combine eating with trying to rip each other to bits. They sleep snugly curled up with their great bushy tails wrapped over their snouts.

North American Indians often cross their huskies with timber-wolves, allowing bitches in season to run loose when there are wolves about. Timber-wolf-dogs are in great demand as leaders of teams of pure huskies. Not only are they very strong and have exceptional powers of endurance, but they have a great capacity for intelligent leadership, are loyal to their drivers and are easily disciplined. Although they make ideal kings of teams of other breeds, there are, however, no teams composed entirely of timber-wolf-dogs, for they are incapable of working in harmony with their own.

Huskies bring their drivers home safely through the darkest nights and the worst possible blizzards. When snow has effaced all signs of a trail, drivers sometimes have to give their lead dogs entire responsibility for finding the way home. On such occasions husky kings have been known to return with eyes swollen and suffering from acute snow-blindness.

These dogs have been widely used by arctic explorers, by trappers, the Hudson Bay Company, the Canadian Mounted Police, and by doctors. In Central Park, New York, there is a bronze statue of 'Balto', the leader of an Alaskan husky team, with a trace hanging from his back. It bears the inscription: 'Dedicated to the indomitable spirit of the sled dogs that relayed anti-toxin six hundred miles over rough ice, across treacherous waters, through arctic blizzards from Nenana to the relief of a stricken nome in the winter of 1925. Endurance—fidelity—intelligence.'

Huskies certainly love their work and they find the cold exhilarating. Those brought up in harness fret when left out of it, and if deprived of their work altogether usually die. Their training only shallowly covers the instinctive behaviour of the wolf pack, and some people believe it is the desire for leadership that is responsible for their willingness to toil—if necessary till they drop.

The relationship of a driver to the king of his team of huskies is a very close one. At most times he is presumably in the position of pack leader to the leader of the pack; but in the worst blizzards when he hands over responsibility to the team's king, he is demoted to the status of, at best, the other dog that runs alongside the bitch!

4) *Entertainment*

BULL-BAITING In addition to all the dogs that hunt and work for man, there are those that entertain him. One of the earliest, and most gruesome, forms of entertainment by dogs was bull-baiting. A Roman poet referred to 'the British hound that brings the bull's head to the ground', for when the Romans landed in Britain they were very impressed by the quality and courage of the English mastiffs which they found being used for bull-baiting. They set up an official at Winchester to search out the best specimens and send them to Rome, where they were set in the arena—four against a lion, three against a bear and one against a gladiator. The seventeenth century was the heyday of bull-baiting in England. It was very popular with the nobility and not only every town but almost every hamlet had its bull-ring. In London the Paris Garden on the Embankment was the popular centre of bull- and bear-baiting. The normal complement of the Garden was seventy mastiffs. There was scaffolding for the spectators, kennels for the dogs, and ponds where injured bears could bathe. Contemporary literature contains many references to the clamour of the spectators, the unmatchable courage of the mastiffs and the reek of blood.

The object of bull-baiting was to grip the tethered bull in the tender part of its face, to hold it still or to throw it. The bulldog was selected for its holding power: it would not let go of the head of its adversary until it was killed or made insensible by strangulation. Tremendous power of jaw was necessary, and the nostrils were set far enough back to allow normal breathing without letting go. Bull-baiting was divided into 'let-go' and 'turn-loose' matches. In the 'let-go' matches dogs were let go alternately, each dog having its second that ran towards the bull with it to goad it on; while in the 'turn loose' dogs were liberated two or three at a time. Some bulls would dig a hole in the ground into which they put their noses for protection. The bull's horns were blunted or padded, for they were liable to toss dogs thirty or forty feet high, and the dogs were bred with bow-shaped bodies and legs as short as possible to enable them to keep close to the ground beneath horn-level. Bull-baiting was not always an organized sport. It would often consist of a bull being tethered to a stake or ring in a roadway, tortured by a crowd of people till it was roaring in a paroxysm of rage, when the dogs would attack its head, seizing it by its nostrils. Most butchers owned a bulldog capable of bringing a bull to the ground, for a baited bull was believed to make the most tender eating. This diabolically cruel sport was forbidden by law in 1853, and it seems extraordinary that animals bred for such savagery can be as gentle and docile as bulldogs are today.

TRICK PERFORMING For the less bloodthirsty, poodles have provided much amusement as dancers, acrobats, actors and performers of tricks. Elizabethan clowns had performing dogs known as 'tumblers', and in the seventeenth century the scholar Dr Caius describes how the dogs of 'vagabundicall masters' were taught to dance to music, 'showing many pretty tricks by the gestures of their bodies—as to stand bolt upright, to lye flat upon the grounde, to turne rounde as a ringe holding their tailes in their teeth'. Performing poodles walked about on their hind legs wearing petticoats and carrying parasols. As highly intelligent dogs and good mimics, poodles learned to perform most complicated tricks. Paris was the home of the 'learned poodles', and here they were to be found playing cards or dominoes, spelling words and doing sums. The well-known poodles of *Pont Neuf* used to soil the boots of passers-by, so that their master, a boot-black, would be employed to clean them.

ACTING   A great vogue for dog dramas swept Europe and America in the early nineteenth century, culminating in '*Le chien de Montargis*', first performed in Paris in 1814 and translated into many languages. It ran in England for over one thousand one hundred performances.

Among the most popular of performing dogs is Dog Toby of the 'Punch and Judy' puppet show. Although this was first performed in Covent Garden in 1662, it was not until the eighteen-twenties that a showman trained his dog to perform with the puppets in the booth, and a live dog became the most popular feature of the show. Toby wears a ruff garnished with bells to frighten the Devil away from his master, and his function is to sit on the playboard and bite Punch's nose at the appropriate cues. He is also sometimes expected to shake Punch's hand, to smoke, and even to sing. Dogs appearing in films these days have a little training, but trick photography and cutting play an important part in their production.

Most dogs have exhibitionistic tendencies, and enjoy their training as actors—which is largely based on their capacity to associate performance with reward. In this dog-man relationship man takes a comparatively passive part and most of his amusement lies in watching dogs behaving as if they were men.

5) *Companionship*

OF EX-HUNTERS AND EX-WORKERS   There only remains the class of dogs that are bred purely as companions to human beings. All hunting and working dogs incidentally provide their masters with companionship, but this is not their *raison d'être*. Dogs such as chow chows, Dalmatians, elkhounds and poodles were once used for sport or work of some kind, but, having long since ceased to fulfil this purpose, are now bred as pets.

The chow chow was originally a hunting dog, and this ancient Chinese breed shares with the polar bear the distinction of having a bluish-black tongue. (The chow chow puppy is actually born with a pink tongue, but it has one black spot on it which gradually spreads over the whole area.) It was also bred for its fur and for culinary purposes. Elkhounds were bred in Scandinavia for hunting elk, and their coats are so thick that they feel neither cold nor heat. They love snow, and in this country will leave a warm room to go and tunnel through it, even carrying out newly born puppies to make a nest for them in the snow. Dalmatians were once used as carriage dogs, for they trotted alongside horse-drawn carriages to protect their owners against highwaymen. They travelled long distances, keeping an easy pace with the best horses, and are said to have been as fond of being among horses as are collies of being among sheep. In France these dogs were known as 'Little Danes', but they are natives of Dalmatia, not of Denmark. Poodles were originally water dogs. The German name '*Pudel*' denotes 'splashing in water', and they made most conscientious fowlers, being quite prepared to stay in icy water all night if a single duck was missing. Four hundred years ago poodles received lion clips, not for fashionable but practical purposes. In Germany and France it was claimed that the shaving of their hind parts gave them swiftness and lightness in water. The bracelets on their legs were left to protect their joints against rheumatism, while the pompons on their tails constituted periscopic signals enabling their owners to follow their course in water. In eighteenth-century England poodles became known, on account of these clips, as lion-dogs. In fashionable circles today they can be found wearing jewelled collars, and with their coats dyed to match those of their owners!

OF 'COMFORTERS' AND LAPDOGS Some dogs of the companion class are thought of as comforters. The King Charles spaniel was originally known as 'the Comforter' for, according to Pepys, Charles II derived more pleasure from his dog than his ministers. He kept a stud of innumerable little spaniels, and delighted in having them in his bedchamber, where, we are told, 'he often suffered the bitches to puppy and give suck, which rendered it very offensive and indeed made the whole court nasty and stinking'! The tiny chihuahas, known as pillow and ornament dogs, were used by Aztec priests as hot-water bottles. The Australian dingo is still used by aborigines as a comforter, for on cold desert mornings the women carry them across their hips for the warmth of their bodies.

Dr Caius spoke of the 'spaniel-gentle', which he said was 'sought for to satisfie the delicateness of daintie dames and wanton womens witts, instruments of folly for them to play and dally withal'. He explained how the smaller they were the more pleasure they gave, for their mistresses bore them in their bosoms, fed them at table, nursed them in their laps and let them lick their lips as they rode in wagons. They also used them to 'assuage the sicknesse of the stomacke, being oftentimes thereunto applied as a plaster preservative'.

Lapdogs have had their place in human lives for many centuries. In ancient Rome most aristocratic ladies kept Maltese terriers. Pugs are popular toy dogs which originated in the East. Their name is believed by some people to derive from the Latin *'pugnus'*—'a fist', for their profiles may be seen to resemble the shadow of a clenched fist. Others maintain that, since in the seventeenth century pugs were bred with monkey faces and the word 'pug' meant 'monkey', the resemblance of these little dogs to monkeys led to the word 'pug' being applied to them. In China, elasticity of the skin was considered one of the most important characteristics of pugs, and the point most sought after by breeders was the 'prince' mark—a vertical bar in imitation of the Chinese character for 'prince' being formed by wrinkles on the pug's forehead. In the cruel days of eighteenth-century England, when no fashionable woman went out without her pug and negro page, the ears of pugs were cropped off in order to produce the desired wrinkling and puckering of the forehead. Nowadays a 'diamond' or black 'thumb-mark' on the forehead of pugs is considered desirable. Pekes are one of the most popular of toy breeds, and are distinguished by their bulging eyes, rolling gait, lion-shaped bodies and by their tails which they wave like standards and hang over their backs. They were first brought over to this country by British soldiers after the Pekin up-rising in 1860. More will be written about them in subsequent chapters. Lapdogs have little opportunity for bringing any of their instincts into play. They have no lives of their own, and the aim of most of their owners is to make them become as much like human beings as possible.

No other animal provides man with companionship comparable to that of a dog, for not only is it a constant source of joy, comfort, amusement and interest, but it is enormously responsive, loyal and affectionate, and obviously derives pleasure from the company of human beings.

PART III

The Depth of Dog

Having tracked dog back through time and across space, we now start a descent into dog. Dogs of quite a different order emerge—two-dimensional creatures that operate out of time and space—for they are not physical, but psychic, phenomena which reveal themselves to human beings at twilight. In 'digging the dog' we will track down its image wherever it lurks, allowing ourselves to be drawn into the depth of dog.

PHANTOM DOGS

1) *Ghosts* The dog-ghost is a common type of psychic phenomenon which sometimes haunts people and sometimes haunts places.

PERSONAL The personal dog-ghost is one that haunts individuals. Many people see the ghosts of dogs that were once their faithful companions. These creatures usually behave in much the same way as when they were alive, and sometimes are seen playing with their three-dimensional successors. Ghosts of people who were in life very attached to their pets are often seen accompanied by dog-ghosts.

There are numerous ghost stories of people haunted by deceased relatives whose spirits have taken canine form. The main body of these tales comes from Texas, where the dog-ghost is usually benign.

Typical are those of people who return from the dead to protect their bereaved children. An orphan boy was guarded every night by a large white dog. It emerged from a puff of smoke that blew in through his window, and was said to be the ghost of his mother. Then there is the story of a Dallas boy who, when he was orphaned, went away and started to live with women. He spent many evenings with a married girl whose husband worked at night, until, one evening, having been tipped off by neighbours, the husband stayed away from work and waited in hiding for the Dallas boy. When he arrived the girl's husband grabbed him and was just about to cut his throat when a huge white dog appeared 'wid eyes shinin' lack balls of fiah'. The attacker collapsed and dropped the razor, which immediately 'ketched fiah an' burnt clean to pieces'. He remained unconscious for a week and the boy returned to Dallas, his life having been saved—it was said—by the spirit of his dead father. (It is interesting to note here that natives of the West Indies are protected by ancestors who often take the form of dogs.)

Sometimes the Texas dog-ghost brings healing. A woman and her daughter had lived together for fifty years and everyone wondered how the younger woman would manage when her mother eventually died. At seventy-two years old the mother passed on, and the day after the funeral her daughter was smitten with severe pains in the head. No medicine did her any good and she did not recover, but just tossed and turned in bed day and night. After three months of this she got up one night and went into the back-yard for fresh air, hoping it would relieve the pain. While out there she felt a puff of wind and, looking round, saw a big white dog staring at her. The dog had a bandage with pills stuck all over it on its head. It pointed with a paw to the pills, so she took one and swallowed it. The headache immediately vanished, and, when she saw the bandage was made of the same material as the dress in which her mother was buried, she knew the dog was the ghost of her mother who had come back to heal her.

Help in the form of bringing food was also given by a dog-ghost. A little boy of five had lost his mother and was brought up by an old lady. No matter what food she produced he would not eat, and he soon began to suffer from starvation. In bed one night he was woken by a hot wind blowing on his face and, as he watched a white puff of smoke coming in through the window, it turned into a big white dog. The dog coughed up a lot of teacakes on the floor, then disappeared the way it had come. The boy immediately ate some of the cakes and stowed away the rest in a sack. He tucked into them again later, but however many he ate the sack was full again next morning and, since the teacakes were identical to those his mother used to bake, the white dog was assumed to be his mother's ghost.

At other times it was wealth that the dog-ghost brought to those who had been closest to it during life. A Bastrop farmer who had made a lot of money selling cotton and corn did not believe in banking it, and would only tell his wife that it was hidden 'on de place somewhars'. One day he was thrown by a horse and killed and, since his wife did not know where he had hidden his fortune, she had to sell mules and pigs to pay for his funeral. Each night the farmer's wife, her brother and two sisters took a lantern and made their way to the bathroom which was 'way down crost a thick patch of timber in de lowuh pastur' of dey farm'. The night after burying the farmer they were on their way to the bathroom, when they found they were being followed by 'a big white dawg wid red eyes jes ashinin' '. Never having seen a dog around the premises before, they chucked rocks at it. The same thing happened every night for about a month. Then on Saturday evening when they attacked the dog following them it did not run off, but continued trotting towards them with the rocks passing straight through it. When, however, they turned round to go back to the house the dog did not follow them, but stood by the bathroom looking towards a big clump of trees. It appeared to want to show them something, so when it started walking towards the clump they decided to follow it. On reaching the biggest oak it started to scratch the ground, but when they joined the dog it looked up at them and disappeared, smoke floating up into the sky where it had been. So the farmer's family marked the spot where it had scratched and, fetching a big shovel, started digging. About five feet down they found boxes full of gold and silver and 'dey was mo'n three thousan' dolluhs in de boxes all tol' '. The white dog was said to be the farmer 'what done comed back to show his fam'ly what he done statched 'way his money'.

It will be noted that in these Texas stories people simply accepted the phantom dog and its gifts, and it was not until later that they deduced it must have been the ghost of a deceased relative.

FAMILY   The family dog-ghost haunts the houses of certain families—often through several generations—and its appearance usually portends the death of a relative.

Belief in the howling of 'solid' dogs as a death omen is very widespread. Dogs often appear to be more sensitive to psychic phenomena than are humans, and there are Jews and Moslems who believe they howl because they see the Angel of Death, while in some parts of Germany it is said they see coffins in the air. Someone who has heard this death omen and seen its fulfilment has described how the dog is very restless until it can get near the room where the doomed person is lying, and if it cannot get into the garden of the house, it will run round the premises or pace up and down in front. If able to force an entry it will stand under the window of the sick-room howling horribly, then after three tremendous barks, will hurry away. South American negroes maintain that if a dog howls twice it predicts the death of a man, and if three times the death of a woman. According to Missouri folk-lore, howling dogs point their heads in the direction of the doomed person and people are very relieved if the dogs howl with their backs to them. A dog in a German village foretold so many deaths that it became an object of terror and was eventually killed. In Ireland the cry raised at funerals was called the 'Caoin' or 'Keen'—probably derived from the Greek κυνός, 'a dog'—and the howling of a dog was considered to be the first note of a funeral dirge and a sign that death was imminent.

Family dog-ghosts resemble three-dimensional dogs. They are often described as brushing past a person who sees them, and where there is a 'real' dog in the family the two are apt to be confused. Typical is the case of a woman who ran upstairs after a dog that had rushed past her, believing it to be her own, but she found on arrival that it had completely disappeared and her dog was still chained up in its kennel outside the house.

A white dog-ghost appears before a death in some families. A woman was sitting chatting with a man friend in his garden one day when she saw a little white dog run under his chair. When they got up and looked for it, it had mysteriously vanished and the man explained that in his family the dog's appearance invariably presaged death. An uncle of his died that night.

More often the ominous family dog-ghost is black. Leeds Castle in Kent is haunted by a dog like a Labrador retriever which appears to be solid until it suddenly fades through walls, windows or doors.

On the island of Mull in the Inner Hebrides a dog-ghost known as the 'Black Dog of Ardura' is an omen of death to anyone living at Lochbuie House. When, in 1909, the chief of the Maclaines lay dying there, he was visited by his doctor from Oban, who, unable to get home, stayed overnight in Lochbuie House. Early next morning, when the doctor was opening the front door to let himself out, a big black retriever pushed past him into the house. When he mentioned to the driver of his trap, a local man, that someone must have left the dog out all night, he was very alarmed and warned the doctor that if he had, in fact, let this black dog in there was no hope of the chief's recovery. In 1914 a doctor who had been visiting an ancient retainer of Lochbuie heard an uncanny howling in the woods as he motored home up Ardura hill, and a black retriever emerged and ran for some distance in the light of his headlamps. He was called back that night when the old man died.

A man whose family was haunted by an ominous dog did not tell the woman he married about it, hoping to avoid causing her anxiety. They had a family and all was well until one of the children contracted smallpox, but the attack was slight and not considered to be dangerous. Then one evening, during dinner, the man's wife got up to see how the baby was, and returned with the news that it was asleep, but there was a large black dog lying on the cot which she was unable to shift. Her husband rushed upstairs to find what he feared and expected, for the dog had vanished, but the child was dead.

'Solid' dogs are usually very frightened of dog-ghosts and often see them when human beings only feel their presence. In France police were once called in to deal with a dog-ghost which was causing trouble in a house it haunted. They set two of their dogs on the ghost, but without effect, for one became too cowed to attack and the other died.

2) *Death demons* The majority of phantom dogs are not, however, attached to people or their homes but to sites such as roads, churchyards and rivers. They are demonic in appearance, so are less easily confused with 'solid' dogs, and they usually either presage death or inflict it.

THE BLACK DOG In Europe belief in the black dog is very widespread and this demon varies greatly in its habitat, appearance, behaviour, degree of malignity and in its effect on people. In Great Britain the main concentration of black dog-phantoms is to be found in East Anglia.

The Lincolnshire dog appears to be the only one that is virtually innocuous and indeed is often felt to be protective. It is described by people still alive who have seen, heard and felt it, as being black, 'table high', thin, with a long neck and a pointed snout. It often trots alongside people returning home at night in country lanes, and it will brush past their legs, or bound into the road from a field, running ahead of them, then leaping back over a gate farther on. A farm labourer describes how he was always joined by the phantom dog at a certain spot in a lane: 'If 'e passed you an' you watched 'im, 'e'd go into th'edge which'd crackle just as if a gurt bullock was pushin' 'is way thruff.' He says that no matter how dark the night is 'you can allus see the dog because 'e's so much blacker'. It is claimed that the dog is only seen by 'good folks' and, since no harm has ever come from meeting this phantom, it is not feared.

In Suffolk, although the phantom dog is called 'Black Shuck' (from *soucca*, Anglo-Saxon for 'Satan'), it still appears to be comparatively mild. People do not see this dog, they only feel it, and they firmly believe that if they did see it they would die. Usually they become aware of its presence, then feel it brush against their legs as it trots past, or when it is travelling faster, whip off their caps. (Often a man becomes aware of the phantom's presence through the reaction of his own dog when it appears terrified and bolts.) Although Suffolk people are not very afraid of Black Shuck, since meeting it is not considered dangerous, the experience is unpleasant enough to make them avoid lanes, churchyards and paths haunted by it whenever possible. The same dog appears to run Essex and the Cambridgeshire fens, but in the fens people who shun certain banks at night say: 'he run silent an' come up ahint ye. An' as sure as yew see him yew up an' die.'

In Norfolk, Black Shuck is far more satanic, and by many people is greatly feared. It is described in these parts as a dog 'big as a calf', with a long, black, shaggy coat; with eyes that burn like coal and are the size of saucers; and as emitting an unearthly howl. It pads silently across desolate marshes, along lonely footpaths, in the shadow of hedges and has for many years bounded across the same points in certain lanes. It is said that drivers on Norfolk roads suddenly jam on their brakes as Black Shuck crosses in front of them. This demon leaves no footprints and fishermen say that on stormy nights when it runs the cliffs its yells, which make the blood run cold, can be heard above the howling gale and roaring waves. They say it is wise to shut your eyes if you hear it howling, for no one survives whose eyes meet those of Black Shuck. It sometimes tracks the steps of lonely wayfarers, and when cottagers returning home after dark hear it padding along behind them and feel its freezing cold breath on their backs, they never turn round, but hurry to the nearest shelter. To meet Black Shuck means death within the year, for, it is said, 'there ain't a man living what can see that owd dog and live. Do he does, he'll go scatty.'

Nearly four hundred years ago Black Shuck made a notorious visit to the parish church of Bungay, a town near Norwich. This was vividly described in a sixteenth-century tract as a 'Strange and terrible

3d Fairy dog with jewel-producing paw (p. 75)

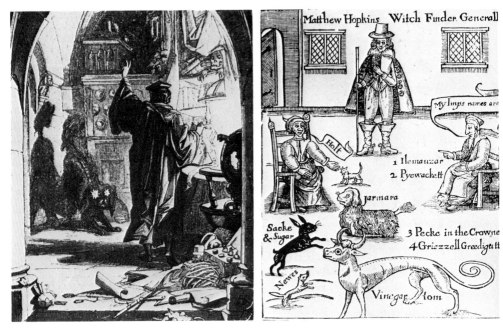

3e Mephistopheles as a black poodle (p. 77)   3f Witches with their dog-familiars (p. 79)

4a Heracles dragging Cerberus out of Hades (p. 92)

4b Hecate as a whelping bitch (p. 106)

4c Scylla, the sea-bitch (p. 88)

4d Jackal-god guiding soul through the Underworld (p. 95)

4e St. Margaret guided by dog to her dead lover (p. 96)

4f St. Roch and his dog (p. 100)

Wunder' (Plate 3a) wrought on August 4th, 1577, 'in a great tempest of violent raine, lightning and thunder, the like whereof hath ben seldome seene'. The church, it was said, quaked and staggered, and members of the congregation were terrified out of their wits, for 'immediately there appeared in a most horrible similitude and likeness to the congregation then and there present, a dog as they might discern it, of a black colour', with 'fearful flashes of fire'. This black dog, 'or the divil in such a likeness', ran 'all along down the body of the church with great swiftnesse and incredible haste among the people', and 'passing between two parishioners kneeling in prayer, it wrung their necks and they died immediately'. It gave another man 'such a gripe on the back that there withal he was presently drawen togither and shrunk up as it were a piece of leather scorched in a hot fire'. In some places it is said that, when spots where Black Shuck has been seen are examined, they are found to be scorched and smelling strongly of brimstone.

In Blythburgh, Suffolk (where the dog is said by some to be the ghost of a dog drowned in a local shipwreck), a similar story is told of a storm bursting over the church there on the same date. The minister, it seems, was reading the lesson when a strange and terrible tempest 'strake through the wall of the same church into the ground almost a yard deepe, drave down all the people on that side above twenty persons'. Then it 'cleft the dore', rent the timber of the steeple, broke the chimes, and fled across the marshes to Bungay, where it did the damage already described. In Blythburgh a man and a boy were struck dead, and others were scorched. It has always been said that the Devil was in that storm and that when he went out of the north door on his way to Bungay he burnt it as he touched it with his hot fingers. When the whitewash and dirt of centuries were cleaned off the door scorch marks were found and remain there for anyone to see. Although the legend was originally told about the Devil, the local people all maintain it was Black Shuck, and that the scorch marks were made by his paws. And, while the vicar will tell you that the notice on the church gate forbidding dogs to enter is to prevent the church being fouled, the villagers 'know' dogs are not allowed in, lest one of them should turn out to be Black Shuck again.

(The Devil has attacked churches in the form of a dog before. In A.D. 857 a bishop was celebrating Mass during a thunderstorm at Trèves when the bell tower was struck by lightning, darkness descended, and an enormous black dog was seen running round the altar in circles. Similarly, in 1341, a diabolical dog entered the cathedral at Messina and proceeded to destroy the objects on the altar.)

In East Anglia people say of someone sullen and bad-tempered: 'The black dog's walked over him', or '. . . is on his shoulders'; and, of someone dying of an incurable disease: 'The black dog is at his heels.'

In the North of England dog-phantoms haunting roads, church-yards and the hills are always ominous. In Lancashire the dog is known as 'Trash' or 'Skriker'—'Trash', because of the splashing sound made by its broad feet which resembles someone walking in heavy old shoes along a muddy road, and 'Skriker' because of the peculiar screech it utters. If followed by anyone it walks backwards, keeping its eyes on the pursuer, then either plunges into a pool with a splashing sound or sinks into the earth with a frightful shriek. Trash portends death either to the person who sees it or to a member of his family. If the dog is seen distinctly death follows quickly, while if the image is faint and nebulous some months of life may still remain. In Swaledale a headless dog foretelling tragic events haunts a hump-backed bridge, gliding silently on to it and over the edge. In Preston a similar hound runs about the streets when the town is threatened by misfortune, while Westmorland has large demonic dogs which are headless and resemble mastiffs.

In southern England the black dog has different habits. There is one in a Devonshire village that rushes between the church and school at midnight, knocking down the corner of the old schoolhouse. (Although the building has never shown any sign of damage, the villagers insist they hear stones falling as it tears by every night.) Everyone knows about this demon, but it is considered bad luck to speak of it. In another village the hound is distinguished by walking each night on its hind legs past the door of a cottage where someone was once murdered. Then there is a huge, shaggy, black, fiery-eyed lane-haunting dog in a Dorset village, which, as people watch it, grows bigger and bigger until it is as tall as the trees, then, swelling into a large cloud, vanishes.

This recalls the phantom dog of Scandinavia and Germany, for in northern Europe at least a sixth of all dog-demons are black poodles which reveal their satanic nature by a similar increase in size. The black poodle usually appears first as a normal three-dimensional dog, then, rapidly swelling, becomes more and more fiery-eyed and demonic.

Another practice of these northern dogs is to run round people in circles. A legend from Thuringia tells of a large black fiery-eyed dog with chains round its neck that impedes travellers by encircling them. Its victims are completely immobilized until one o'clock in the morning, when, with the end of the hour of bewitchment, its power fades. But perhaps the most unpleasant of all their habits is that of riding people. A typical Danish legend tells of a man who felt a great weight pressing on his shoulders, and when he stabbed at it with a pocket knife saw it leave him in the form of a large black poodle with glowing eyes. Another Dane was riding home one dark, foggy night when a huge black dog sprang on to his horse behind him. He was unable to chase it away, and as it became heavier and heavier his horse kept sinking to its knees, but fortunately, as he neared home the demon suddenly vanished. In Bavaria people who walk by a river at night are often mounted by river-poodles which press so hard on their backs that they cannot remain upright.

To return to British dogs—in addition to ominous and molesting phantoms, there are some that are considerably more violent in their attacks, or their effect, on people. Black dogs often haunt spots of violent death—the beheading stone, for instance, in Stirling Castle. Near Tring, in Hertfordshire, the place where a gibbet once stood is haunted by a black dog, and last century a village schoolmaster described his experience of it. Returning home one night in a trap, as he approached this spot he saw on the roadside 'a flame of fire as large as a man's hat'. When his trembling horse came to a dead stop an immense black dog appeared, lying in the road just in front of it, with eyes like balls of fire and huge teeth. The demon opened its mouth and seemed to grin at the schoolmaster, but after a moment or two it sank into the earth, and the trap was driven over the spot where it had lain.

More disastrous was the experience of a Buckinghamshire farmer. This man kept his cows in a field some distance from a village near Aylesbury, and when, every night and morning, the time came to milk them, he made his way across a field and through a gap in a hedge. One night he found the gap occupied by a large, black, fierce-looking dog with fiery eyes that grew larger as he watched it. So he turned aside and walked through a gate at the end of the field. Night after night he found the same dog in the gap and abandoned the short cut through the hedge. One night, however, he had a friend with him and was determined that if he found the dog he would attack it and drive it away. Finding it standing in the gap, looking larger and fiercer than ever, the farmer put down the milk pails, raised the yoke in both hands and struck at the dog with all his might. The dog vanished, but the farmer fell senseless to the ground and, although he was carried home alive, he remained speechless and paralysed to the end of his days. It seems that nothing could be more dangerous than attacking these phantoms; it is said that when a man struck at the black dog of Hatfield Peverell, in Essex, he, his horse, his wagon and its load were all burnt to ashes.

One of the most lethal of all black dogs was the famous 'Mauthe Doog', a demonic spaniel that haunted Peel Castle in the Isle of Man. In the seventeenth century, when the candles were lit in the guard-room each night, it came and lay down there in front of the fire. Although the soldiers became accustomed to its presence, they never lost their fear of the Mauthe Doog; and never did anything they thought might annoy it. This phantom came and went by a passage which was used by the soldier who delivered the keys every night to their officer-in-charge. The man on duty always took someone with him through the passage for fear of meeting the Mauthe Doog alone. One night, however, one of the troopers got very drunk and, with false courage, snatched the keys and insisted on going through the passage alone, swearing that he would find out 'whether it were dog or devil'. There was a great commotion outside, and when the braggart staggered in he had been struck dumb by the horror of his experience, and he died three days later writhing in agony. After this no one would venture through the passage, so, in 1666, it was closed up and the Mauthe Doog was never seen in Peel Castle again.

Another account of a death-dealing black dog-phantom comes from Devonshire. A man returning home across Dartmoor late one winter's night heard the patter of feet behind him and, a few moments later, a huge dog like a Newfoundland appeared at his side. Being fond of dogs, he tried to stroke it, but his hand passed straight through its body. It gazed at him with great glassy eyes, and when it yawned a stream of sulphurous vapour issued from its throat. Very frightened, the man started to run, but the dog chased him, never losing speed, until they reached cross-roads. Here he heard a loud report, and a blinding flash struck him senseless to the ground. It was said that the ghost was that of a dog which, because its master had been murdered on Dartmoor, was doomed to haunt the spot and kill every man it met until the murder was avenged.

THE CELTIC DOG The Welsh coast is haunted by dog-demons called 'Gwyllgi', which are not black and look rather like mastiffs. They have blazing eyes, baleful breath and emit blood-curdling screams. Gwyllgi are dangerous to meet, for the glare of their fiery eyes and the sound of their unearthly howls so terrify people that they usually fall down senseless. An eighteenth-century writer tells of a Pembrokeshire man who, walking through a field where there were two ancient stones said to be haunted, called the 'Devil's Nags', was suddenly seized and thrown over a hedge. The next day he returned to the site with a powerful mastiff (a 'solid' one) for protection. As they approached the 'Devil's Nags' the dog-demon appeared again, but, when the man tried to get his own dog to attack it, the three-dimensional mastiff crouched by his feet too terrified to move. When he picked up a stone to throw at the Gwyllgi, a circle of fire suddenly surrounded it, lighting up the gloom and revealing its grinning teeth, a white snip down its nose, and a white tail. This convinced the man that the dog was infernal.

Scotland is famous for its faery dogs (*cu sith*), which are described as being the size of a two-year-old heifer, and sometimes white, but more usually green, with tails either flat and plaited or coiled over their backs. These demons are greatly dreaded in the Highlands and Western isles. On dark nights it is said they silently and rhythmically glide from place to place, always moving in a straight line, and leaving immense footprints in snow, mud or sandy beaches. They have a loud clamorous bark which is repeated three times, and at the third bark anyone they pursue is overtaken by them and destroyed, unless he has been able to reach a place of safety. Since there is an interval between each bark, people rush, terror-stricken, to any refuge in sight. 'Solid' dogs that chase *cu sith* are liable to return home with all the hair scraped off their backs (except for their ears) and they usually die soon after.

DEALING WITH DEMONIC DOGS Many indications have already been given as to the best way of dealing with demonic dogs. These include keeping away from the dog's regular beat; closing your eyes when you hear it howling to avoid seeing it; turning your back on it and running for shelter; and waiting until 1 a.m., when its power diminishes. A further hint is contained in an account of the Devonshire

dog that haunted the road running between Copplestone and Torring-
ton. When it appeared running round with its nose to the ground,
barking loudly from time to time, horses shied and bolted and car
drivers braked hard. A van driver told how he got used to 'the gurt
hound' on this road, but 'dursn't touch him nor speak when he were
by'. Apparently the phantom remained harmless so long as no one
spoke when it appeared, or cried out when they heard it panting
behind them.

Although attempts at striking demonic dogs usually prove
disastrous, there are occasions when this seems to be the right thing
to do. A German legend tells of a man who, when he met a black dog-
phantom, hit it hard on the head with a stick and, when it did not
move, gave it a blow in the teeth. The dog then grew alarmingly large
and, gazing at the man with its fiery eyes, said: 'Hit once more.' The
man knew this would be unwise, and by refusing to do so deprived the
demon of its power. It has also been shown how successful it can be to
stab at the weight on your shoulders when ridden by a demonic
poodle.

Dog-demons can be laid by the power of Christianity. A Tyrolean
peasant climbing a wooded hill suddenly became aware of a big black
dog with glowing eyes running around him in diminishing circles. He
could not move, but when the dog came close to him he struck it on
the back with a much-blessed rosary. Sparks of fire flew out in all
directions and the dog ran away howling. A Bavarian once rid himself
of a river-poodle by leading it towards a crucifix. And when a
Pomeranian who was being followed by a black dog the size of which
increased as it approached him, exclaimed (with his hair standing on
end): 'Lord God help me', the demon dwindled until it disappeared
altogether. Naming a devil is also a means of eliminating it. At
Lübeck, in 1687, a house was haunted by a large black dog that would
not move and could not be lifted, but departed as soon as it was recognized and named 'devil'.

THE SPECTRAL PACK Packs of dog-demons are also omens of
death, and legends of the Wild Hunt are widespread throughout
northern Europe. The original Wild Hunt was led by Woden, the
Teutonic storm-god, who was nightly to be seen rushing across the
skies surrounded by shouting and hollering huntsmen with a large pack
of baying hounds, in pursuit of a phantom boar, horse or woman. The
Wild Hunt came out of mountains, forests and lakes and disappeared

into them again when the Hunt was over. Wherever Woden rode hedges crashed down, and roads opened up, before him.

When hounds were heard baying in the woods, on heaths or at cross-roads, people took it as a sign that Woden was hunting, and, since they were in danger of being carried off or of having the hounds turned on them, they threw themselves face downward on the ground or, if there was time, hurried home. In Mecklenburg a peasant going home through the forest one night heard the cry of the Huntsman and the baying of hounds in the air; then a voice called out 'in the middle of the road, keep in the middle way and then will the dogs not bite thee.'

The horses of the Wild Hunt were often the souls of women who had sinned with priests, and the hounds were human souls transformed into air. Woden's hounds talked like men, but, as wind, they were continually howling and tore to pieces any linen hung out to dry. (In old German engravings the wind is depicted as the head of a wolf or dog from which blasts issue.) When on earth they could not pass over graves and had to be lifted over. They greedily devoured everything that came their way, including the ashes on peasants' hearths, and the safest thing to do was to give them a bag of meal. During the twelve nights of Christmas it was wise to keep linen in and doors closed, for the hounds tore any linen hanging out, and Woden and his pack passed through any houses whose doors were left open, consuming all the food they could find. According to a North German legend, Woden once entered the house of a poor peasant and his hounds devoured everything. When the victim asked what compensation for the damage to expect, he was assured he would be paid in full. Woden later appeared dragging a dead dog behind him and told the peasant to throw it into his chimney. When he did so the dog's skin burst open and gold coins poured out.

Woden rode at such a speed that the hounds often had difficulty in keeping pace with him, and sometimes a panting, howling dog would be found left behind in the road, or on the hearth of a household through which the Wild Hunt had passed. The hound on the hearth lived on ashes, and it howled and whined incessantly for a whole year. If it was picked up it became a lump of coal and there was only one way of ridding a house of it and that was by brewing beer in eggshells. The hound would watch this operation and exclaim:

> Though I am now as old as the old Bohemian wold,
> Yet the like of this I ween, in my life I ne'er have seen.

Then it would vanish and return no more. Otherwise it had to be tolerated until the Hunt reappeared, when it suddenly stopped howling, jumped to its feet, wagged its tail and rejoined them.

In some parts of Europe the legend of Woden has been transferred from a divine to a human being, the Huntsman being the soul of a wicked man doomed to hunt for ever with the storm. Sacrilege was the sin which usually brought this punishment. According to Basque tradition, a hunting abbot was saying Mass one Sunday when a hare ran past. The abbot's hounds caught the scent and rushed out howling after it and a moment later the abbot deserted the Holy Sacrament to join them. At death he was condemned to endless chase and can still, it is said, be seen whirling across the plains behind baying hounds, never to run down the quarry. (In some versions of this story, the hare is the Devil.)

A wealthy woman, Fru Gode, loved the chase, and hunted frequently with her twenty-four daughters. One day, in full gallop and wild with joy, she shouted: 'The chase is better than heaven.' As these profane words left her mouth her daughters were transformed into baying hounds, and they all rose to the clouds, where they have hunted ever since. It is said that during the twelve days of Christmas Fru Gode directs her course to human habitation and if she finds a door open will send in one of her hounds. This creature will not only whine and moan unceasingly for a year, but is liable to bring disease, fire and even death to its reluctant hosts. Nothing will appease it or drive it away: if anyone kills it, it turns into a stone which, if thrown away, returns to the house as a dog again. On the other hand, Fru Gode once left a hound lying in front of the door of a poor farmer, who took it in, fed and cherished it for a year, and when it suddenly disappeared he found in the bed he had made for it a large lump of gold.

The flying Huntsman appears throughout Denmark. People who have seen, or heard, the Wild Hunt in a tumult of horns and baying hounds galloping through fields and forests in pursuit of unseen quarry, usually shudder in describing it. Peasants who hear it approaching hide behind trees, or lie face downward on the ground (to avoid either seeing or being seen) until it has passed. The Huntsman sometimes orders human beings to hold several of his hounds on a leash while he goes off to kill someone. On returning he asks for a drink, then gives the victim what is known as 'drink money'—coins which burn a hole through his hand.

In Seeland, King Valdemar is the Huntsman. He rides a white horse and rushes through the air amidst much shouting, cracking of whips and baying of hounds; as he rides through farms all gates fly open at his approach. When his hounds sniff around on the ground they are seen to be black with red-hot tongues. King Valdemar rests at various places in the country. At Vallö castle, where he has a bed-chamber with a ready-made bed, he spends the night in the form of a black dog. When he meets anyone he commands them to hold a couple of his hounds, either making them stand with them for several hours or alternatively loose them on hearing a shot. Sometimes he pays with what looks like a gold coin, but burns a hole through the recipient's hand, falling like coal to the ground; but on other occasions, when an old man or woman has held his dogs for hours, he throws them an object that looks like coal, but, when examined, is found to be a lump of pure gold.

Sometimes the Huntsman is the Devil himself, as in Normandy, where the Wild Hunt is known as the *'Chasse du Diable'*. In Lower Normandy the *Chasse Hennequin* is nightly led by the Devil with untamed horses mounted by the souls of monks and nuns who forni-cated and died unrepentant. In some parts the power of these Hunts can be counteracted by sacrificing to the hounds, or by prostrating oneself on the earth face downward (so that no contact is made through the eyes). The Hunt can safely be observed from a stump marked with three crosses (three, as a divine number, gives protection to the soul), or from cross-roads; but by far the most effective means of circumventing the evil is by tracing a circle round oneself with a stick (they cannot enter and will disappear with a shriek), and by prayer. The story is told of a *curé*, living near Courteuilles, who was over-taken by the *Chasse Hennequin*. Protecting himself with a magic circle, he asked what they were pursuing, and was told they sought the soul of a woman who had committed adultery with a priest. The *curé* suggested meeting them an hour later at the village where the woman lived, then, praying hard, he ran there as fast as he could. When the demons appeared they complained that their journey had been in vain, for, thanks to the *curé*'s prayers, they were cheated of their 'rightful gain', the Virgin Mary having arrived first and taken away the woman's soul.

In the British Isles also the Wild Hunt presages death. The Welsh *Cwn Annwn* (Dogs of Hell), or *Cwn y Wybr* (Dogs of the Sky), are a pack of spectral hounds belonging to Annwn, King of Hell, whose mount is a black horse with fiery eyes. The hounds are sometimes black, but are often a luminous white with red ears. Their voices resemble those of beagles, and a deep hollow voice like a monstrous bloodhound's is often heard among them. They are peculiar in that, as they approach man, the volume of sound decreases, while the more distant they are the louder their baying becomes. These hounds are usually heard during winter accompanying a howling wind. Although the *Cwn Annwn* are comparatively harmless in themselves, since their cries are a certain omen of death they strike terror into peoples' hearts. They fly to houses of the fatally ill, and bark several times as the sick person dies. In some parts of Wales the colour of the hound is significant: if a white dog appears near the home of a dying person it means his soul will be saved, while a black dog indicates that his soul will be subjected to everlasting torment. (In Somerset, where they are called 'death hounds', they are seen rushing through the air with flames issuing from their mouths, and are heard on windy nights 'coming for the wicked'. Since it is unlucky to name them, they are usually referred to as 'they dogs', and if you meet them and want to avoid death you must fling yourself flat on your face, and remain on the ground with hands and feet crossed until they have passed. In this area there is a strong prejudice against white dogs. Children are forbidden to play with strange ones, and on New Year's Eve, when the *Cwn Annwn* hunt the ghost of a drunken squire, all white dogs are shut up.) Some people maintain that the *Cwn Annwn* are hell-hounds that hunt the souls of the wicked as soon as they leave the body; others that they lead a cavalcade of doomed souls to hell. Sometimes these demons follow funerals, but as funeral dogs they are known as *Cwn Maman* (Mother's dogs).

Although the *Cwn Annwn* are heard when travelling as a pack by air, they are visible only when they appear singly on the ground. One member of the pack, it is said, once fell on a tombstone, but no one was able to catch hold of it. Sometimes a hound will be found sitting howling by a stream, but the sound is so unearthly that anyone finding it loses his senses. The King of Annwn once left a hound in an old Glamorganshire barn, for three weeks it remained there defying all attempts to dislodge it. Then one stormy night when the shouting and baying of the Wild Hunt were heard above the howling wind, the dog emerged from the barn, jumping about with joy and, with one wild bound, vanished and was never seen again. People who are kind to abandoned hounds are usually rewarded. An old Welsh woman who found one lying on the ground in an exhausted state carried it home in her apron, made a soft bed for it, and placed a brass pot over the dog. Henceforth her cows gave more milk than those of any farms in the neighbourhood. Other legends tell of people who, as a result of their cruel or negligent behaviour to members of the *Cwn Annwn*, received pursefuls of valueless coins or, in some cases, fell down dead.

An Anglo-Saxon Chronicle describes the Wild Hunt in England as seen by monks in the deer park in Peterborough, Northamptonshire. Here twenty or thirty 'black, huge and hideous' huntsmen rode on black horses with hounds that were 'jet black with eyes like saucers and horrible'. In the West Country the Hunt is sometimes believed to consist of demons that hunt the souls of the damned; sometimes of souls of wicked people driven for ever by the Devil; and often of the souls of children who, having died unbaptized, suffer eternal restlessness. In the twelfth century, during the reign of Henry II, the Wild Hunt manifested itself in a meadow in broad daylight. The shouting and blowing of horns drew people from the neighbourhood, many of whom recognized dead friends among the huntsmen, but, as they spoke to them, the whole host rose in the air and vanished into the River Wye.

Dartmoor is famous for its wisht hounds ('wisht' being a word now meaning 'uncanny' and 'melancholy', and thought to be derived from 'Woden'). A black huntsman leads this pack, which consists of black, blood-sprinkled, fire-breathing hounds. They do not fly high, and since they choose cloudy nights for their hunts they are seldom seen in the air—but can often be heard. Their yelping is said to be as loud as that of bloodhounds, but sharper and more diabolical. If 'solid' dogs hear it they die, and it foretells the death of human beings. On the moors wisht hounds are frequently seen running round in circles.

A horrid story is told of a moorman who was riding home from Widecombe Fair one night when he had no sooner heard the sound of a horn than a pack of jet-black hounds followed by a dark spectral huntsman swept past him. The moorman called out to the Huntsman, asking for some game. 'Take that,' replied the Huntsman, tossing a bundle to him. The moorman caught it, but could not see what it was in the dark. When he arrived home he called for a lantern to throw light on the bundle, and found that the game hunted by the demons was his own child. It vanished as a servant came up to break the news to him that his son had recently died. Another legend tells of two children together on the moors—one asleep, and one lying awake. The Wild Hunt passed overhead, and a voice called out: 'Shall we take it?' 'No,' came the reply, 'it will come of itself shortly.' The next day the sleeping child was dead.

This Devonshire pack are also known as Yeth hounds ('Yeth' being the word for 'heathen' in local dialect). It is believed by some that the spirits of unbaptized children, having no admittance to paradise, unite in a pack of 'heathen', or 'Yeth', hounds to hunt the Devil, whom they blame for their dilemma. Others say the children are hunting for their souls; or hounding their negligent parents; or, alternatively, that the hounds are not themselves the children, but demons eternally hunting the souls of the unbaptized.

In some areas King Arthur is the Wild Huntsman. In Northumberland it is said that King Arthur and his pack are spellbound in the subterranean hall of the castle of Sewingshields, waiting to be released by someone who blows a horn at the entrance and, with the 'sword of the stone', cuts a garter beside it. No one knows where the entrance is, but one day, some years ago, a farmer came upon it accidentally. On entering the hall he found a fire blazing in the centre of it: King Arthur, the Queen and their court reposing on thrones and couches, and a deep-toned pack of thirty couples of hounds lying on the floor. Seeing on a table the spell-dissolving horn, the sword and garter, the farmer cut the garter with the sword. As he drew it their eyes opened and they all sat up, but, since he had not blown the horn, as soon as he sheathed the sword they all returned to sleep, and the farmer was never able to find the entrance to the hall again. Around Plymouth, Sir Francis Drake has this honour, for, according to tradition, he was able to destroy the Spanish Armada only because of the help he received from the Devil. He can be seen driving a hearse into Plymouth every night with headless horses, and a pack of headless hounds, the baying of which causes the death of any earthly dogs that hear them.

In the North of England the spectral pack are referred to as 'Gabriel' hounds, for they are said to be the wandering ghosts of sinners hunted by Gabriel, the Prince of thunder and lightning and Angel of Death. Gabriel hounds are sometimes described as monstrous dogs with human heads. They not only presage death to those who hear them, but they fly towards homes of the fatally ill and bark as they die. Typical is the story of a man who was suddenly summoned to the bedside of a relative. As he set out he heard the sound of hoofs overhead, and the Wild Hunt accompanied him throughout the journey until the destination was reached, when it came to a standstill and the hounds yelped loudly over the house. On entering he found the sick relative had just died. Near Leeds, in Yorkshire, where they are known as 'Gabble Retchet', the pack are believed to be the souls of unbaptized children doomed to flit restlessly near the homes of their parents, and to hover around the house when they die.

In Cornwall the spectral pack are essentially avengers. In the village of St German's there was once a very wicked priest called Dando who, we are told, worshipped sensuality, spent his nights in dissolute company and drank too much. He also habitually hunted on the Sabbath. One Sunday, after a long run, the Devil appeared to Dando disguised as a hunter and offered him a flask of infernal liquor. As soon as Dando was intoxicated the Devil lifted him up on to his black steed and made off with him, the hounds bringing up the rear. When they reached the banks of the Lynher, horses, riders and hounds leapt into the middle of the river and disappeared in a blaze of fire. It is said that on Sunday mornings the hounds are still heard in the area, and in St German's church the Bishop's chair has the images of Dando and his dogs carved on it so that his wickedness shall never be forgotten.

The story is told of a young herdsman who was walking across the moors one windy night when he heard the baying of hounds among the tors, and, recognizing the ominous chorus of the Devil's 'Dandy-dogs', took to his heels and made for his home three or four miles away. The holloa of the Huntsman came nearer and nearer, and he turned to see a black fiery-eyed figure with horns, tail, and a clawed hand carrying a hunting pole, surrounded by black fire-snorting dogs. When the hell-hounds were about to rush on the herdsman, he fell on his knees in prayer. At the first holy word, the pack stood at bay howling; the Huntsman shouted: 'Bo shrove' ('the boy prays'), and they drew off and disappeared.

Tregeagle is the name of a Cornishman said to have been diabolically wicked. He was a tyrannical magistrate, a rapacious and unscrupulous landlord who lived near Bodmin, and eventually murdered his sister, wife and children. When he died the Devil came to claim his soul, but, in terror, Tregeagle consigned all his wealth to the priest-hood, so that they would fight the evil spirits and save his soul from hellfire. The power of the Church prevailed in so far as that the demons were unable to harm him so long as his spirit was in perpetual toil; the tasks set him were to extend into eternity, their object being to soften his hard heart by repentance. The most famous task imposed on Tregeagle was the emptying of the bottomless lake on Bodmin moor known as Dosmery Pool. He was provided with a holed limpet shell to bale out the water, but, although day and night, summer and winter, year in and out, Tregeagle could be seen bent over the waters of the lake, they remained at the same level. The Devil watched over the doomed spirit, knowing that if Tregeagle paused in his labours he could seize and secure his soul. On one occasion he raised a wild tempest and succeeded in driving Tregeagle from his work. The spirit fled round the lake hotly pursued by demons, then sprang shrieking across Dosmery Pool; sped over the moors, and, as they were about to overtake him, reached a chapel, the sanctity of which gave him temporary protection. Tregeagle is said still to be hunted over the Cornish moors by the Devil and his hell-hounds. Their baying and his yells for mercy disturb the night as he races across the heather, leaping over boulders just ahead of the pack.

3) *The Devil* In addition to all the folk-lore and legends in which the phantom dog is associated with disaster and death, there are many in which it is associated with evil. In this context when the dog-demon is specially diabolical it is said to be the Devil (a reputation it may perhaps have inherited from the wolf, for according to a twelfth-century bestiary, 'The Devil bears the similitude of a wolf . . . darkly prowling round sheep folds of the faithful so he may afflict and ruin their souls.')

HIS REACTION TO PIETY The Devil is often incited by concen-trated piety, as in the case of the church services at Bungay and Blyth-burgh, where, assuming dog form, he brought death to a number of parishioners. When St Stanislaus Kostka was preparing for admission into the Society of Jesus, the Devil is said to have appeared to him in the form of a terrifying black dog which thrice seized him by the throat trying to throttle him. He drove it away with the sign of the cross. From the Outer Hebrides comes the story of a priest's dog which lay on the hearth while its master heard confessions. One day it was suddenly unable to bear the pious atmosphere any longer and, springing up, it exclaimed: 'If you liked me before you never will again', and vanished in a shower of sparks. (In this case the dog was not specified as being the Devil, but its fieriness and its oversensitivity to piety reveal its identity.)

'HIS OWN' Many legends are based on the assumption that sin invites the Devil's appearance, and more often than not on these occasions he manifests himself in the form of a dog.

In northern Europe card-playing and dancing have been regarded as sinful. In card-playing—the 'Devil's own game'—the fourth at a table is commonly believed to be the Devil in human form; but in some accounts the Evil One is found under the table in the form of a black phantom dog. In North Germany it is told how, at a certain inn, peasants who played cards day and night disliked playing with the landlord, who repeatedly won, but dared not refuse him a game. One night one of the players dropped a card and, stooping to pick it up, he noticed a great black fiery-eyed dog sitting under the table at the landlord's feet. When the clock struck 1 a.m. a violent wind swept through the building and the satanic dog vanished. In Norway and Sweden the Devil is often seen among dancers in the form of a black phantom dog. The fiddle is the 'Devil's own instrument', and some say good fiddling can only be learnt from the Devil. A man who went to the Devil for such tutelage by the sea watched black dogs emerge from the water and dance as he played.

Reading books on black magic often invokes the Devil in the form of a large black dog, and so does cursing. In the Rhineland a woman who was in a wood with a five-year-old child started cursing it, saying: 'The Devil shall take you away.' A black dog immediately appeared, but she was able to rid them of it by calling on the power of the Holy Trinity. The Devil appears in dog form when married couples quarrel, and wherever there is lying, theft or cheating.

According to an Apocryphal gospel, Judas Iscariot was possessed by the Devil, and, after he had struck Jesus, Satan went out of the traitor in the form of a dog.

Not only does the dog-phantom accompany sinners, but it also plagues them. In London there is a public house adjoining Newgate Prison called 'The Black Dog', and the prison is said to be haunted by one. According to the original story, when England was gripped by famine in the thirteenth century many people in London starved to death and the prisoners in Newgate Prison were reduced to eating one another. One day, when a scholar was sent to jail on suspicion of conjuring—for it was said that 'by charms and devilish witchcraft he had done much hurt to the king's subjects'—the prisoners killed and ate him as 'passing good meate'. Shortly afterwards they began to hear strange cries and groans as of a creature in torment, and every night they saw the scholar in the shape of a black dog with ravening jaws, pacing up and down the prison ready to tear out their bowels. Driven to desperation, they killed the keeper and escaped, but wherever they went the black dog pursued them. In a seventeenth-century pamphlet entitled 'The Discovery of a London Monster called the Blacke Dogg of New-gate' (Plate 3b), the author explains that the black dog is a black conscience—'haunting none but blacke conditioned people'. This 'rugged curre', he says, abides in the 'bosom of Traytors, Murtherers, Thieves, Cut-purses, Cunny-catchers and the like', and he describes it as being:

> A Cerberus, nay worse, he thrice as wide did gape,
> His haires all snakes curling, they will not part.
> Cole-blacke his hew, like Torches glow his eyes,
> His breath doth poyson, smoke from's nostrils flyes,
> His foaming mouth still gaping for his prey.

It is said that this black dog walked the prison when the sessions were held, and the prison yard on nights of execution. When condemned criminals were taken to Tyburn to be hanged Newgate's black dog sat beside the driver of the cart.

On the other hand, the Devil also looks after 'his own'. In Poland he guards the property of wicked people. In Argentina, where it is commonly believed the owners of sugar mills are allies of the Devil, each mill is guarded by a fiery-eyed black dog-phantom which lies in the cellar all day and silently circles the building at night.

The Devil fetches his allies when their term of agreement has run out. A Frisian legend tells of a sea-captain who was a Freemason—and Freemasons were commonly believed to be in league with the Devil. On the high seas one day a black poodle appeared swimming towards the ship, and jumped on board despite the sailors' efforts to stop it. It went directly to the captain's cabin, where the sound of a great struggle was heard, and when they finally emerged the poodle chased the captain overboard and both disappeared in the waves.

The Devil often comes in the form of a black dog to the death-bed of 'his own', where he waits to receive their souls which are 'his due'. At such times it is possible for a clergyman to drive the Devil off. (A Danish legend tells how a wicked and cruel man was unable to die because of a black dog that lay in bed with him. When, however, a priest drove the Devil out of a window the man's soul was immediately released.)

In Scandinavia the Devil in dog form follows people who intend to commit suicide, and in Switzerland the black dog will appear at a dance where there is going to be a fight in which someone will be killed. A big black mastiff rushed past a Scottish farmer, who was strolling across his fields one Sunday morning, and entered a farmhouse where two brothers lived. The farmer followed it and as he arrived one brother shot the other dead.

Funerals of the Devil's allies are guarded by him in the shape of a black dog; he sits near the corpse or runs alongside the cortège, for although he cannot prevent a Christian burial he does his best to counteract its effect. In Germany it is said a black poodle is often seen on the graves of priests and clergymen who have not been true to their faith.

THEIR GHOSTS After death the Devil's allies often themselves become phantom dogs, and haunting in this form is regarded as God-inflicted punishment. Only people who have committed such heinous crimes as murder, suicide or blasphemy receive this fate. Blasphemers are liable to be struck down instantaneously, and their spirits condemned to eternal wandering in the shape of a dog. A Polish legend tells of a nobleman who was very cruel to his subjects, taking away their cattle which provided them with a livelihood. One night the wrath of God struck him by killing off all his cattle, and in a rage the nobleman shouted that whoever had killed the animals could eat them. No sooner were these blasphemous words out of his mouth than he was transformed into an ugly black dog and started devouring the carrion.

The English dog-demon that haunted Hergest Court in Herefordshire and appeared as a death warning to the Vaughan family was believed by some to be the ghost of Black Vaughan himself. Vaughan was apparently a very wicked man and after death was unable to rest. When asked by a parson why he was so fierce he replied: 'I was fierce when a man, much more so now a devil.' He inhabited a room at the top of the house which no one dared enter, and at night was heard clanking his chains.

In the British Isles some of these dog-phantoms have the additional punishment of impossible tasks to perform. In the seventeenth century Lady Howard of Devonshire, who was apparently a very beautiful, wealthy and talented woman, disposed of four husbands and treated her daughter with great cruelty. When she died her spirit was transformed into a dog which was condemned to spend every night running between her old residence and Oakhampton Park, carrying a single blade of grass in its mouth until every one had been removed from the park—a task unlikely to be fulfilled before Judgement Day.

In some parts of the West Country people believe that the souls of the wicked haunt pools and river beds in the form of phantom dogs, and their yelping is so dreadful that all who hear it go mad.

Although such ghosts are usually beyond redemption, there are exceptions to this rule. In Catholic countries, after receiving absolution from the Pope, or after a member of his family has made a special pilgrimage, a dog-spirit will occasionally regain human form. In Wales there was the case of a greyhound phantom, chained to the ground, that was asked by an Anglesey parson, who had been thrown from his horse by it, why it molested passers-by. The spirit replied that its unrest was due to having stolen, during its lifetime, a silver groat belonging to the parish church and hidden it under a stone. When the clergyman had found the groat and paid it over to the Church the greyhound was immediately released.

GUARDIAN OF TREASURE According to northern European tradition the Devil takes dog form when he is guarding buried treasure. The treasure is often secreted in a castle or a cave where it is guarded by a black phantom dog which scares off, and sometimes even kills, treasure-seekers.

From the Austrian Tyrol come legends of treasure hidden in the vaults of castles. Once two peasants were foolhardy enough to enter the underground passage of the ruined castle of Maultasch, where treasure lay. The Devil in the form of a huge black dog rushed upon them, and since they fled terrified no one has ever tried again to discover the treasure. Incalculable riches are said to be buried in the vaults of the castle of Sigmundsburg, guarded by a hairy black dog that has the appearance of a luminous mass. The key to the door of the treasure room is to be found in its mouth, but no one knows the conditions under which the treasure can be attained.

In the North of England a Tudor mansion, called Dobb Park Lodge, has a 'Dog Court' and is haunted by a talking phantom dog. According to local tradition, a doorway off the Dog Court is the entrance to a passage leading to a dungeon in which treasure lies. A local man once decided to risk exploring the recesses of the building and, having fortified himself with strong drink, disappeared down the passage. He rambled a long way through twisting corridors and was beginning to feel fatigued when sweet music struck up and so enchanted him that he lost all apprehension and all desire to turn back. Following the sound of music, he came to a room with a great fire blazing away and before the fire stood a black dog, the size of two or three mastiffs, which appeared to be master of the place. Opening its mouth, the dog spoke with a human voice and informed the man that if he wished ever to see daylight again he must perform one of three tasks, namely to drink all the liquor in a certain glass, to open a certain chest, or to draw a certain sword.

The man then saw a great chest bound with iron bands and huge locks, but he had no tools with him to open it. From a peg above him he noticed there hung a heavy broadsword, but he knew nothing of sword work and was afraid of cutting himself. On the chest stood a long-stemmed glass full of liquid so, feeling thirsty, he decided to try the drink. The dog-phantom glowered at the man with fiery eyes the size of pewter plates, and when he lifted the glass to his mouth the liquid scalded his lips and tongue. The moment he tasted it up flew the lid of the chest with a bang, revealing it to be crammed full of gold; and an invisible hand drew the sword, which glittered and flashed like lightning. The man then banged down the glass, spilling the liquid, and immediately all was pitch dark: the fire went out, the music ceased, and the place was filled by howling and yelling as if hundreds of dogs were being beaten. He fell flat on the floor in a swoon, and when he eventually came round, scrambled along the passages and dragged himself out. Since then no man has ventured into the vaults of Dobb Park Lodge, and the treasure remains intact, waiting for someone to brave the terrors of the talking dog.

In Normandy treasure-guarding dog-phantoms bury their teeth in the flanks of the horses of any riders who stray near their treasures after nightfall, and they do not release their hold until the morning.

Occasionally the Devil's part is played by a wicked man, as in the case of a German usurer who was much feared because of his enormous wealth and avarice. He was believed to have acquired all the gold and silver in return for handing over his soul to the Devil. One day, during a terrible thunderstorm, the usurer was killed by lightning and his home was buried in the depths of the earth. His ghost haunted the spot and he is still to be found, once every twenty-five years, in the form of a big black dog sitting on his coffer of money. It is said that anyone who strikes the dog at the right moment with a blest rosary will both redeem the usurer and receive all his money.

Another means of counteracting the power of the black dog treasure-guard is revealed in a story of treasure buried in the locality of Baden. A local woman decided to lift this treasure one night. So, first praying, she went into the forest with her two sons, arriving at the site as the clock struck twelve. The boys worked hard with pick and shovel until they unearthed an iron box, but a big black dog with fiery eyes immediately appeared and sat on it, growling. When, however, the mother picked up a stick, made the sign of the cross over it and struck at the dog, it promptly vanished and they opened the box to find it full of silver coins.

In Denmark the treasure is believed to belong to trolls—those dwarfs who live underground and in the hills. A legend is told of the treasure of a troll-smith who had a workshop in a large mound in the parish of Buur. (Anyone who wanted a piece of iron forged used to lay it on the mound at night together with a silver skilling, and return next morning to find the money had disappeared and the work was completed.) One night the people of Buur determined to dig up the troll's treasure, and they assembled for this purpose with spades and pick-axes. They dug in silence until they came to a spacious stone chamber, and there lay the treasure before them in the form of a large copper kettle full of gold coins. Beside the kettle an enormous black dog lay asleep, so one of the men took off his coat and, picking up the dog, laid it gently on it. But, unfortunately, as they were about to remove the treasure they broke the strict rule of silence, and consequently were all immediately projected some distance away. So the mound closed up behind the people of Buur and the troll's treasure remains buried.

Sometimes, however, silence is maintained and the dog allows the treasure to be removed. In a Danish valley called Lodal a light was seen burning brightly every night, and it was revealed in a dream to a Holsteiner that treasure was to be found at the spot where the light burned. So the dreamer made his way to Lodal and, after digging for some time, found a large copper kettle full of gold. But on top of the gold lay a large black poodle with a ring round its neck, so the Holsteiner carefully lifted the dog off the kettle and laid it on his over-coat. He then took the treasure, distributed some of it to peasants who had helped him, and departed. The light, it was said, ceased to burn in Lodal, and the black dog was sometimes seen running about the valley.

In Hans Andersen's fairy tale of the 'Tinder Box' treasure was guarded by demonic dogs. The soldier who descended into the hollow of a tree to obtain the tinder box found in the first chamber a chest on which was seated a large black dog with eyes the size of saucers. This he was able to remove by spreading on the floor a magic apron given to him by the witch, and placing the dog on it he then opened the chest to find it full of copper coins, and helped himself to them.

In the next room there was a chest surmounted by a large black dog with eyes the size of dinner plates, and the soldier removed the creature the same way, thus securing the contents of the chest, which were silver coins. When, in the third chamber, he found a black dog with eyes the size of mill wheels guarding a chest of gold coins—he dealt with it as before and returned to the surface heavily loaded with treasure. After this whenever he lit the tinder the phantom dogs appeared and they carried out his every wish.

In some legends the dog-guard not only allowed the treasure to be taken but anxiously awaited the unearthing as the only means by which it could be released from the haunting to which it was con-demned. There are many variants of the German fairy story, 'Schlangenjungfrau', and in most of these it was an enchanted maiden that awaited release by the raising of treasure which was guarded by a black phantom dog. Typical is one from Lower Saxony in which a young man appeared at a castle haunted by a beautiful maiden dressed in white, who walked with a bunch of keys hanging from her waist. She gave him the keys and begged him to redeem her by taking the seventh one, opening the doors of the castle with it, and taking the coins he found there, for she could have no peace or rest so long as the treasure remained undiscovered. She warned him not to be alarmed by what he would find lying beside the treasure, and above all not to speak. When the young man found a large black dog lying by the money, looking as if it was going to bite him, he became terrified and called out. The money immediately disappeared and so did the dog, who was the Devil; and the maiden cried in despair: 'Now for a hundred years no one will be able to redeem me.' In a Swiss version the maiden waited in a dark passage under a castle with a set of golden skittles at her feet guarded by a big black dog. She could be redeemed by receiving three kisses from a young man, but the dog would allow only pure young men to approach. Spirits can be released from enchantment by blows as well as by kisses, and there are versions in which, to release the maiden, the man must strike the black dog-guard. In one case the black dog is the form taken by the maiden herself, and the hero has the choice of either kissing the dog or striking it three times on the head.

There are also legends in which the phantom dog leads the way to hidden treasure. Just outside Lyme Regis in England there is an old Dorset farm-house with a huge fireplace and wooden seats either side of the chimney. It is said that, many years ago, when the farmer settled himself in one of the chimney seats every evening a large black dog-phantom took possession of the other. When neighbours told the farmer he should drive the demon away he insisted that it did not interfere with him in any way, but, in fact, it oppressed him greatly and cast a gloom over his life. One night, inflamed by taunts and having had a few extra drinks, the farmer returned home to find the black dog in its usual seat, so he seized a poker and rushed straight at it. The phantom sprang from its seat and fled upstairs into the attic and, panting after it, the farmer arrived just in time to see it disappear through the ceiling. When he struck the boards through which the dog had passed with a poker, a small box fell down which was full of gold and silver coins. From then on the dog ceased to trouble the farmer, but has ever since haunted the lane leading to the farm-house. (A small inn near by displays the sign of 'The Black Dog', and the lane is now known as 'Dog Lane'.)

In this case the black dog inadvertently led a man to hidden treasure, but in some stories the help is more direct and intentional. There are black dog-phantoms in Normandy, for instance, which, if given food and drink, will lead their benefactor to a spot where treasure is buried, and stand on guard until it has been raised.

From Japan comes a popular legend which tells of an old couple who had a dog called Shiro. One day Shiro sniffed and barked at a spot in the garden with such insistence that the old man dug the earth there and found a number of coins. Envious neighbours tried to persuade Shiro to lead them to wealth, but, finding only filth where he sniffed, they killed him and buried him under the root of a pine tree. His owners were very distressed, and during the night Shiro's ghost appeared to the old man telling him to cut down the tree and make a rice mortar of its trunk. This he did, and found the rice mortar was endowed with the property of turning each grain of rice into a gold coin.

La Fontaine describes a dog that actually produced treasure, for his story 'The Little Dog' tells of a spaniel that secreted riches in its paw. It fulfilled the wishes of whoever it served, and when its paw was squeezed, gold, diamonds, pearls and ducats were scattered over the ground. According to this story there was once a beautiful woman called Argia who was married to an old Mantuan judge. During his absence from home a handsome youth called Atis fell in love with Argia, and 'grudged no pains could he possess her charm'. A fairy, who appeared to Atis promising to help him with this beautiful woman, transformed herself into the little dog. So Atis disguised himself as a pilgrim travelling with bagpipes and a spaniel, and the little dog did everything it could to delight Argia, dancing before her and fawning on her. Argia was very taken with the dog and offered to pay any price for it, but the pilgrim refused, because it was not her money that he wanted. However, he promised:

> If she'll a night permit me in her bed,
> The treasure shall at once to her be led.

At first Argia was outraged at such a suggestion coming from a 'paltry pilgrim', but after the dog had scattered pearls among the servants, who immediately strung them, and the pilgrim had 'gallantly fastened them around her arms', Argia bought the dog and bestowed on the pilgrim a kiss (Plate 3d) 'as earnest of the promised future bliss'. When night arrived Atis became himself again, and when Argia, lying in his arms, discovered who the pilgrim really was, 'she scarcely could her joy contain'; and the treasure-secreting dog served her well for the rest of her life.

In popular tales such as these the dogs are no longer demonic, but like the Devil dogs they have supernatural powers and are treasure-orientated.

WORSHIP   A famous sixteenth-century theologian writes of the Devil as 'barking after the manner of a dogge', and many references have been made to worship of the Devil in his dog form in Europe during the Middle Ages.

In Scotland, we are told, Highland witches were seen holding their sabbath meetings on a pool enveloped with flames. Hundreds of these hags used brooms to steer themselves to and fro in their riddles and each held a torch of blazing fir in her left hand. Shrieking and yelling, the witches swirled themselves into a row from which they made profound obeisance to a 'large black ugly tyke' perched on a lofty rock. The Devil graciously acknowledged these expressions of their devotion by 'bowing, grinning and clapping his paws'.

A young Frenchman who wanted to attend a sabbat meeting described the Devil as a large black dog with long curly hair, eyes glowing like live coals, and great pointed fangs. He prowled round the meeting-place of the witches, guarding it so that the young man was unable to enter.

According to a seventeenth-century record, a Guernsey woman who wanted to renounce the Catholic faith went to a castle where sabbats were known to be held. The Devil met her in the form of a horned dog and, taking her hand in his paw, called her by name and welcomed her to the meeting. Then, standing on his hind legs, he made her kneel down to denounce her former faith and worship him.

The initiation of a male witch has been described in an early account of a sabbat meeting. The Devil marks him, 'in the brow, neck or shoulder, but commonly in the more secret parts', with the stamp of 'the foot of a blacke Dog'. Thus branded, the witch becomes the Devil's slave and vassal for life.

Freemasons were, as we know, commonly believed to have sold their souls to the Devil, and he was said to be present at their meetings in the form of a black poodle to which they paid homage by kissing its posterior.

From confessions made by witches during the seventeenth-century trials it appears that the Devil frequently visited them in the form of a dog.

In 1566, Agnes Waterhouse, of Hatfield Peveril, confessed to having called on Satan, who then came to her as a black dog to ask what she wanted. She told him she wished to frighten a child that annoyed her and offered him a red cock by way of payment. The

Devil, however, replied that this was not enough and he must have her body and soul; so she consented and he went off to frighten the child. According to a confession by a Lancashire witch, Anne Whittle, the Devil came to her in the form of a spotted bitch promising her gold, silver, worldly wealth and the power to hurt people if she became his subject and allowed him to suck upon her body. A woman known as 'Old Demdike', who had been a witch for fifty years, confessed to suckling the Devil, and she described how this had first started. She was sitting, she said, snoozing with a child on her knee one Sabbath morning when the Devil came to her in the shape of a brown dog and forced himself on to her knee to drink blood from under her left arm. She was only wearing a smock, so he succeeded and, although she called out 'Jesus save my child', she was unable to pray for her own soul to be saved, because she had already given it to the Devil. The famous witch of Edmonton suckled the Devil in the form of a black-and-white dog. She explained that he first visited her in this form when he came to seek a contract with her blood, bringing her the power to blight the countryside and take revenge on her enemies. It was said 'the Devill leaveth marks upon their body and these the Devill makes to be insensible, and being pricked will not bleed'.

One of the most famous of all sorcerers to whom the Devil appeared in dog form was Faust, for, according to Goethe, Mephistopheles took the shape of a black poodle. The behaviour of this poodle was consistent throughout the play with that of the demonic dog of oral tradition. Faust and Wagner first became aware of it when they were walking in the cornfield on Easter Day, and it scampered round them in diminishing circles, leaving a fiery track behind it. In Faust's study it took up its position on the hearth behind the stove, and, unable to tolerate piety, constantly interrupted Faust as he translated the Bible. When the magician tried to rid himself of the distracting poodle it revealed its demonic nature by greatly increasing in size. Recognizing the Devil in dog form, Faust exclaimed:

> In length and breadth how doth my poodle grow; (Plate 3e)
> With bristling hair now doth the creature swell
> Huge as a hippopotamus,
> With fiery eye, terrific tooth,
> Ah! now I know thee, sure enough.

Although, as often, the poodle shifted its shape to human form, Faust addressed Mephistopheles: 'Hound! Execrable Monster', and bade him:

> Cease thus to gnash
> Thy ravenous fangs at me! I loathe thee.

One of the occult powers received by witches and sorcerers from the Devil was the ability to transform themselves into animals, and there were reports from all over Europe of witches taking the shape of dogs. It was said of a witch tried at Salisbury and sent to the gallows in 1653: 'She could transform herself into the shape of a Mastive Dog', and old crones often displayed wounds they claimed to have received while in the likeness of dogs. Typical is an account coming from Prussia of strange noises heard in the house of a family of Freemasons, and black dogs seen in their granary. One day when a maid milking a cow was molested by a black dog she picked up the stool and hit it until it went away. The next day the master of the family was seen with a head wound, and he told the maid: 'Do not do such things again or something bad will happen to you.' In France, near Niort, a farmer, seeing from an upstairs window a strange black-and-white greyhound molesting his dogs one night, shot at it. Next morning he went out to examine the corpse in the yard, and finding the body was that of a beautiful bejewelled woman, realized that he had unknowingly killed a witch.

FAMILIAR SPIRITS When a woman first made a compact with the Devil he gave her a demon in the shape of a small animal to wait on her, advise her and carry out her malicious errands. As a reward, for constant attendance, the witch allowed her familiar to suck her blood, thus renewing its strength and creating a close bond between them. All imps craved human blood and witches fed them from their fingers, or more often from teats on their bodies (which formed prima facie evidence of witchcraft). These creatures were quite distinct from the Devil, or the witch, in animal form; for familiars were spirits that witches sent out as animals, while themselves retaining the shape of human beings. Many references have been made to the dog-familiars employed by witches. A witch called 'Ludlam', who lived in a cave near Farnham in Surrey, had a dog-familiar, and the proverbial saying 'Lazy as Ludlam's dog' arose from the reputation it acquired of never bothering to bark when anyone approached the cave. The status of dog-demons was apparently higher than that of cat-demons, for some say that, whereas the cat-familiar remained an inmate of the witch's house at all times, the dog-familiar only appeared on special occasions—usually at crises of the witch's career.

During their trials witches confessed to various different types of dog-familiars. One had 'a spirit like a black dog, named Suckin'; another, 'a spirit of white colour in seeming like to a little rugged dog'; and a third, 'a brown dog which she called 'Ball' '. Best known of all dog-familiars were those of Elizabeth Clark, a seventeenth-century witch, who confessed to having had carnal connexion with the Devil three times a week for seven years. The familiars she suckled were Jarmara, a white spotted dog, short-legged like a spaniel (she said she kept him fat by suckling good blood from her belly); and Vinegar Tom, a long-legged greyhound with a head like an ox (Plate 3f). Alison Device confessed to allowing a black dog-familiar to suck at a spot below her left breast, for which favour it lamed for life a pedlar who had annoyed her by refusing to sell her pins. Her brother, James Device, confessed to being responsible for the death of four people by willing Dandy, his dog-familiar, to kill them.

In the Congo people in a primitive stage of culture have used and probably still use—dog-magic. A nail-fetish in the form of a double-headed dog was believed to have magical power focused in the great mound on its back—its 'medicine'—which consisted of parts of plants and of animals cemented together. This was not strictly speaking a dog-familiar, but it was inhabited by a spirit which, when nails were driven into it as offerings, would go out and attack its owner's enemies.

In seventeenth-century China dog-familiars were used by sorcerers in much the same way as in Europe. These instruments of revenge, which were known as '*inu-gami*' (dog-gods), were terrible weapons in the hands of wicked people, for they inflicted sickness, madness and even death. If a man who owned a dog-god hated someone, he would send his familiar to possess that person so that the victim immediately became ill, mad, or died. (If, however, he carried a fox-tooth in his pocket, the dog-god could not possess him.) If a dog-god owner coveted the possessions of another, he used dog-sorcery—that is, he sent his familiar to possess the owner of the envied object until he was prepared to give it up, upon which the dog-god was withdrawn and he recovered.

One early work describes how a dog-god was obtained. A 'solid' dog was loosely tied with a rope to a pillar, and a vessel with food was placed so that it could only just reach it with the tip of its nose. When the dog had died of hunger its soul was worshipped, and, since the power of the dog-god was equivalent to the intensity of the live dog's hunger, its head would be cut off at the moment when its desire for food was keenest. An old Chinese woman buried her pet dog, leaving only its head above ground, then, cutting it about with a bamboo saw, said: 'If thou hast a soul kill so-and-so and I will make thee a god.' The person she wanted to eradicate died, and from then on the dog-god dwelt in her house and wrought, we are told, many wonderful curses.

Dog-gods were handed down through the generations within a family, and descendants could not disown them even if they wanted to. Employers of dog-gods did not mix with, or marry, others. In the province of Awa all female members of a family in which a dog-god had been passed down were called *'inu-gami'*. They were all poor, and were disliked because they were believed to extort food from others by means of their dog-gods, and also because they were often attacked by a form of madness known as 'dog's curse'. At temple festivals these women often fell into ecstatic trances, dancing wildly and beating people out of their way with supernatural force. If a priest read sutras on their behalf, the *'inu-gami'* danced incessantly, spoke gibberish and fell on the ground, but it was virtually impossible to drive the dog-gods out of them. In the province of Shikoku, where each village had several dog-god owners, they were shunned by their neighbours; and the first inquiry matchmakers always made was whether any relatives were dog-god owners, for no villager married into such families. These families are gradually dying out, but since no one dares pull down the old houses they occupied they are still to be found all over the place.

Dog-familiars have been employed (or are believed to have been employed) by some famous people. Simon Magnus, the sorcerer of the Apocrypha, sent to Peter the Apostle 'certaine devils in the likenes of dogges to devoure him'. These dog-devils were put to flight by pieces of consecrated bread thrown at them by the Apostle. On another occasion Simon Magnus tied up a great black dog with instructions to strangle Peter when he arrived, but when the Apostle made the sign of the cross over it the dog-devil became meek and tame.

Faust, as portrayed in sixteenth-century chapbooks, had a dog-familiar, which was shown on murals sometimes as black and sometimes white. According to the *Faustbuch* tradition, Faust was a magician who had made a pact with the Devil, as a result of which all earthly pleasures were bestowed on him for many years. His dog was a helpful spirit that waited on him, and possessed the power of prophecy. It was said that doors magically opened before this dog as it approached them, and Faust used it to demonstrate his occult powers, as when, for instance, he changed the colour of its coat by running his hand over its back. The scholar, Agrippa, had a black dog-familiar, called 'Monsieur', in constant attendance on him, which wore a collar decorated with magic characters from which, it was said, he derived all his knowledge. (Some maintain the dog had a devil tied to its collar.) When Agrippa lay dying he removed the collar from his dog's neck with the words: 'Depart, unhappy beast, the cause of eternal damnation'—at which Monsieur fled and drowned himself in the Saone.

The dog-familiar that received the most publicity was probably Prince Rupert's white poodle. When the Prince was imprisoned at Linz, Lord Arundel gave him a dog which he named 'Boye', and after his release he brought the poodle with him to England to take part in the Civil War. He became very attached to this dog and it is recorded that when in council Prince Rupert had Boye sitting on the table by him and that he often turned to kiss the dog during a debate. King Charles fell victim to the poodle's charms, allowing him to sit in his chair and to play with his children, and he continually fed him at mealtimes. When Boye went to church he was reported to have conducted himself 'most popishly and cathedrally'. After Royalist victories Prince Rupert and his officers sat up all night drinking the health of Boye, whom they believed brought them good luck. The Puritans, who saw the white poodle bounding beside the Prince as he rode at the head of his army, always escaping death, were convinced that Boye was his familiar spirit, and pamphlets were written on the dog's supernatural powers.

Prince Rupert's dog was pronounced by them to be 'a divell', once a 'handsome white ladye now a handsome white dogge'; and they tried to destroy him 'by poyson and extempore prayer'.

In a pamphlet published in London, 1643, and entitled: 'A Dialogue or Rather a Parley between Prince Rupert's Dogge whose name is Puddle and Tobies Dog whose name is Pepper', Boye converts a

Roundhead dog to Royalist views. Puddle calls the Roundhead 'a foolish snarling cur', 'a rebellious dog, and wilt barke against the king'. Pepper called Prince Rupert's dog 'no better than a witch in the shape of a white Dogge', 'a Popish profane Dog, more than halfe a divell, a kind of spirit', and declared Boye was 'whelped in Lap-land or else in Fin-land where there is none but divells and sorcerers live'. Pepper accuses him further that 'at Edghill you walked invisible and directed the bullets who they should hit, and who they should misse, and made your Mr Prince Rupert shott-free, and it is known that you would rather heare Masse at Oxford, than come to our private prayers or conscionable sermons'. In another pamphlet of the same date Puddle was addressed: 'I hear thou art impenetrable and likewise besmeared over with inchanted oyle, so that no weapon, bullet, nor sword can enter thee to make thee bleed.'

The poodle was eventually killed at Marston Moor, where he followed Prince Rupert into the hottest part of the fight and fell on the field. After this Royalist fortunes ebbed and Prince Rupert's luck began to fail him. The death of the 'accursed cur' caused great rejoicing in the Roundhead camp, and Puritan poets broke out into verse. The best-known work is probably 'A Dog's Elegy, or Rupert's Tears', which was published in London on July 27th, 1644. The title-page shows an engraving depicting the death of Boye at Marston Moor (Plate 3c), the caption reading: 'where his beloved Dog, named Boy, was killed by a valiant souldier who had skill in Necromancy.' It begins:

> Lament poor Cavaliers, cry, howl and yelp
> For the great losse of your Malignant Whelp.

It claims that Boye, with all his 'Tricks and Feats', was whelped of a 'Malignant Water-witch', and that within two years the poodle

> Excelled his Mother in her Witcherie,
> And in his black and gloomy Arts so skill'd
> That he even Hell in his subjection held.

It describes Boye's master as the

> Prince of Robbers, Duke of Plunderland,

who was determined

> To kill, burne, steele, ravish, nay anything,
> And in the end to make himself a King.

This pamphlet also includes the following invitation:

> Sad cavaliers Rupert invites you all
> That doe survive, to his Dog's Funerall,
> Close mourners are the witch, Pope, and Devill,
> That much lament your late befallen evill.

4) *Man's confrontation with phantom dogs* So the nature of man's experience when he confronts the dog in its two-dimensional form is determined partly by the type of phantom it is and partly by his attitude towards it.

When the dog he perceives is a 'personal' ghost, provided he is not alarmed by the presence of psychic phenomena, the experience will be either an indifferent, or a pleasurable, one.

If the dog-ghost is attached to a family or their residence it will probably be an omen of death. These ghosts are easily confused with three-dimensional dogs, and experience of them is not unpleasant in itself—the shock and anxiety coming only with realization of their significance.

Phantom dogs that haunt certain sites may be comparatively innocuous 'spirits of place'; evil spirits that are in some way associated with the area, or—most impersonal of all—the Devil himself who could be anywhere, but happens to be there. Experience of them, therefore, varies from being mildly disconcerting to unspeakably horrific, and while some are omens of death others appear to be actual spirits of death.

The dog that guards treasure may be the ghost of an actual dog, a fairy, an enchanted maiden or man waiting to be released, but most likely will be the Devil. So, although the treasure-seeker may be guided by a phantom-dog to where treasure is buried, or may find a dog protecting it in only a half-hearted way, the chances are his experience will be of the incarnation of all evil.

Confrontation with a pack of spectral dogs may be with the souls of wicked people or of avenging demons hounding them; with the souls of unbaptized children or of demons hunting them, or with hell-hounds leading the dead to the inferno. The huntsman may be a wicked man who is allowed to hunt for ever as a reward for selling his soul to the Devil, or is condemned as punishment to hunt until Dooms-day; or he may be the Angel of Death, God of the Dead, or the Devil. The experience is always frightening, because it constitutes a warning of impending death. There may also be the minor annoyances of torn linen, devoured food, and a whining hound on the hearth, or the major disaster of being carried away by the hunt or torn to shreds by the pack.

The blackness and whiteness of phantom dogs does not necessarily indicate the nature of their intentions, for, as has been shown, both coloured dogs can be innocuous or malign. It is significant that, in Suffolk, Shuck was described as being black, even though never seen, and that in many parts of England it is said that the only visible hounds of the Wild Hunt are those single ones left behind on the ground.

Many dog-phantoms are not seen at all, but only felt or heard. When the noise made by spectral dogs is specially emphasized in accounts given by people who have experienced them it often appears vital that they should not be seen, for those who hear them are warned to shut their eyes if they want to survive.

This account of the nature of man's confrontation with dog-demons applies in cases where his soul is still his own and consequently the Devil constitutes for him a horrifying threat. But for those who are in league with the Devil, experience of him in dog form is quite different. The potential witch may be frightened by the first approach of the satanic dog, but once she hears what it has to offer she shows little hesitation in handing over her body and soul. Since every sin invokes the Devil, he is her frequent companion, and her experience of the demonic dog is, on the whole, most desirable and satisfying. Although the Devil's demands on her are considerable, there is little evidence that she finds them excessive.

So much for two-dimensional dogs that appear to human beings at twilight. They seem to vary as much in type, behaviour and in their relationship with man as do those more solid creatures of daylight reality.

MYTHICAL DOGS

If we now delve even deeper, moving from twilight—*entre chien et loup* —to an area of total darkness, we find ourselves confronted by images of dogs that have no external reality, but whose appearance, nature and activities are described in myths. These creatures are naturally two-dimensional and belong to the Underworld, but at times three-dimensional dogs appearing in broad daylight have been believed to be incarnations of canine gods or spirits.

5a Egyptian priest worshipping the dog (p. 109)

5c Bhairava, with his dog-vehicle (p. 114

5b Hermanubis, the Alexandrian dog-goc
(p. 111)

5d Holy dog of Parsi funeral rites (p. 125) 5e Dogs licking the sores of Lazarus (p. 136)

5f Buddhist lion-dogs (p. 118)

5g Pekes of The Imperial Palace (p. 130)

1) *The Hell-hound* The most famous and the most terrifying of all mythical dogs is undoubtedly the Hell-hound, for the Hound of Hell is that great ferocious devourer whose chops are, for men, the 'jaws of death'.

ITS ANCESTRY Hell-hound myths probably spring from the dog's lupine ancestry. In Norse mythology the 'jaws of death' are those of Fenris—a cosmic wolf, son of Loki the Devil. The gods chained and fettered Fenris, fastening him to a lofty crag where they left him until the end of the world. At the hour of doom, when chains snapped and the wolf broke loose, he led the forces of evil and destruction against the gods. It has been described how Fenris galloped towards them with flames issuing from his eyes and nostrils; with his ravenous jaws agape, his upper fangs scraping heaven and his lower raking the earth. At the final battle, it is said, the World Tree trembled as Odin came to grips with Fenris, and after a fierce combat the king of the gods was struck down in all his splendour and devoured by the avenging wolf. A milder version of this incident is found in a myth telling how, at the twilight of the gods, the offspring of Fenris—two wolves known as Skoll and Hati—swallowed the sun and the moon.

On the other hand, Hell-hound myths may also owe something to the mythical jackal. In ancient Egypt, where this animal nightly prowled among the tombs, the god of the dead was Anubis, the jackal, and, although this deity is not particularly ferocious, he is closely associated with decay and decomposition.

THE DEVOURER In ancient Greek mythology Cerberus is the Hound of Hell. This monstrous dog has been described by some as having three heads, and by others as having fifty. He has a mane of serpents' heads, a dragon's tail, and was said to be 'bronze-voiced'. He is an offspring of Typhon, god of evil, and lies chained to the gates of Hades, where he voraciously devours both intruders from the outside world and anyone trying to escape from the Underworld. (Hecate, goddess of death and queen of Hades, was also portrayed as triple-headed, and was often referred to as 'The Bitch'.)

In Hindu mythology Yama, god of the dead, sometimes assumes canine form, and he has two insatiable dogs called Çyama and Çabala —the offspring of the goddess, Saramâ, who was known as 'The four-eyed Bitch'. These two Hell-hounds are described as having four eyes each and huge wide nostrils, and as being fierce, very strong and long-winded. Çyama, who is the moon-dog of the night, is black, while Çabala, the sun-dog of day-time, is spotted or brindled. According to those sacred writings, the Vedas, day and night destroy the lives of men: they are encircling arms of death, and Çyama and Çabala are, therefore, death-hounds.

There is a famous Buddhist story which tells how Sakka, King of the gods, observing the suffering of men and the decay of Buddhism, decided to terrify mankind in order to restore religion. So the god disguised himself as a hunter, and transformed his charioteer into a huge black hound 'having tusks as big as of a woman ready to be delivered of a child'. He fastened the vast dog with a fivefold chain and, placing a red wreath on it, led it into the city. As Sakka shouted: 'The world is doomed to destruction', people scattered in all directions taking refuge behind locked doors. When the black hound had cleared the streets, it searched out the royal palace and, putting its paws in a window it 'roared a great roar', the sound of which reached from hell to heaven. The terrified king asked: 'Ho, huntsman why did your hound roar?' Told it was because it was hungry, the king fed it with his own food and that of the whole household. But the hound made one mouthful of the lot and then roared again. It was not until the creature had devoured all the city's food and roared again that the king realized it was a supernatural being, and it was explained to him that the black hound came not to hunt game but to punish the enemies of the god. These included false brethren, usurers, adulterers, robbers, and those who neglected aged parents. 'When brahmins, skilled in sacred books and holy rites, shall use their skill to sacrifice for pelf, the Black Hound shall go loose'—threatened the Hunter. 'When men with hearts of evil full, false and deceitful men, walk in and out the world about, I'll loose the Black Hound then.' When he saw that the multitude were terror-struck, Sakka threw off his disguise as a hunter, and rose blazing in the air. And thus it was that by declaring the Law, and warning the people to be vigilant, he strengthened the waning power of religion so that it lasted another thousand years. (Buddha is said to have told this story, and in doing so he explained that at the time he was Sakka.)

In Celtic mythology Arawn, King of Annwn, the Underworld, has a hound, but not much is known about it.

THE AVENGING PACK OF THE KING OF HELL In addition to the single Hounds of Hell with their numerous eyes and heads, there are also packs of death-hounds belonging to the kings of the Underworld. Celtic mythology describes the experience of Pwyll, a Welsh prince, who met King Arawn with his pack when out hunting one day. Pwyll ruled over Dyfed (a county which included the whole of what is now Pembrokeshire and most of Carmarthen), at the centre of which was said to be 'The Dark Gate'—an entrance to the Underworld. One morning the prince set out on a hunt, unleashing his hounds and blowing his horn. As he followed his pack he suddenly heard the baying of hounds different from his own and coming from the opposite direction. Pwyll arrived at a glade to see a stag start up, and he watched hounds from the other pack overtake it and bring it down. These hounds had luminous white coats and glistening red ears, and the prince was driving them off and setting his own on the stag when the huntsman came up mounted on a pale horse. He revealed himself to be Arawn, and Pwyll then descended into the Underworld, where he replaced the king, reigning there for a year.

In British mythology Gwynn ab Nudd was the god of the Underworld, and had a pack of hounds with which he hunted the souls of the dying. The most formidable of his hounds was one called '*Dor-Marth*' —'The Gate of Sorrow' or 'Door of Annwn' (and in south Cardiganshire death is still referred to as 'The Gap, or Pass, of the Dog's mouth'—that is, the 'jaws of death').

When a pagan religion was suppressed by Christianity, Christians often relegated the king of its sky-gods to be ruler of the Underworld. Hence Odin (or Woden), king of the Norse gods, appears as the Wild Huntsman whose pack of hounds hunts the souls of the doomed, while in France, it will be recalled, it was the Devil who, as the Wild Huntsman, led the hunt with his death-hounds.

THE AVENGING PACK OF THE QUEEN OF HELL In Greek mythology Hecate, Queen of Hell, was known as 'Our Lady of the Hounds' and 'She who rejoices in the barking of dogs', for every night this death-goddess led a swarm of ghosts through the Underworld, accompanied by demonic barking dogs.

As vehicles of the Terrible Mother-goddess, Hecate's pack of hounds were avengers. (Her companions, the Furies or Erinyes— those revengeful spirits who hounded Orestes for the sin of matricide —were dog-headed and serpent-maned, and their approach was heralded by barking.) The well-known myth of Actaeon tells how Artemis, the virgin goddess of the hunt, was bathing in a stream one day when a young huntsman, Actaeon, accidentally beheld her naked. She promptly transformed him into a stag and tore him to pieces with his own pack of hounds. Although this story is told of Artemis, the hounds were undoubtedly those of the Terrible Death-goddess, for Artemis was a much earlier deity than Hecate and in the more archaic myths she plays a dual role.

The name of 'Hecuba', who was wife of Priam, King of Troy, is thought to have been an alternative form of 'Hecate'. When Troy was captured by the Greeks the hero Odysseus won Hecuba and carried her off as a slave, but apparently she uttered such hideous invectives against the Greeks that they had no alternative but to kill her. Her spirit, it is said, took the form of one of Hecate's fearful black bitches, and leapt straight into the sea. The place of the burial of Hecuba came to be known as 'The Bitch's Tomb'. (According to another version of this myth, Hecuba assassinated the King of Thrace in revenge for the murder of her son. When pursued by an angry mob towards the stormy waters of the Hellespont, 'attempting to speak out, her jaws just ready for the words, she barked', and 'in the semblance of a dog, leapt the cliffs to be engulfed in the depths'. The city of Cynomessa was built in her honour and a monument engraved with the words 'The Tomb of an Unhappy Dog' became a landmark for lost sailors.)

HECATE'S CANINE OFFSPRING   The Empusae—filthy demons whose habit was to frighten travellers—were children of Hecate who often took the form of bitches.

Scylla, Hecate's daughter, was often known as 'The Sea-Bitch', and the name 'Scylla' means 'puppy' or 'she who rends'. According to one myth, Poseidon, god of the sea, fell in love with Scylla, and his wife filled her womb with puppies out of jealousy. Another myth states that the same jealous goddess changed her into a canine monster with six heads and twelve feet, that whimpered like a newborn puppy and barked like a young bitch. According to a third account, barking dogs appeared in her groin (Plate 4c), as the result of washing in a fountain the waters of which had been corrupted by the enchantress, Circe. Scylla is often depicted as a beautiful woman to the waist, below the waist as a dog, and below the hips as a fish. She dwelt in a cave under a rock, from which she would seize sailors, crack their bones and slowly swallow them. When, during his wanderings, the hero Odysseus steered too near to Scylla (in order to avoid the whirlpool Charybdis), she snatched six sailors off the deck, one in each mouth, whisking them away to rocks where she devoured them at her leisure. (An ancient Greek vase shows, on one side, Poseidon's wife standing by a pool which is occupied by a dog-headed monster, on the other side, a drowned hero caught between two dog-headed triads of goddesses at the entrance to the Underworld.)

2) *The Guard* The Hell-hound is not only a devourer but also a janitor whose duty it is to guard the entrance to the Underworld.

OF THE ENTRANCE TO THE NORSE, GREEK AND HINDU SPIRIT-WORLD In Norse mythology a great wolf-dog, called Garm, with a bloody chest was chained at the entrance to the infernal regions until the end of the world. On the day of doom, when the watchdog broke free, the way out of hell gaped wide open.

Cerberus, as controller of the exits and entrances of the Greek Underworld, was perhaps the greatest of all watchdogs. When people died their ghosts descending to the Underworld had first to be ferried across the Styx, river of death, and then to contend with Cerberus the Guard. (They had usually been provided with a coin for the ferryman and with honey cakes to use as a sop to Cerberus.) The poet, Orpheus, was one of the few live heroes successful in evading the Hell-hound, for when he set out to rescue Eurydice, his wife, from the Underworld, although he was greeted by fierce growls at the portals of Hades, Cerberus was so charmed by his music that he was able to make his descent. Theseus and Peirithous, two other Greek heroes who descended into Hades, appeared to have successfully avoided Cerberus by making their way down through a back entrance. But when the King of the Underworld heard their outrageous request, which was to give his wife, Persephone, to Peirithous as a bride, he offered them a seat on the Chair of Forgetfulness, and as they languished there for years unable to rise they were continually mauled by the Hell-hound.

In Hindu mythology the sun- and moon-dogs of Yama (whelps of Saramâ, the watchdog of Indra, king of the gods) guarded the gates of the kingdom of the dead by day and by night. These fierce guardians were said to 'watch the road observing men', and a Vedic hymn prays for a departed soul—'that he may be able to pass safely beyond the two dogs, sons of Saramâ, having four eyes, spotted, who occupy the right path'.

OF THE ENTRANCE TO THE SPIRIT-WORLD OF OTHER ANCIENT CIVILIZATIONS It will be recalled that in British mythology Gwynn's devouring hound was called '*Dor-Marth*' and, since the first part of the word meant 'Door' or 'Gate', this dog presumably was also a janitor. In the Avesta—the sacred book of the ancient Persians—reference is made to a yellow-eared dog that guards the rainbow-bridge which spans the gloomy depths between this world and the next, and with its barking drives the Fiend away from the souls of the righteous ones. According to Aztec mythology, souls of the dead had to cross the nine rivers of Chicunoapa, which were guarded by a dog (to whom they had to give slips of paper by way of toll); and Mohammed's bridge of El Sirat, over which only faithful Mussulmans can pass, is said to be guarded by a dog.

The Koran also contains a legend of a dog-guard, Mohammed having borrowed an apocryphal story from Christian traditions and embellished it. This is the story of the Christian youths in Ephesus who, to avoid persecution by the Emperor Decius, hid in a cave where they slept for a great many years. According to the Koran, when they fled to the cave they were followed by a dog and tried to drive it away. But God caused the dog to speak to them, saying: 'I love those who are dear unto God; go to sleep, therefore, and I will guard you.' When they settled down in the middle of the cave, the dog 'stretched forth his forelegs in the mouth of the cave', and they did not wake up for three hundred and nine years. During this period entry of the cave was forbidden even to the Prophet, and when the taboo was eventually broken by soldiers they were immediately struck dead by a burning wind. (Mohammedans have a great respect for this dog—which was said to have been endowed with the gift of prophecy—and it is one of the ten animals admitted into their paradise. They have a proverbial saying which refers to a covetous person as one who 'would not throw a bone to the dog of the seven sleepers'.) This story of the long sleep and the waking after so many years is said to represent the resurrection of the dead, and so once again a dog is found lying at the entrance to the world of life after death.

OF THE ENTRANCE TO THE SPIRIT-WORLD OF PRIMITIVE TRIBES Such watchdogs are also to be found in the mythologies of people still in a primitive stage of culture. A dog guards the gates of the paradise of the Massachusetts and Eskimos, and people of North Borneo believe in a fiery dog that guards the gates of paradise and lays claim to all virgins. In many cases it is believed that the soul has to cross a river of death, contending with an evil spirit, often in the form of a dog, which guards the bridge. The Iroquois and Hurons believe souls have to cross a deep swift river by means of a bridge formed by a slender tree guarded by a dog, while members of the Algonquin tribes of North American Indians see the river of death as being spanned by a snake-bridge of which there is a warder in the form of a great dog. Finally, the soul of a Menomeni Indian is said to travel westward for four days before reaching the home of his creator. As he approaches the village of the dead he comes to a swift river with a slippery log across it for a bridge. A great dog guards the log and decides whether or not he lived a good enough life to enter the spirit-world. In passing the dog the Menomini has to cross the log without falling in, and if he succeeds he is joyfully greeted by the old people of the tribe with radiant vermilion-painted faces, and will remain happy for evermore.

OF THE FIRST CREATED MAN AND WOMAN Dogs have played their part in creation myths, for God sometimes set a dog on guard in paradise. An Indian myth tells how, at the beginning of the world, God spent twelve hours moulding a man and woman, then went to sleep. During the night, however, a serpent came and it destroyed his first human couple. Next morning the deity re-created them, but his handiwork was again the victim of the serpent's cunning. So, on the third day God rose early, and created a guardian in the form of a dog before remodelling the man and woman. That night, when the serpent glided through the long grass, it was so horrified by the sound of the watchdog's growl that it abandoned its intentions once and for all.

These primal watchdogs were, unfortunately, not always incorruptible. One in a Russian myth, whose duty it was to guard paradise, on being thrown a bone admitted the Devil. A Western Asiatic myth tells of an equally untrustworthy dog. According to this, after creating the body of the first man God returned to heaven to fetch a soul, leaving a naked dog on guard. During his absence the Devil bribed the dog with a coat, and it permitted him to approach man and defile him.

ITS THEFT IN GREEK MYTH Cerberus, the Guard of the Greek Underworld, was eventually captured and removed from the realm of Hades by Heracles—a hero of superhuman brawn and strength. In order to attain immortality, Heracles served King Eurystheus of Mycenae, who imposed on him twelve dangerous and apparently impossible tasks. The twelfth labour on which the hero embarked was to bring Cerberus up from the infernal regions, and before setting out he partook of the Eleusinian Mysteries. When he had been cleansed and prepared for the ordeal by these rites, he was guided by the goddess Athene and by Hermes, messenger of the gods, to the Underworld. On arrival Heracles found his friends Theseus and Peirithous fastened to the Chair of Forgetfulness, but, although he managed to wrench Theseus free, he was forced to leave Peirithous behind. When the hero stood before the King of Hades demanding Cerberus, he received the reply: 'He is yours if you can master him without using your club or your arrows.'

On finding the monstrous dog chained to the gates of the Underworld, Heracles resolutely gripped Cerberus by his throat, from which sprang three heads each maned with serpents (Plate 4a). A barbed tail flew up to strike the hero, but he was protected by a lion-pelt and did not relax his grip until the watchdog choked and yielded. (Some, however, say Heracles first gave Cerberus a narcotic cake which relaxed the Hell-hound's vigilance.) With Athene's assistance he then crossed the River Styx with Cerberus bound by chains—half dragging and half carrying him up to the earth. (According to one account, Cerberus strongly resisted—barking furiously with all three mouths, and his saliva, as it flew across the fields, gave birth to the poisonous plant, Aconite.) Eventually Heracles fulfilled his task by presenting Cerberus to King Eurystheus at Mycenae.

OTHER VERSIONS OF ITS THEFT The myth of the struggle with, or theft of, the Guardian of the gates of the Underworld appears elsewhere in thinly disguised form. In Greek myth the tenth labour imposed on Heracles was to fetch the Erytheia, the famous herd of cattle which belonged to Geryon. Geryon was a three-bodied maneating monster who owned fine red cattle which were the object of widespread envy. They were guarded by Orthrus, his watchdog, which was born of the same parents as Cerberus, had two heads of its own and, in addition, some say, seven serpents' heads and a serpent's tail. When Heracles approached Geryon's herd, Orthrus rushed barking at him, but the hero struck the dog lifeless with his club, and then fought in single combat with Geryon. When he finally succeeded in overcoming Geryon by shooting a single arrow through all three of the monster's bodies, Heracles drove off the cattle and presented them to Eurystheus. There is also a myth telling of the 'unsleeping and unapproachable' dog guarding the cattle of King Phylacus, which

Melampus, the first mortal to receive prophetic powers, tried unsuccessfully to steal.

Finally, we come to the theft of the golden mastiff belonging to
Zeus, King of the Greek gods. When Zeus was an infant in Crete,
Hephaestus the divine smith created a golden mastiff to watch over
him, and it subsequently became the guardian of Zeus's temple at
Dicte. A Cretan, named Pandareus, stole this sacred mastiff from the
precinct of Zeus, and, not wishing to be caught with it in his possession,
gave it to his friend Tantalos to keep for him. But when, after the hue
and cry had died down, Pandareus asked Tantalos to return the dog,
he swore he had neither seen nor heard of it. Zeus ordered his
messenger, Hermes, to investigate the matter and to recover the
golden dog for him. This he did and, as a result, Pandareus perished
miserably in Sicily, while Tantalos received eternal punishment in
Hades, where an enormous crag threatened to crush his skull. (In
other versions of this myth it was Tantalos who stole Zeus's mastiff,
and Pandareus who was entrusted with it. When the latter denied
having received the dog-guard, he was destroyed by the angry god—
or turned into stone.)

The labour of Heracles is, however, more directly reflected in the
myth of Cuchulain—a Celtic warrior famous throughout Ireland and
Scotland. It is described how a great smith of Ulster, whose name was
Culain, had an enormous watchdog which was unbelievably savage
and cruel and had the strength of a hundred normal dogs. When unchained it would allow no one but Culain past it, and it was said there
was no man in Ireland whom it could not drag down. One day the
smith gave a great feast for the King of Ulster. The king was on his
way there when, passing his seven-year-old nephew, Setanta, who was
playing with other children, he called out to him to come along to the
feast. The boy said he wanted to finish his game, but would follow in
the king's chariot tracks later. Arriving at the smith's house, the king
received a great welcome and was regaled with songs and the recital
of poems and of laws. Then Culain instructed his men to raise the
drawbridge which spanned the deep black moat surrounding the city,
and he unchained his great watchdog. It sprang over the moat,
careered with fearful baying three times round the city, then stood at
the edge of the moat watching, listening, and occasionally growling.
As soon as the smith returned slamming and bolting the folding doors,
the feast was brought in and they all began to celebrate.

Culain toasted heroes of the past and, proposing to drink to future heroes, inquired of the king about his nephew. When he heard that Setanta was due to arrive any minute, the smith was horrified, for he knew that the child would be torn to small pieces. No sooner had they realized what had happened than the earth quaked with the baying of the hound. Short furious yells were heard, followed by sibilant gasps and the sound of breaking bones—then silence. A few moments later there was a knocking at the door and, to their astonishment, the little boy stepped in out of the night—his tunic tattered and dripping with blood. The smith's men fetched in the watchdog, with its skull, ribs and backbone in pieces and torrents of blood gushing from its mouth. When they saw what had become of their wonderful guard they were very angry and started fighting the men of the King of Ulster, but Setanta rushed in between and managed to part them.

The pale-faced boy then explained that it was only in defence of his own life that he had killed the hound. 'Three times he leaped upon me with white fangs bared and eyes red with murder, and three times I cast him off.' But when, the fourth time, the dog rushed at Setanta like a storm, he took it by its throat and legs and flung it against a rock, intending only to stun it. Filled with remorse, the boy promised that, if a whelp of the same breed existed in Ireland, he would find it and rear and train it until it was as good as the one he had killed. Meanwhile he said: 'I, myself, will be your watchdog, to guard your goods, your cattle and your house.' His offer was accepted, and as the king's leach dressed the gashes made by the beast's claws, he murmured healing incantations over Setanta. The boy served the smith for many years, and Culain and his people taught him a great deal and grew very fond of him. A druid renamed him 'Cuchulain'—'The Hound of Culain', and later he became known as the 'Hound of Ulster'.

3) *The Guide* Guide and messenger dogs also appear in mythology, and many of them are responsible for conducting souls of the dead into the lower regions.

ITS ANCESTRY The ancestor of the mythological guide dog was probably the jackal. In Egypt the jackal is the pathfinder of the desert, and in dynastic times it was the duty of the jackal-god, Anubis, to superintend the passage of souls from this life to the next. In the Underworld he guided souls on their way to the kingdom of Osiris, judge of the dead (Plate 4d), a duty which he sometimes shared with Apuet, another jackal-god (in which case the Underworld was divided into two, and one of the gods ushered souls through the northern and the other through the southern part). Both jackals were spoken of as 'Openers of the Way' to the gates of the kingdom of Osiris.

OF SOULS TO, AND THROUGH, THE UNDERWORLD When the Greeks arrived in Egypt with their own gods they were so impressed by the Egyptian deities that in many cases they became assimilated with their own, and they gave them Greek (or partly Greek) names. Anubis, the jackal-god of dynastic Egypt, was identified with Hermes, the Greek psychopomp and usher of souls, and became known as Hermanubis, the dog-god of Alexandria.

In the Gnostic system, of the first six centuries of the Christian era, in which souls on their way to paradise were believed to follow the paths of the planets, it was Hermanubis who guided them. He also possessed words of power which enabled him to pass through all the gates, and to overcome on their behalf the resistance of any opposing spirit.

In Hindu mythology Saramâ, the mother of Yama's dogs, guided Indra, King of the gods, on his way. She also sometimes helped human beings who were lost in forests or dark places. Yama daily sent Çyama and Çabala as messengers of death to the earth, where they searched out doomed men and guided them to the Underworld. (Although these infernal dogs guarded the graves of the spirit-world, they were not, like Cerberus, chained there, but, far more mobile, sallied forth into the world to claim their victims.) In so far as they acted as guides these dogs were not destructive to man, for, we are told, they guided his departing soul safely through 'the howls and pursuit in the other world'. In Hindu myth, where heaven and hell merge, those searched out by Çyama and Çabala joined their fathers, who, it is said, were 'having an excellent time in Yama's company'. Furthermore, the dogs were ordered to take charge of the dead, and to furnish them with health and prosperity.

Babylonian myth tells of a dog belonging to the god Hea that conducted souls to the Underworld, and the Etruscan moon-goddess, Tana, had a dog as her messenger. In the fifth century, during the Gothic war, it was popularly believed in Germany and Bretagne that Britain was the island of souls. It was said that, at the moment of death, mens' souls presented themselves to the parish priest of Braspar and his dog escorted them to Britain. The 'soul-car', a cart overloaded with souls of the newly dead, was often heard creaking in the air as it set out on its journey guided by the priest of Braspar's dog.

OF THE BEREAVED TO THE DEAD BODIES OF THEIR LOVED ONES In Egyptian mythology Osiris was the sun-god and deity of vegetation as well as judge of the dead, and he was married to Isis, the Great Mother-goddess of the earth and moon. Osiris was murdered by Set, the Devil, and his body was broken up into pieces and scattered throughout the land. When Isis set out on her lengthy travels to hunt for the limbs of Osiris she was assisted in her search, we are told, by a dog.

From ancient Greece comes the myth of Icarius, who was famed as the first cultivator of the vine, and had a hound devoted to him called 'Maera'. Icarius was eventually slain by a drunken peasant and buried under a pine tree. Maera, who saw it happen, set up a howl and, catching hold of the clothes of Erigone, Icarius's daughter, led her to the grave and dug up the corpse. In despair Erigone hanged herself, and the image of Maera the hound was set up in the sky, where it became known, according to one version of the story, as the Lesser Dog-star.

Then there is the Christian legend of St Margaret of Cortona. Margaret was a beautiful thirteenth-century Umbrian peasant who, at the age of seventeen, was seized and carried off by a young nobleman. She had a son by him before he met a mysterious death—a tragedy of which she was informed by her lover's dog (Plate 4e). She later became a Franciscan tertiary, and her son a Franciscan friar.

CYNOSURE AND CYNOSARGES A 'cynosure' is, as we know, something that attracts attention by its brilliance, and serves for guidance—a 'Guiding Star'. The word comes from 'Kynosaura'—'the dog's tail'—a name given to the Pole Star, or to the tail of the constellation of the Little Bear which contains the Pole Star.

The word 'Cynosarges' means 'the dog's yard'. A Greek myth tells how a man called Diomus was sacrificing to the god Heracles in Athens one day when a white dog snatched up the victim and ran off with it. Diomus consulted an oracle about this, and was told to find out where the dog had deposited the animal and to build an altar to Heracles there. The place to which the dog guided Diomus came to be known as 'Cynosarges', and the dog was recognized as a sacred messenger sent by the god to declare his will.

4) *The Hunter* In many mythologies gods are commonly portrayed accompanied by the dogs they hunted with, but there are certain myths in which the hunting dog plays a particularly important part.

HOUNDS OF THE GODDESS OF THE CHASE Artemis was the Greek virgin-goddess of the chase, and she obtained her hounds from Pan, the god—half man, half goat—of the woods and pastures. When she made her way to Arcadia where Pan bred hunting dogs, she found him feeding his bitches and their whelps. He gave her three lop-eared hounds, and two parti-coloured, and one spotted, hounds which were together capable of dragging even live lions back to their kennels. She also received seven swift hounds from Sparta.

Artemis once made a gift to King Minos of Crete of a wonderful hound, called Laelaps, that never failed to catch its quarry. When the king later wished to seduce an Athenian princess called Procris, whose husband had been unfaithful to her, he gave her Laelaps and also a dart that never missed its mark. Procris then, disguising herself as a boy, joined her husband on a hunting expedition. He coveted her hound and dart and, not recognizing her, offered her a huge sum of money for them. But Procris refused to part with them 'except for love', and only when he took her to bed did she reveal herself as his wife. Artemis was, however, furious at having her precious gifts bandied about by mercenary adulterers and she plotted her revenge. She made Procris suspect that her husband was still unfaithful to her, and follow him one night when he went out hunting. The hunter thought he heard a rustle in the thicket behind him, and when Laelaps growled and stiffened he let fly the unerring dart in the direction from which the sound came, transfixing his unfortunate wife. Some time later Laelaps was lent by Procris's husband to the King of Thebes to hunt a vixen that was ravaging the land and demanding the monthly sacrifice of a child. The vixen was, however, divinely fated never to be caught, as was Laelaps to catch whatever she pursued. And Zeus, eventually fed up with the pair of them, transformed both vixen and hound into stone.

STELLAR HOUNDS There was once a Boeotian hunter called Orion—a giant of immense size, strength and beauty, who had no fear of any animal alive. He promised to rid the earth of wild beasts and monsters, and his exploits rivalled those of Heracles. Artemis, whose enjoyment of the chase the giant shared, fell deeply in love with Orion, and they roamed together over the mountains every evening in search of game. Artemis's brother, Apollo the sun-god, was furiously jealous, and tricked the goddess into shooting her giant through the head. Broken-hearted, Artemis carried the body of her lover up to the heavens and set it amidst the stars. Here Orion can still be seen striding across the sky, wearing a star-studded belt and a lion-skin, and carrying a shining sword and a huge club. Following Orion are his two favourite hunting dogs—Sirius (the Greater Dog-star), sitting behind his feet, and Procyon—or Maera or Laelaps (the Lesser Dog-star), behind him at shoulder height.

Other stellar dogs are the two hunters (*canes venatici*) of Boötes. Boötes, who is often identified with Icarius, is the huntsman who eternally chases the Bear in slow flight around the axis of the Pole, accompanied and assisted by his hounds.

HUNTING DOGS OF CELTIC HEROES In Celtic myth most of the outstanding heroes had wonderful hounds, some of which were said to be larger than wild oxen, fiercer than dragons, and swifter than eagles, and all caught every wild beast they saw. The most famous Celtic hunting pair were Finn and his dog Bran. Bran was unequalled not only in size but also in speed, for she was 'swift as a march wind and could overtake wild geese'. The Fenian princes are believed to have indulged in magnificent hunts in which a thousand knights wearing silken shirts, green mantles, purple cloaks, golden diademed helmets, and carrying javelins, set out accompanied by three thousand hounds which were led by Bran as the fleetest and wisest of them all. On one occasion, when each hound brought down two deer, Bran killed on her own six thousand and one, while on another, when many famous hounds chased a witch, Bran was the only one to return unscathed. Most impressive of all, however, was the story of the time when Finn and his men were out on a hunting expedition in a forest and started a great boar. The monstrous creature broke through the trees with eyes blazing like fire, white tusks red with gore, bristles standing up like rods, froth flying like snow from its mouth, and it tossed many hounds over its head, trampling and maiming them for life. Then Finn slipped Bran, and so swiftly did she fly at the boar that 'her track was like a black and yellow flash' over the green turf, and the distant mountains rang with her baying. When she overtook the boar she seized it by its throat, and shook it as a puppy shakes a rag until it was dead.

One Celtic myth tells of three green hunting dogs: one of which was called 'Knowledge' because it knew where the deer were; one was called 'Swiftness' because it always caught them; while the other was called 'Heaviness' because it brought them home. But these dogs turned out to be enchanted princes—young men who had been put under spells by their stepmother.

ARTHURIAN HOUNDS The legendary King Arthur was a great huntsman, and he had a hound called 'Cavall'. ('Caball' means 'horse', so it may have been given this name because it was large. Famous Celtic dogs were often compared to horses: they would be described as having a 'crest like a horse' or a 'horse-like chest'.) It played an important part in Arthur's epic hunt of an enormous boar which was laying waste the countryside. It is said that during this hunt Cavall left a paw-print on a stone and Arthur placed a heap of pebbles under it. A tenth-century historian refers to a heap of stones with one on top bearing the footprint of a dog; and 'Carn Cavell' is a mountain in Breconshire with cairns scattered over it, one of which is capped by such an engraved stone.

The heroes of medieval legends who searched for the Holy Grail usually took a dog with them. In a French version of the Percival legend a beautiful damsel lent the knight her hound, demanding that, as proof of his devotion, he should find and capture a white stag.

5) *The Faithful Companion* The Greek poet, Aelian, writes of the 'unsurpassable loyalty' of dogs, and of the 'unbreakable affection which dogs have for those who keep them', and myths and legends from all parts of the world describe the fidelity shown by dogs to their masters. Many of the mythical watchdogs, hunting dogs and guides were incidentally faithful companions: outstanding in their loyalty were the dogs that guarded the seven sleepers for three hundred and nine years; the deep-baying hunting dog of Arthur, and the hound of Icarius that guided his daughter to his corpse. There is, however, also a body of tales in which the fidelity of a dog plays a central part.

OF CHRISTIAN SAINTS When, in the thirteenth century, Europe was smitten by plague, St Roch (who was born with a birthmark in the shape of a cross on his chest) travelled as a monk with his dog throughout Languedoc, ministering to peasants. He worked among the sick and healed many people, until he was finally himself smitten by the plague. When near death the monk crawled out of the city to neighbouring woods and, while he laid under a tree, his dog went off to search for food. According to the legend, it discovered a castle where a nobleman was carousing with friends, entered, helped itself to a loaf of bread and walked out. Day after day St Roch's dog returned for a loaf until, astonished by its regular theft, the nobleman decided to follow it. When he saw the dog drop the bread at the feet of the prostrate man, and tenderly lick his plague spots, he was so moved, both by the animal's devotion and the saint's holiness, that he forsook his wealth and self-indulgent habits and entered the Church. 'St Roch and his dog' (Plate 4f) has become a proverbial reference to people who are inseparable companions.

St Simon Stock, a twelfth-century saint, was also brought bread daily by a dog. He lived in the trunk of a hollow tree in the forest of Toubersville in Kent.

The Old Testament Apocrypha describes how, when Tobias set out on his journey to Media with an angel, he was also accompanied by his faithful dog.

OF HEROES The dog is (like the jackal and fox) to be found among those animals that assist heroes in danger, and in the performance of the difficult tasks that bring them wealth and happiness.

Typical is a Swedish legend, 'The Three Dogs'. This tells of three beautiful princesses who had been imprisoned by giants in the mountains, and whose father promised that any man who rescued them should have one for a wife and half his kingdom as a wedding present. Many wealthy warriors set out with horses, servants and costly weapons to search for the princesses. The news of the king's distress at the abduction of his daughters also reached the ears of a young man who lived alone with his mother in the depths of a wood. This lad had three large dogs: one called 'Holdfast' that, if told to hold, would hold whatever it might be; one called 'Tear' that would tear anything into pieces; and one called 'Quickear' that could hear what was taking place many miles away—and he set out with his faithful dogs to try to find the princesses. After travelling a considerable distance, Quickear heard one of the princesses spinning within a high mountain; he also heard the hoofs of a giant's horse some ten miles away. The boy ordered the dogs to break open the door into the mountain, and inside there was revealed a beautiful maiden spinning gold thread. When the giant returned the dog called Holdfast threw itself at him, holding him until Tear took over and tore him to pieces. The same thing then happened in the case of the other two princesses, who were also imprisoned in mountains. When they all had finally been released the lad took the horses, a golden chariot full of treasures, and the princesses home to their father's palace. He married the youngest of the king's daughters and when the king died he was chosen to be ruler of the land.

MAGICAL PROPERTIES   Many of the faithful companions of Celtic gods and heroes were magical dogs. The sun-god Lugh had a magic hound—a bitch—which turned into a ball of fire every night. She was said to be irresistible in battle; to be 'better than wealth ever known', and to turn any running water in which she bathed into wine.

Bran, the faithful companion of the hero, Finn, was in Irish myth described as being a bitch, but in Scottish myth as a male dog. The name 'Bran' means 'raven black', 'an avalanche' and 'a mountain stream', but it has also been claimed that she was given this name because, as a whelp, she ate a carpenter's shavings. Some say Bran was born of Finn's aunt, who had temporarily been transformed into a hound; others, that Finn had stolen her as a puppy, from a giant he had overcome. This elfin dog has been described as having yellow paws, a broad speckled back, black sides, a white belly and red sharp-pointed ears. She was also said to be small-headed and white-chested, and to possess the eyes of a dragon, the claws of a wolf, the vigour of a lion and the venom of a serpent. An account of Bran's prowess as a hunter has already been given, and in addition she was gifted with foreknowledge of evil. Most descriptions agree in claiming that Bran had a venomous claw in her right paw, the scratch of which inflicted certain death. But, although when enraged she was as ferocious as a tiger, when she lay at Finn's feet she was as gentle as a lamb. Usually the venomous, death-dealing claw was kept covered by a silver 'shoe', and Finn led her by a silver chain attached to a collar of gold. Her life was dedicated to that of her master, and when the Fenians were beaten in battle it is said that she wept bitterly.

One myth tells of the great heroic combat of Finn with a sea-monster. He was wrestling with the creature and was almost over-come, when Bran uncovered her venomous claw and plunged it into the monster's back, tearing out its liver and heart. On another occasion, when Bran was challenged to a dog-fight, she was losing badly, for no one had remembered to remove her 'shoe'. Suddenly, the Master of the hounds realized what had happened, and, lying down alongside Bran's foot, took the 'shoe' off. She lifted her venomous claw immediately and killed the other dog outright.

The accounts of how Bran met her death vary. According to one, she was killed by Finn when they were hunting one day following a fawn. The fawn called out: 'If I go into the sea below I will never come back again, and if I go up into the air above me it will not save me.' 'Go through my legs,' said Finn, believing the fawn to be his mother under enchantment. As it did this, Bran followed and got caught between her master's knees, where she was promptly squeezed to death. Finn suffered great grief when he discovered that, in saving his mother, he had killed his most faithful hound.

In an account in which Bran is referred to as a male dog he lost his life hunting a witch deer, for, it was said, although he had the venom of a serpent he had none of its wisdom. When he was out hunting one day with Finn and the rest of the hero's pack, a snow-white hart was started with hoofs that shone like gold. Bran led the hounds and they pursued the hart for many hours, until, one by one, they dropped off through weariness and Bran alone continued the chase. Eventually the hart headed for a lake and, reaching a high cliff, plunged over it and down into the watery depths. Bran leapt in after the hart, and seized it as it rose to the surface. But his prey immediately changed into a beautiful woman, and drew Bran down under the water, where they disappeared together, never to be seen again.

Finn also possessed three other venomous hounds, of whom it was said fire could not burn them, water could not drown them, and no weapons could wound them.

Then there was the huge multi-coloured hound put at Finn's disposal by the princes of Iruath. This creature, we are told, wore a chain ridged with red-gold round its neck, gave off the scent of mead, and whenever Finn needed money it threw out of its mouth fifty ounces of silver and fifty of gold. It protected Finn from his enemies by encircling and licking him three times a day, and when any enemy approached it sent under them a blast of wind which blew them out to sea. One stipulation was, however, made by the princes of Iruath and that was that no one should attempt to see them at night when they withdrew with the magic hound behind walls of fire. When, eventually, two princes of Ulster broke this taboo, penetrating the walls of fire and gazing at them, the great hound appeared to be no bigger than a lap-dog; and, while one of the princes of Iruath watched over the creature with a sword in his hand, another held a silver vessel to its muzzle—for there gushed out of the dog's mouth any drink they desired. When

one of them told the multi-coloured hound of the treachery Finn had
allowed, it turned towards the princes of Ulster and 'a dark Druid
wind' blew their shields and swords into the wall of fire. The three
princes of Iruath then slew them, and the hound breathed on them,
burning their bodies to ashes.

According to one version of the medieval romance of Tristan and
Isolt, Tristan was given, while in exile, a magic dog called 'Petit Crû'
that came from Avalon, the earthly paradise. It was an extraordinarily
beautiful little creature that shone with innumerable colours, for from
one angle it appeared white, black and green, while from another, it
looked as red as blood. Petit Crû was gentle, delicate, agile and
obedient, and it wore a little bell on a golden chain round its neck
which, when it shook its body, tinkled with such a sweet sound that
Tristan forgot all sorrow and even his love for Isolt. Consoled, and
filled with joy, he sent Petit Crû to his beloved to free her from her
grief at his absence, but Isolt reproached herself bitterly for feeling
gay while her lover was (as she imagined) so sad. When, over-
whelmed by feelings of guilt, she tore the bell from the dog's neck, it
immediately lost all its magic power. (There are many references in
Celtic literature to coloured animals: when St Ciaran blessed some
blue dye for his mother, we are told that 'it made blue the dogs'.)

MISUNDERSTOOD There is a series of legends in which the actions
of a faithful hound are misunderstood by its master with dire results.
Typical of these is one which tells of the deer-hound, Gellert, belonging to a Welsh prince called Llewellyn.

When Prince Llewellyn was away one day he left Gellert to guard
his baby son. On his return he found, to his intense horror, the cradle
empty, the child's clothes bloodstained, and the dog's chops dripping
with gore. Concluding that Gellert had devoured the child he had been
entrusted with, Llewellyn in a paroxysm of rage drew his sword and
killed the deer-hound outright. A few minutes later the prince heard a
cry from behind the cradle, and found the baby lying there uninjured.
He also discovered the body of a huge wolf which, on entering the
house with the intention of devouring the child, had been killed by the
courageous Gellert. Llewellyn, suffering great grief and self-reproach,
erected a monument in Carnarvonshire on the spot where his faithful
hound was buried, which is known as 'Beth Gellert'—the grave of
Gellert.

Different versions of this popular tale appeared in medieval

Europe, many of which are included in the *Gesta Romanorum*—a collection of legends made by fourteenth-century monks. A French version tells of a greyhound and falcon belonging to a knight that were left in charge of a child while its parents and their servants attended a tournament. During their absence a serpent glided into the room, and the falcon, spotting it as it crawled towards the cradle, fluttered its wings until it woke the greyhound. The dog then attacked the serpent, and, after a grim struggle in which it was seriously wounded, succeeded in killing the reptile. When the nurses returned they found a general state of disarray, with the baby missing, the cradle upturned and the greyhound trailing blood. The parents were greeted with the horrifying story, and, as the wounded dog tried to rise to welcome the knight, it was stabbed through the heart by him. When the knight later found his child uninjured and the dead body of a serpent near by, he broke his sword in two in disgust and set out on a pilgrimage to the Holy Land. These folk-tales originated in India, where, in their most common form, they tell of a faithful hound that saved its master's child from a wolf and was killed owing to misinterpretation of appearances.

Japanese legends go even further in describing the lengths to which a dog's fidelity will stretch. Popular ones tell of a man who falls asleep under a tree and is woken by his dog barking and pulling at his clothes. In a fit of rage he draws his sword and cuts off the animal's head. Undaunted, the dog's severed head jumps up and kills a snake on the tree above him, and the man realizes all too late why his faithful companion had tried to rouse him.

'. . . TILL DEATH' There are many legends of dogs whose fidelity has continued after the death of their owners, and of those that have died out of love for their masters. (In these the dog's character appears partly to be natural and partly supernatural.)

Aelian tells the following story about King Pyrrhus of Epirus. The king came upon the corpse of a man who had been murdered three days before, and whose dog had remained guarding him—unfed since his death. So the king gave orders for the man to be buried, and for the dog to be fed and housed. Some time later the king was watching a review with the dog beside him, when it suddenly attacked a couple of men, barking and clawing them. When the king had the men seized and put on the rack, they confessed to being the murderers of the dog's master.

To illustrate further what he calls the 'peculiar goodwill' which dogs bear to their masters, Aelian tells of a trader of Colophon who was making his way one day to Teos, with money, a servant and a dog. In stopping for a rest *en route*, the servant put down the money and forgot to pick it up again, so that when the trader eventually arrived at Teos to do business he found he had no money with him. Retracing their steps, they found the money where the servant had left it with the dog lying on it hardly breathing, and as it moved off the money-bag it died from starvation.

The proverbial saying 'The black dog's day will come' derives from the legend of a dog that saved its master from a supernatural being at the expense of its own life. This was the black dog of a Scot, MacPhee of Colonsey, which was lazy—seldom leaving the fireside and refusing to follow the chase. MacPhee often spoke of having it destroyed, but his cook was fond of it and said: 'Never you mind, the black dog's day has not yet come'—which, indeed, turned out to be true.

Homer's *Odyssey* contains the well-known story of how Ulysses returned from his wanderings to be greeted by his dog, Argus. The hero had disguised himself as a beggar in order to spy on his wife, whom he suspected of infidelity. On entering the courtyard of the palace he saw his old hound lying stretched out on a dunghill, mangey, decrepit, and tormented by lice. Recognizing his master after twenty years' absence (and in spite of his heavy disguise), Argus, although he had not the strength to rise, wagged his tail with joy, drooped his tattered ears—and then died.

There are numerous stories of dogs that jumped on to pyres and were burnt to death with their masters. The lapdog of a Greek harp-player threw itself on its master's coffin and was buried with him; and the hound of Eupolis, the writer, pined, we are told, through grief and starvation when its master died, finally expiring on his grave. (The place of its death is known as 'Hounds Dirge'.)

A Japanese legend tells how, when a rebel who had two faithful dogs killed himself, the Emperor ordered his body to be cut into eight pieces and distributed over eight provinces. One of the rebel's dogs knew its master's body so well that it could distinguish the pieces from those of the many others who were killed in battle. It found them all, put them together, then guarded them until they were put into a coffin. The other dog took its master's head in its mouth, put it in an old grave, then laid down by it and died. The Emperor was apparently so moved by this action that he ordered the man and dog to be buried side by side.

6) *The Suckling Bitch* In Greek mythology various gods were said to have been suckled by bitches.

ITS ANCESTRY The myth of the suckling bitch probably derives from that of the suckling wolf. In Greek mythology Apollo, the sun-god, who was born of Leto, a goddess known as 'the she-wolf', sent wolves to suckle those of his children whose mothers were human beings. In Roman myth the foster-mother of Romulus and Remus, the founders of Rome, was a she-wolf, and so was the foster-mother of the founder of the Turkish nation.

MOTHER-GODDESS The great Japanese rice-goddess, Inari, took the form of a vixen, and various other Mother-goddesses took the form of a bitch. (The Greek word '*Cyon*' means not only 'dog' but also 'begetter'.) Hecate, the Greek goddess of the Underworld, was depicted as a whelping bitch (Plate 4b). She was here confused with the Ephesian many-breasted Artemis, hence the overemphasized teats of the bitch; the Roman Earth-goddess, Ceres, sometimes took bitch form; Ceridwen, the Celtic Earth-goddess, transformed herself into a greyhound bitch; and Isis the Egyptian Great Mother was at times identified with the dog reputed to be her guide. Then there was an Aztec goddess of childbirth called Xochiquetzol, who was commonly known as the 'Bitch-mother'.

NURSE Zeus, king of the Greek gods, was usually believed to have been suckled by a goat, cow or bee, but on Cydonian coins a bitch is depicted as his foster-mother. The Cydonians, of western Crete, claimed Zeus was born on their territory, and, according to their tradition, the infant god was suckled by a bitch which was later transformed into a bear.

Asklepios, the Greek god of healing, was also, it seems, reared on bitch's milk. It is told how his mother exposed the infant on a mountain (which came to be known as 'Titthium'—'nipple'), and he was found by a goatherd who was searching for the she-goat and the bitch that guarded his herd, both of which, he had noticed, were missing. When he eventually found them they were taking turns to suckle a child, and, seeing a bright light radiating from the infant's head, the herdsman withdrew, realizing it was divine. (According to another version, the herdsman rescued the child and gave it to Chiron, the centaur, who reared Asklepios and taught him the art of medicine.) Neleus was another bitch-suckled god. This son of Poseidon, god of the sea, was also exposed on a mountain, but it was said that he acquired a savage nature from the bitch that served as his foster-mother.

THE RELATIONSHIP BETWEEN PHANTOM AND MYTHICAL DOGS

Man's experience of phantom, and of mythical, dogs is quite different. Phantom dogs are only seen at dusk, and they either appear to be two-dimensional or else temporarily appear to be three-dimensional but are proved to have been two-dimensional. Mythical dogs usually appear to living men in daylight as three-dimensional creatures, which are believed either to have been sent by deity or to incarnate it. Unlike phantoms, they are never attached to persons, families or places, but are essentially impersonal beings. Only at death do they appear two-dimensional—at the moment, that is, when man is himself about to change his dimension. After death, when man's spirit is confronted by dog, it is by an entity in the same dimension as himself.

Phantom and mythical dogs seem to have much in common: the Wild Hunt exists both in folk-lore and in myth; man can be protected and guided by black dog-ghosts, as can spirits, heroes and gods by mythical dogs; he can be helped, fed, and healed by white phantom-dogs, as are saints and others by mythical dogs; the dog-familiars of witches and sorcerers serve their owners in much the same way as do those magical hounds that are the faithful companions of gods, goddesses and heroes, for in both cases all desires are fulfilled, including the acquisition of wealth and the death of enemies. Both phantom and mythical dogs can be demonic—described as fiery, ferocious, horrifying, monstrous and lethal. Black dog-phantoms usually portend death, but both types are, at times, virtually incarnations of death. The black dog-phantom was worshipped by its sorcerers and witches, as was the divine dog of myth by its priests and priestesses.

Some people believe that dog-phantoms derive from myth: that the black dog-ghost of East Anglia arrived with the Vikings, and constituted a regional version of the mythical Hell-hound. This theory is, however, untenable—at least from an historical and geographical point of view—for dog-ghosts appear prolifically in parts of England uncontaminated by Nordic beliefs. Nevertheless phantom and mythical dogs certainly merge to a considerable extent, and, since their relationship operates within the sphere of man's perceptions, it will be investigated more deeply in the final chapter.

PART IV

Cult of the Dog

Having explored the nature and behaviour patterns of solid dogs and the many aspects of their relationship with man, and having investigated numerous forms of two-dimensional dogs, the time has now come to try to discover the nature of those solid dogs which were believed to be divine, sacred, ominous, or possessing some other form of supernatural power. We must examine the behaviour of man in relation to dogs thus endowed and, in some cases, note the relationship of ordinary dogs to those more 'spiritual' hounds.

DOG-DEITIES

Many gods have taken canine form and, during periods of dog-worship (Plate 5a) dogs have often become the centre of religious ritual.

1) *Their ancestry* Before dogs were venerated, wolves and jackals had their cults.

In ancient Egypt the people who built Lycopolis were wolf-worshippers (the name deriving from the Greek *lukos*, a wolf), and they practised ritual eating of sheep in imitation of the natural habits of their god.

In ancient Greece, Apollo was a wolf-god. He often took lupine form and the wolf was his sacrificial animal. In Delphi, where he was worshipped, sacrificial wolf-skins were found near his altar, and wolves were kept in some of his temples, where they received sacrifices from his worshippers. In Arcadia, Zeus was worshipped as a wolf-god. When, once every nine years, the festival of Zeus was celebrated, a boy was sacrificed and his guts were mixed in soup with those of sheep and goats and served up to shepherds. The shepherd who had the misfortune to eat the human guts was immediately transformed into a wolf and remained in this state for nine years. He became human again only if he had abstained during this period from eating human flesh.

In Rome homage was paid every year at the festival of the Lupercalia to the she-wolf that suckled Romulus and Remus, twin-founders of the city. The feast of the wolves was conducted by priests known as the *Luperci* in a cave at the foot of the Palatine Hill where the twins were originally deposited. (It is maintained by some scholars that the twins were suckled not by a wolf but by a whore, for the word *'lupa'* means 'prostitute', such women being thought of as rapacious. Brothels were known as *'lupanaria'*—*'lupa'* + *'nares'*, a cave—and Livy stated that they were suckled by the wife of the shepherd who found them, and that she was called *lupa* because she was 'free with her favours with herdsmen'.) The wolf rites included the sacrifice of two goats and a young dog outside the holy cave. It is not known why a dog was sacrificed, but it is thought probable that it was because the dog is the wolf's enemy. In 296 B.C. a cult statue depicting the twins beneath the dugs of a wolf was placed near the cave.

The worship of the jackal-god, Anubis, was very general in dynastic Egypt. Anubis was sometimes represented as a black jackal, and sometimes as a human being with a jackal head. He guarded cemeteries: the places where jackals wandered, and where wailing women brought offerings for the dead before dawn each day, yelping the jackal's cry to invoke the god to accept their gifts. Anubis presided over tombs and was the god of embalming.

The rites of embalmment were usually carried out by priests (wearing jackal masks, thus personifying the god they served). The day of the funeral, magical rites were performed outside the tomb where the deceased was to be buried, in which the living powers of the body were revived. In one vignette in the Book of the Dead, Anubis is shown standing at the door of a tomb, receiving a mummy; in another, he bends over a mummy on a bier, laying protective hands on it.

In judgement scenes Anubis is Guardian of the Scales of Truth in which the hearts of the dead are weighed. His duty is to place a vase representing the actions of the deceased in one scale and a figure, or emblem, of truth in the other, at the same time protecting the body against the monster which waits to devour the dead.

2) *Hermanubis* During the Graeco-Roman period in Egypt, Herman-

ubis, the Alexandrian dog-deity, inherited most of the characteristics of Anubis, but they received a different emphasis. Whilst Hermanubis was a funeral deity and a judge of souls, since the Greek Hermes was psychopomp and messenger of the gods, the primary duty of the Alexandrian was to guide souls of the dead through the Underworld. The dog-god was sometimes known as 'The Pregnant One', and was a protector of parturient women; he was also addressed in love charms by men who wanted to win womens' love, so presumably was associated with sexual power.

Hermanubis was depicted with a dog's head and was commonly known as 'latrator', 'the Barker'. On bas-reliefs, gems, and coins, he is usually shown dressed in Roman fashion, wearing a tunic to his knees, a large enveloping cloak falling over his shoulders. He wears winged sandals (Plate 5b), and holds a palm branch in one hand and a caduceus (the staff, with two snakes entwined round it, borne by heralds) in the other.

When the cult of the dog-god was at its height people turned up in thousands at the Anoubeion in Alexandria, which was one of the most prosperous temples of the ancient world. On feast days they brought hecatombs, and offered up to the god ingots of gold. Treasures found in this temple included gold libation bowls, a golden caduceus and silver figures of Hermanubis.

The Anoubeion of Philadelphia was virtually a kennel, for it was full of dogs sacred to the Alexandrian god, which were tended and ritually fed by priests.

In the annual ceremonies of Isis, the great Earth Mother, Hermanubis played an important part as the guardian, guide and companion of the goddess. (According to myths of the Classical period, Anubis was the son of Osiris and Nephthys, his wife's sister. Nephthys exposed the child, but Isis, the wife of Osiris, searched, with the help of two dogs, for the infant, and when she found him brought him up as her own. He received the name of 'Anubis' and was reputed to 'protect the gods as dogs protect men'. Plutarch maintained that Isis represented all that was above the earth and visible, Nephthys all that was beneath and hidden, and it was because a dog can see both by day and night that the child was called 'Anubis' and given the form of a dog.) In Italy, figures of Hermanubis have been found with several altars dedicated to Isis. In one Isis is replaced by a serpent; another, an engraved stone, shows the dog-god leaning on a palm while a serpent, whose tail he holds, coils around his arm and raises its head above his shoulder.

Apuleius gives a vivid description, in his book 'The Golden Ass', of one of the great processions of Isis. First to appear were women dressed in white clothes and garlands, some of whom sprinkled the pathway with herbs, balm and precious ointments, while others carried mirrors and ivory combs with which to adorn the goddess's hair. Next came men lighting the way with their lamps, torches and candles; the white-clad initiates of both sexes. Priests and leaders of the religious appeared wearing white surplices and bearing relics and small shrines of the most powerful of the gods. Finally, behind the priests, the gods themselves followed on foot. Towering above them all was the figure of Hermanubis—'messenger of the gods, supernal and infernal, his dog's head and neck rearing on high, displaying alternately a face black as night and one golden as the day, he bore the caduceus in his left hand and in his right waved a green palm branch aloft'. The procession moved triumphantly forward to the music of pipes, flutes and trumpets, and to the singing of white-clad youths. (As a guide to heaven and leader of souls to Osiris, Hermanubis was a beneficial god; as the incarnation of death and decay, he was a being who inspired terror—hence the black and golden aspects of his face.)

Priests of Hermanubis wore wooden dog-masks with black muzzles and ears and wide black stripes drawn across the neck, and they usually carried the herald's staff. It is recorded that in Rome, about 43 B.C., a man who wished to leave the city unrecognized borrowed a dog-mask from a friend who was an Isiac initiate, and made his way through the streets mimicking those celebrating the mysteries of the goddess. It has also been described how the Emperor Commodus once followed a procession of Isiacs, with shaven head and carrying in his arms an image of the dog-deity which unfortunately he kept allowing to topple over, knocking priests on the head with its muzzle.

Priests who were members of a college dedicated to Hermanubis regularly carried in procession a huge statue of their god. The body was painted black, revealing the funereal character of Hermanubis; the eyelids, nostrils, mouth, ears and mane were gold, or golden-striped; and it was dressed in white linen grave clothes. Many terra-cotta images representing this statue have been found buried in the Delta. A rite performed daily at the Anubeion in Alexandria was the 'showing' of the image of Hermanubis. Early in the morning, in an inner sanctuary of the temple where the laity were never allowed, the sacred statue in which the dog-god was represented standing with fists against his chest was painted, dressed and perfumed. Then priests carried it into the outer courtyard and *showed* it to the faithful gathered there.

Gnostic sects superimposed Christian doctrine on the old teachings of the mysteries, and their members sometimes identified figures of Hermanubis with those of Christ. Gnostic gems show the dog-god with his arms outstretched in the form of a cross: a graffiti scratched on a wall of a Roman house showed a dog-headed man holding a cross, with someone standing in front worshipping him. Hermanubis was, like Christ, a judge of the quick and the dead; like Christ he was a psychopomp and raised souls out of purgatory.

Throughout the cult of Hermanubis dogs were venerated (but were never considered to be divine as were cats), and the city of Cynopolis was the centre of the dog cult. Here dogs were ritually fed on food provided free by the city inhabitants. When a dog died a natural death members of the household shaved their heads and bodies (when a cat died they shaved only their eyebrows!) and threw away any food present in the house at the time of its death. The funeral rites of dogs were performed with great solemnity. An inscription at Giza records how the burial of a dog which guarded the King of Egypt was carried out with all the ritual ceremony due to a great man. The king presented the dead dog with a coffin, with linen for the wrappings, with incense, and a jar of perfumed ointment to be placed in the burial chamber. The tomb was constructed by the royal craftsman—all in order that the dog 'might be honoured before the great god Anubis'. The bodies of the dogs of Cynopolis were prepared by embalmers, wrapped in linen and ritually deposited in tombs allotted to them at public expense; while mourners uttered loud lamentations and beat their chests in grief. Dog-mummies were often placed in wooden coffins formed in the shape of dogs, their eyes being reproduced in paste, obsidian or glass. In other Egyptian towns graveyards were to be found devoted entirely to dog-mummies.

So although, during the cult of Hermanubis, dogs were not officially worshipped as actual incarnations of the god, they appear to have participated in much of the sanctity and power attributed to the deity.

3) *Bhairava* Hindus worship a dog-god called Bhairava, whose name

means 'The Terrible', and who is one of the blood-thirstiest forms of their great god Siva. Bhairava is sometimes incarnated as a black dog, and he is commonly portrayed as either riding on, or being accompanied by, one (Plate 5c). He is typically depicted with three eyes, dishevelled, matted hair, protruding teeth, a dark, or red, body, and numerous arms. He is sometimes encircled by a serpent, or wearing snake ear-rings or armlets, and may wear a garland, or collar, of skulls, and a girdle of tiny bells round his waist. His symbols are a trident, sword, noose and kettle-drum, and when riding a dog he is often followed by demons and spirits. At night the god is reputed to set out riding a black horse and accompanied by a black dog. Like Siva, Bhairava is untouchable.

In some ancient temples Bhairava is sculpted with his dog-vehicle behind him, and a five-hooded serpent overhead. In one temple the dog is biting a human head held by the god; in another Bhairava is holding a human head and a cup of blood with two dogs in attendance. He is often painted deep blue-black on temple walls. The image of Bhairava with his dog is found acting as a sort of warden in Siva temples, and sweetmeat-sellers, at the entrance, make little images of the dog in sugar which are presented to Bhairava as an offering. In Bombay the dog is much worshipped and no one will lift a hand against it.

In northern India a village god called Bhairon is depicted as a black, or dark-blue man, dressed with a cloth round his loins, a serpent round his neck, and accompanied by a black dog. He is sometimes confused with the priestly Bhairava, and attributes of the great god were transferred to the peasant god, who was purely a personification of the field genius. Bhairon is one of the most popular deities of agricultural communities. He is worshipped as the protector of fields, cattle and the homestead; and offerings of milk and sweetmeats are made to him. One way of conciliating Bhairon is to feed a black dog until it is surfeited: a barren woman (who regards Bhairon as a fertility god) will feed a black dog with pieces of bread that have a series of numbers written on them. Dogs are worshipped in connexion with the cult of Bhairon, and his temple in Benares is the only one into which a dog is admitted.

4) *Tribal gods*   Many dogs are to be found among tribal gods. Members of some south American tribes worship a dog as the 'Opener of the Day', for they claim that primeval man was originally

released from the Underworld by a dog scratching away the earth.

When the Incas invaded Peru they found, in the province of Huanca, the figure of a dog installed in temples as the highest deity of the inhabitants. (In the British Museum a Peruvian pot shows a hairless dog seated on a throne.)

The Kalangs of North Borneo worshipped a red dog and each family kept one in their house. They prayed to wooden images of this dog, and burnt them a thousand days after anyone close to them died. At nuptial ceremonies the brides' and bridegrooms' bodies were rubbed over with the ashes of a red dog's bones.

In northern India certain Dravidians served a dog-god. In Nepal a dog was worshipped at a festival called 'Khicha Puja', during which garlands of flowers were placed round the necks of every dog in the country. At Lohary, in the Punjab, a dog's grave is greatly respected by Hindus: a chief of the Thakuns had a dog which did noble service in battle, seizing the throats of wounded warriors and slaying them. When it was itself finally killed it was buried to the beat of drums, and its grave has been an object of worship and homage ever since.

In Sicily river-gods often took canine form—both rivers and dogs being thought of as 'runners'. (In Hungary dogs were often given the names of rivers.)

Chinese and Japanese mountain-gods were sometimes dogs. At Chichibu, where the protector of the mountain was a dog-deity, two sacred dogs (one white and one black) were in attendance at his shrine, receiving the homage and sacrifices of pilgrims. A temple was built in Japanese hills to a god who was the patron of dogs. It was lit by many lamps, and a priest struck its bells with iron hammers. A large white plaster dog stood on the altar consecrated to this deity. A celebrated temple outside the city of Foochow also contained the image of a large dog. Children placed bread, cakes and biscuits in its mouth and then ate them as a preventative against colic. A dog was worshipped in a sixteenth-century Shinto temple on a mountain known as 'The Dog's Head and Tail'. This shrine was erected in memory of the occasion when a dog, in spite of having been decapitated by its angry master, saved his life when it was threatened by a snake.

SACRED DOGS

There were various reasons for dogs being considered sacred. In some cases they were sanctified by association with divinity, in others by participation in religious ritual.

1) *The lion-dog of Buddha*   The attributes and lore of Chinese, Japanese and Tibetan toy-dogs are closely interwoven with those of the Buddhist lion.

In the first century A.D. many people in China were converted from Confucianism to Buddhism, and by the fifth century the latter had become the state religion. Buddhism came to China from India, where its supreme symbol was the lion. The Lord Buddha had, it was said, by the might of his holiness, brought into abject submission this creature which appeared to be an incarnation of all the most terrifying powers of darkness. Tamed and subdued, the lion first became Buddha's faithful servant and companion, and later, sanctified by its association with the master, was endowed with his attributes. As a symbol of Buddhism the image of the lion was proliferated throughout Buddhist countries.

When the Chinese embraced Buddhism they took over its symbolism, but to them the lion was largely a mythical beast for, although they were familiar with tigers, most of them had never seen a lion. Before long, however, it was observed that the Imperial dogs of Pekin resembled the drawings of Indian lions and gradually the pekes became invested with many of the attributes of the sacred Buddhist beast.

In art the Chinese drew upon the known for the unknown, and, combining the features of their pekinese dog with those of the imagined lion, produced a grotesque creature—the lion-dog—which bore no resemblance to any living animal, but became a symbol of Chinese Buddhism. Within a hundred years of the arrival of Buddhism in China, the lion-dog—with its strong, short body, massive legs and rectangular head, its shaggy mane, fantastic curls and bushy tail; and with its decorated collar hung with bells and tassels—rose to great heights of popularity, and the natural lion was recognized as an animal apart.

With the spread of Buddhism the image of the lion-dog appeared in other Eastern nations. When the Japanese were converted in the sixth century they carried reverence for the lion-dog to extravagant lengths. They regarded the Buddhist lion literally as a dog, referring to it as the 'Dog of Fo' ('Fo' being the Chinese name for Buddha),

5h Mass of the dogs (p. 124)

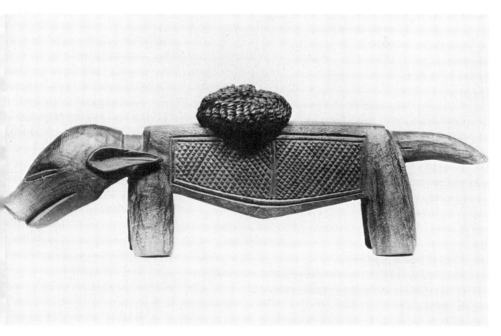

5i Congolese divining dog (p. 139)

5j St. Hubert, patron of dogs, receiving the rabies-curing stole (p. 150)

5k Chinese tomb-dog (p. 157)

5l Talismanic watch-dog (p. 141)

n Mandrake—the 'dog-dragged' (p. 162)

6a St. Dominic 'Sleuth-hound of the Lord' (p. 176)

6b Sorcerers transforming themselves into dogs (p. 167)

and they substituted a dog for the lion in their zodiacal system. The lion which was once the steed of Kwan-Yin, Japanese goddess of mercy, dwindled into a harmless lion-dog which she was depicted nursing on her lap.

Various myths and rationalizing legends arose to account for the image of the lion-dog. In Japan the Buddhist lion was known as 'koma-inu'—'the Korean dog'. According to tradition, when, in A.D. 201, the Japanese conquered Korea, the king of that country promised: 'I and my sons, my grandsons and my great-grandsons will ever remain faithful as a dog. We shall always lend our support in protecting Japan from the invasion of the attacking barbarians.' The following Japanese myth describes the origin of the lion-dog: When a Buddhist retired into the jungle of Korea for meditation all the beasts came to him for advice and consolation in their troubles. The lion was in great distress because he had fallen in love with a marmoset and their difference in size made their union impossible. The Buddhist suggested that, if the lion's love was really so great, he should be prepared, in order to win the monkey, to sacrifice his strength and become the least among the beasts. The lion agreed and the hermit recited a prayer by virtue of which the lion dwindled until it was the same size as the marmoset. As a reward for its steadfastness, although the lion lost its great strength it was allowed to retain its form, its courage, and its dignity, and the playful spirit of monkeys was added to its character. So the lion and marmoset were finally married, and their offspring was the Imperial lion-dog.

By the seventh century Buddhism was established in Tibet, where a new form of it evolved as the religion of the lamas. Here also the images of lion and dog became confused in both religion and art, but the relationship between the two animals appears to have been different from that in Chinese and Japanese Buddhism. According to a Tibetan myth—the Buddha was travelling one day as a simple priest accompanied by a small dog, when he met a Taoist who begged him to obtain for him a vision of the Buddha. After he had sworn that he faithfully kept his vows, the Taoist was told to look up in the sky, and here he saw, where the clouds were glowing with five colours, the pet dog transformed into a mighty lion with the Buddha riding on its back. A Lama gospel explains that the lion is the king of beasts, and that it has the power both to increase without limit and to 'diminish at will and become like unto a dog'. (In practice the lama priests distinguished between 'true lions' which were mountain spirits and dog-lions which were earthly beasts. They taught that the dog-lion was inferior to the spirit-lion, as is a dog to a lion in nature.)

Statues of lion-dogs are often found in pairs at the entrance to Buddhist temples. Tibetan lamas tell how the Buddha, on entering his temple, ordered the two lions accompanying him with doglike devotion to seat themselves on the tables covered with altar-cloths at the door. They awaited his return in motionless obedience, and their images are said to serve as reminders of the subjection of the passions by the Holy Creed. In South China a colossal stone 'lion' that stood in front of a sixth-century tomb posed in the attitude of a playful peke. These creatures, far more canine than feline, were also placed in the doorways of the Imperial palaces of China and Japan.

The pairs of lion-dogs usually wear leads consisting of silken cords or ribbons, and are seated on low ornamental pedestals covered with richly embroidered cloths. The male has his right pad set on a ball covered with embroidered silk; while the female rests her left pad on the mouth of an upturned cub (Plate 5f). (According to ancient belief, lionesses secrete milk in their pads and the cub is supposed to be suckling through her claws.)

Much has been written on the significance of the lion-dog's embroidered ball. There is a passage referring to it in the lama gospels. Apparently lion's milk was considered to be a sovereign remedy against fever and was therefore very sought after. It was explained, in the sacred writings, that, if a man wished to obtain the milk of lions, he must make an embroidered ball of many colours and place it on their path. The lions would be attracted to it and would play with it for a long time, leaving the ball soaked with their milk, which the man could then squeeze out and use. In Korea, pills were sold which were said to contain the milk collected from balls exposed at night near Buddhist temples for the lions to play with.

Some say this ball is the lion-dog's 'chu'—that is, a globular fleshy organ, which it can expel and recall at will and which is the very source of the creature's life. In countries where sun-worship prevailed the lion and sun were closely associated (the stone lion guarding St Mark's Church at Venice has its front paw on the ball of the sun), and it is thought to have been the sun-ball that evolved into the oriental chu. It became endowed with the qualities of the 'dragon's pearl'—the jewel to be found in a dragon's heart which contained the spiritual essence of the universe, and it may also be compared to the luminous globe believed to be found in the hearts or tails of foxes which constituted their soul and the source of their magical power. In Japan the *chu* was known as 'The Brocade Ball of the Lion'. It was hollow and symbolized 'emptiness' or 'pure vacancy', which, according to Japanese teaching, was the necessary condition of the mind if it was to receive wisdom.

By the seventeenth century there was no longer any pretence in China at delineating the symbol of Buddhism as anything but a pekinese dog. The attitudes of the pekes depicted in religious paintings were entirely dog-like, the attributes they had previously shared with the lion having disappeared altogether. In later Japanese art the lion also appeared as a peke, and even when acting as a steed to the Buddha it wore a collar with dangling bells and ornaments. An eighteenth-century manuscript at the British Museum shows the Buddha seated on a rock with a peke lying at his feet.

In the countries that supported a cult of the lion-dog, lion masques were regularly held. In Tokyo the Dogs of Fo which stood in front of Buddhist temples were carried in procession. In China a pair of cardboard lion heads with cloth bodies were carried in procession from certain temples accompanied by a large embroidered ball attached to a staff. When they reached a high place the lions stopped to play with the ball to the delighted applause of a large audience. These Chinese ritual processions were known as 'Exercising the lions', and they were comparable to the old English mystery plays.

The cult of the lion-dog was the cult of the pekinese, and, from the time when the pekes were first recognized as bearing some resemblance to the Indian lion (and images of the latter started to appear more canine), their leonine features were deliberately emphasized in breeding. In Imperial palaces, pekinese were bred by the chief eunuch of the court, who presented only the most leonine specimens to the Emperor. Many pekes were bred with a white blaze on their foreheads in imitation of the little shining sphere between the eyebrows of the Buddha. Since they were guarded as sacred animals, few of these pekes ever found their way into the outside world.

Tibetan lamas also threw themselves with zeal into the production of leonine toy-dogs, and habitually made presents of them to Chinese Emperors. In their old Buddhist monasteries, the Tibetans preserved for many centuries a race of dwarf lion-dogs resembling pekes, but somewhat heavier and with more massive heads. In monasteries where black was not admitted, a light red or biscuit colour was cultivated.

In Japan the chin was bred as the lion-dog—a dog much lighter in weight than the peke. Whether black and white or red and white, the chins all had white foreheads with a black spot in the middle said to be the 'Sacred Island of Japan', or alternatively, the place on which the dog was touched by a Japanese goddess. (Five rules of beauty for the chin are: the Butterfly Head; the Sacred 'V'—a white mark up the centre of the head; the Butterfly's wings formed by the ears; the Bump of Knowledge—a round spot between the ears; Vulture Feet— hair feathering forward to a point; and the Chrysanthemum Tail.)

The Tibetans have tended to refer to any shaggy, long-coated dog as a lion-dog. Their golden apso (see p. 121) is claimed by some to be *the* Tibetan lion-dog; others give this title to the shih tzu—a Sino-Tibetan breed resulting from the cross between an apso and a peke. The creature on the Tibetan national flag is called a lion-dog, but the drawing is highly stylized and shows little resemblance to either breed.

2) *Monastic dogs of Tibet and Mongolia* In Tibet dogs are bred in monasteries and trained by the lamas to take part in religious ritual.

Tibetan spaniels have, for centuries, been considered sacred and have learnt to perform various services. The lamas use prayer wheels —revolving cylinders containing tightly rolled parchment on which is written a Buddhist prayer—and have taught their spaniels to turn these wheels as the result of which they have become known as 'Prayer dogs'. (Each revolution of the wheel is believed to give the prayers an impetus which carries them directly to heaven.)

The spaniels are used as guards, both of the monasteries and their flocks of sheep. They lie along the battlements keeping watch over the surrounding countryside, and if man or wolf approach they set up a shrill excited bark. At this warning signal the gates are flung open, and monks armed with long staves pour out, joined by the sacred dogs, to drive off the intruders. These dogs are also valued by the monks as muffs and hot-water bottles. An abbot will sit on a cushion cross-legged with his hands folded inside the capacious sleeves of his robe, and when he rises a small hairy bundle will often jump out of his sleeve on to the floor.

In ancient times Tibetan spaniels were so highly prized that they formed part of the tribute annually paid to the Emperors of China by successive ruling dynasties at Lhasa. This is how the breed originally became established in China. They were treasured as pets in oriental courts, and are portrayed in early Chinese paintings, tapestries and ceramics. The whole court went into mourning when one of these little dogs died, and there are people who claim that the pekinese derives from a cross between a Tibetan spaniel and a Chinese pug.

In Tibet today these dogs are rarely found outside the monasteries. As sacred animals they are closely guarded, and the monks will never part with a bitch. People owning them in this country say that they make characteristic movements with their paws as if they were still turning prayer wheels.

The Tibetan terrier is, however, supposed to be the original and true 'holy dog of Tibet'—although this is a matter of controversy. (There is a great spirit of 'holier than thou' among Western owners of Tibetan dogs!) The terriers are said to have originated in an ancient seat of learning now spoken of as the 'lost valley of Tibet', and they accompanied as guards the ancient caravans conveying Tibet's tribute to China. (The protection these little dogs gave was due more to their sanctity than their ferocity, for no Tibetan would lay hands on a 'holy dog' or the treasures it guarded.) In addition to taking part in monastic rites, the Tibetan terriers were used to receive the souls of dying lamas and incubate them until they were ready for reincarnation.

Another sacred Tibetan dog is the apso—so called because of its resemblance to the small, long-haired, indigenous goat ('apso' being a corruption of 'rapso', the Tibetan word for 'goat'). From very early times apsos were bred in Tibetan monasteries and also in the palace of the Dalai Lama. It is said that the souls of lamas who have not been as good as they should have been enter the bodies of apsos at death. Apsos have also been presented to Chinese Emperors over the last four centuries, and they are generally accepted as talismanic dogs.

In Mongolia packs of chow-chows are kept in Buddhist monasteries, and, in particular, the beautiful blue variety the breeding of which the lamas keep a close secret. They are used for hunting, for rounding up monastic herds of cattle and to guard and protect the monastery and its inmates.

3) *Greek and Roman temple-dogs* In various Greek and Roman cults dogs were kept in temples where they participated in the religious rites of the gods.

At Etna, in Sicily, the temple dedicated to Hephaestus, god of subterranean fire, had a precinct full of sacred dogs. They appear to have been extraordinarily discriminating hounds, for they fawned upon worshippers who came with pure hearts, bit those whose hands were polluted and chased away such as had recently left a bed of debauchery. The temple of Adranus, a Sicilian war-god, appears to have supported a thousand splendid dogs. During the daytime these sacred hounds took part in temple rites and greeted visitors to the shrine. At night when worshippers had drunk well in the god's honour, they escorted safely home those that were staggering; ripped to bits the clothes of the more noisy and violent ones, and made savage attacks on thieves and pickpockets. Dogs kept in a Roman shrine of Diana, tore to pieces a man who tried to rape a woman worshipping the goddess there. Dionysius was said to keep a pack of hounds in his temple in Sparta which savaged anyone who obstructed his musicians.

Sometimes the duty of these temple-dogs was to guard treasure. At the temple of Dictynna in Crete, dogs 'fierce as bears' were thus employed late one night when the miracle-worker Apollonius of Tyana arrived. Instead of barking they fawned on him, and so unheard of was this that a guardian of the shrine promptly arrested him believing that he must be a wizard who had thrown the dogs charmed food. Sacred dogs were kept in all temples of Asklepios, god of healing. It is told how a thief once entered the Aesculapium at Athens, stole gold and silver offerings and escaped without being noticed by temple attendants. One of the dogs, however, saw him, and having tried unsuccessfully to attract the attention of servitors, followed the thief day and night, never letting him out of sight, until, when the treasures were eventually missed, the police caught up with him. The thief got his deserts, and a decree was passed that the dog should receive food at public expense and that the priests of Asklepios should tend it for the rest of its life.

Dogs appear to have taken part in the Eleusinian mysteries. A sculpture representing the Eleusinian cave shows the Great Mother-goddess attended by a dog, and the aspirant being brought into the cave by a dog.

It is considered probable that sacred dogs were kept in that temple dedicated to Heracles called Cynosarges (see p. 96) to which Diomus had been led by a white bitch.

4) *Dogs of pagan and Christian hunting rites*   Dogs participated in ancient Greek hunting rites. The hunting god, Maleatas, had a sanctuary on a hill outside Epidaurus called Kynortion (the 'Mountain of the Rising Dog'), and here rites of the hunt periodically took place and sacrifices were made to hunting dogs. At the annual festival of Artemis, goddess of the chase, hunting dogs were at the centre of the ritual. After sheep, goats or calves had been sacrificed to the goddess, huntsmen and dogs alike were feasted and the dogs were ritually crowned with garlands of flowers.

The worship of Diana (as the Romans called Artemis) extended to the British Isles, for it is claimed that the custom of crowning and decorating greyhounds that have distinguished themselves in the coursing field with roses and garlands of ribbons was based on the Scots' veneration of her as goddess of hunting. A medal depicts Diana holding a spear, or hunting pole, in her left hand, and a fillet or crown in her right hand above the head of a hunting dog which looks up as if in anticipation of a reward.

In Christianized southern Europe the patron saint of hunting was St Eustace, and on his feast days huntsmen travelled from distant parts to obtain blessing on themselves and their hunting dogs. The greatest of all patron saints of hunting was, however, St Hubert, whose cult was widespread in northern Europe. According to legend this saint was of noble birth and spent his youth in worldly pursuits. He was so keen on the chase that he hunted even on holy days. One Good Friday, when he was hunting in the forest of the Ardennes, he received a vision of a white stag with a crucifix between its horns. Christ spoke to him, asking him how much longer he intended to hunt and amuse himself with mundane vanities, and as a result of this experience Hubert withdrew to an abbey in the solitude of the Ardennes. He later received instructions from an angel to go to Rome, and finally became the first bishop of Liège.

Abbots in the monastery founded by St Hubert bred hounds which took the saint's name and were renowned throughout Christendom for their hunting qualities. (Bloodhounds are their modern descendants).

St Hubert took over many of the sanctuaries of the pagan goddess of the chase, and his rites were superimposed on those of Artemis. In some places the pagan Wild Hunt (see p. 55 ff.) came to be known as the 'Hunt of St Hubert'.

An eleventh-century work on the saint refers to his receiving offerings of huntsmen : 'It had long been the custom of nobles of the entire
Ardennes to offer to the blessed Hubert both first fruits of the hunt of
each season and one-tenth of every kind of game.' From the Ardennes
this custom spread to nobles of neighbouring territories, for they
looked to the saint for protection both for themselves and their hunting dogs.

The feast of St Hubert was the feast of the huntsmen of the
Ardennes, and on this day, 3rd November, every year a mass was celebrated under the name of the 'Mass of St Hubert' or, more popularly,
the 'Mass of the dogs'. It has been described how, at Chantilly (where
until recently the Mass was still celebrated), on the feast day of St
Hubert, the chapel in the castle was decorated with flowers which
would be spread over the floor and over the dogs' kennels. A great procession of dogs would be led towards the chapel by the oldest man
mounted on the oldest horse, followed by the oldest dog, and accompanied by the oldest whipper-in. First in the procession came the great
dignitaries of the kennels : the regulars and reserves of the German
bull-dogs, wearing collars bristling with spikes. Then came the greyhounds with their smooth skins, nervous legs, slim stomachs and
ferrets' muzzles. When all were finally assembled in the centre of the
chapel, and lined up before the portrait of St Hubert, Mass was celebrated. After this, the chaplain climbed into the pulpit and pronounced a
panegyric of the great saint of the hunt; then prayers were offered to
protect all the hunting dogs from bites, stings, wounds and rabies.

A slightly different version of this Chantilly rite was recorded in
the middle of the last century by someone who had recently attended
it. This describes how the Duc d'Aumole, who kept up the tradition,
assembled with guests in the parish church at 3 a.m. on the 3rd of
November. The chief huntsman appeared with the oldest member of
the pack of hounds on a leash, and, seated on the altar steps, it received
holy water and the Orleans cockade, which was attached to its neck.
At the elevation of the Host, six huntsmen sounded the blast of St
Hubert on the trumpet, and on leaving the church gave the 'Reveil de
veneur'.

At Sillé-le-Guillaume, in Sarthe, the 'Mass of the dogs' continued
to be celebrated (Plate 5h) up to the end of the last war, and it was
followed by a ritual hunt. Before the Mass began the piqueurs
assembled on the east side of the church with the hounds, and the pro-

cession was led by a verger who tapped the altar steps three times with a silver cane. Then a priest with a cross came forward and blessed the hound at the foot of the steps, after which the hounds were leashed together as a pack. Finally, the whole hunt was blessed, and when the mass was over they all, with the exception of the hounds, moved off to a meeting-place in the forest. When they had met a horn was blown summoning all hounds in the neighbourhood to join in, and the huntsmen arrived with the pack from the church. As soon as the hounds scented the stag everyone mounted and followed them. When, eventually, the stag was surrounded by hounds, it made for water and the *piqueurs* rushed in and hauled it out. The hounds were trained never to touch the stag until given permission to do so, and it was not until the *piqueurs* had killed it, and the huntsman had blown on the horn a tune called '*l'hallali*'—that they were allowed to tear the entrails—the only part of the stag allotted to them.

On the Saint's day at the church of St Hubert in the Ardennes, horns sounded the reveille at 3 a.m., and huntsman, whippers-in, keepers, trainers and followers set off with the hounds to attend the 'Mass of the dogs', which was celebrated by torchlight. Horns sounded during the consecration and benediction; and afterwards the priest came to the door of the church, where he blessed the whole hunt, including the hounds. This also was followed by a ritual hunt.

These hounds were not sacred dogs in any permanent sense, but they regularly participated in religious rites and received the temporary sanctification of the Mass.

5) *Dogs of Parsi funeral rites* Parsis regarded the dog as a holy animal, for it played a very important part in their funeral rites.

When a Parsi was dying a little dog was placed on his chest, and its muzzle applied to his mouth to receive the departing soul (Plate 5d). At the last moment it would be made to bark twice as if to force the soul to enter it so that it could be delivered to the waiting angel. When a pregnant woman was dying, two dogs would be set before her—one for each departing spirit. (This practice has now been modified into merely bringing a dog into the dying person's room.)

Another Zoroastrian funeral rite, known as '*Sâgdid*', consisted of exposing the face of the deceased person three or four times to the gaze of a brown four-eyed dog, or a white dog with yellow ears. (A four-eyed dog, it is explained, is one with two spots above its eyes.)

According to the sacred writings of the ancient Persians, the first spiritual aim of man is purity. Impurity (or uncleanliness), they maintain, is the state of a person or thing possessed by a demon and so the object of purification is demon-expulsion. Death is considered to be the triumph of the demon and the chief means by which it enters a man: as soon as the soul has parted from the body the corpse-demon comes up from hell and takes possession. Anyone who touches the corpse becomes unclean and will infect any others with whom he comes into contact. The purpose of *Sâgdid*, therefore, was the expulsion of the corpse-fiend, for when the corpse was exposed to the gaze of one of these dogs, the demon inhabiting it bolted back to hell. When a Parsi died a friend of his would scour the neighbourhood for a dog with the necessary markings, and if he found one would bribe it with crusts of bread to bring it as near as possible to the corpse. (The nearer the dog approached, the nearer was the dead man assumed to be to the 'mansions of bliss'). An incontestible sign of his being destined for eternal joy was when the dog jumped on to his corpse and seized from his mouth a piece of bread placed there for this purpose.) The corpse had to be exposed three or four times to the dog-gaze, and the officiating priest supported this rite with incantations. The demon-dispelling dog was sometimes made to go three, six or nine times through the route taken by the deceased between his home and his final resting-place; for no one could safely pass that way until the corpse spirit had been blown back to hell.

All Zoroastrian corpses, whatever had been their rank or dignity in life, were laid in open fields to be devoured by dogs. The corpse of a Magus was not allowed to be buried before it had been attacked either by dogs or birds, and some sects felt burial or cremation to be sacrilegious. (According to the historian, Herodotus, the Bactrians actually called dogs 'buriers'.) If the dogs refused to touch a carcass, this was regarded by relatives and friends as the worst possible sign of the ultimate destruction of the deceased's soul. (In Buddhist monasteries in Tibet large and savage dogs were bred for the express purpose of devouring bodies of the dead, and this was considered to be an honourable form of disposal reserved for monks and persons of high position.)

The *Sâgdid* rite is thought to have been based on myth. The supreme god of the ancient Persians, wishing to protect the body of the first man he had created from the assaults of the Devil, said: 'O thou yellow-eared dog, arise.' The dog manifested itself, shook its ears and barked, and when the Devil saw and heard it, he was frightened and fled back to hell. The dog that guarded the Kinvad bridge was yellow-eared, and it will be recalled how, when after death the souls of the righteous arrived there, they were successfully defended by this dog against the assault of unclean spirits. The image of the four-eyed dog is presumably taken from Hindu mythology, where such dogs owned by Yama steered the souls of the dead safely through the dangers of the Underworld.

Parsis were bidden to put aside for sacred dogs three mouthfuls of any bread they ate; and if a dog died they carried it out of the town, praying for its soul. The correct treatment for a mad dog (or one that bit without barking) was to place a wooden collar round its neck and tie it to a post. If it then succeeded in injuring a man or a sheep it was mutilated. On the other hand, it was laid down that if a dog went mad people should 'attend him to heal him in the same manner as they would do for one of the faithful'.

REGAL AND COURTLY DOGS

Some dogs have been venerated not for their spiritual but for their worldly power; they have been treated not as gods or priests but as kings, noblemen or warriors.

1) *Dog-kings* A Norwegian saga tells how, when Eystein the Bad had conquered Drontheim, he offered the people a choice of being ruled by his dog or his slave. They chose his dog to be their king, as they thought it would allow them more independence. This animal, it is said, had the wisdom of three men, and spoke one word for every two that it barked. A throne was erected for the dog and he 'sat upon a high place as kings are wont to sit'. A collar of gold was made for him and silver chains for his courtiers, whose duty it was to carry the dog-king on their shoulders whenever the weather was foul. One day, however, wolves broke into the royal cattle pens and the courtiers stirred the dog-king to defend his cattle. When he rushed at the wolves in attack he was torn to pieces by them.

An Ethiopian race is said to have elected a dog as its king. It was kept in great state, surrounded by a train of officers and guards, and expressed its pleasure or displeasure by fawning on people or barking.

2) *Imperial dogs* Long before the arrival of Buddhism in China there were pekes in the Imperial palaces; and three thousand years ago, when these dogs were little different in type and character from those bred today, there was a cult of the pekinese in Chinese courts.

The Imperial dogs were bred and reared by eunuchs, and the puppies were suckled by ladies-in-waiting (in place of girl babies, who were considered superfluous)—all under the close supervision of the Emperor. Each Emperor had portraits painted in 'dog-books' of his favourite pekes, and they constituted the only recognized standards in breeding. The eunuchs, of whom there were often a thousand or more in the palace, vied with each other in trying to reach these standards and to secure favour with the Emperor by presenting him with specially fine specimens. These breeders employed various methods of modifying the natural development of the pekes' bodies: to retard their growth the puppies were often enveloped in close-fitting wire cages which were not removed until they reached maturity; or they would be deprived of exercise after the third month to lessen their appetites. Growing puppies were held for days on end in the hands of eunuchs who, by gentle pressure of their fingers, would induce an exaggeration in width between the shoulders. To produce short noses the cartilages of three-to-seven-days-old puppies were broken with thumbnails or chopsticks. Some eunuchs massaged the noses daily to restrain their growth, while others fed the puppies from flat plates or encouraged them to bite pigskin stretched on a board. Protrusion of the tongue was a point much valued in pekes, and the eunuchs rendered the puppies' tongues permanently long by forcibly stretching them. In dynastic China pekes were bred with dark red coats and black masks.

The Emperor's favourite pekinese were given the ranks of the highest mandarins; were created dukes and princes, and granted royal revenues. Imperial guards kept watch over these chosen animals, and officers of state paid them homage. They had hosts of personal servants attending on them: their toilet was carried out with elaborate ceremonial, and after their daily baths they would be sprayed with perfume before being laid to rest on silken cushions. They were taken out for regular exercise, or carried around in sumptuous palanquins. These pekes were the constant companions of the Emperor and of his ladies, who pampered them. They shared the Imperial couch; sat in front of the Emperor's saddle when he rode on horseback; accompanied him in the hall of audience; sat beside him on the throne, and generally played their allotted parts in all palace ceremonies. When, in the court dress of dynastic China, wide sleeves were considered a sign of aristocracy, a certain number of diminutive pekes were bred as 'sleeve dogs'—being carried around in the voluminous sleeves of the long robes which were worn by the ladies and mandarins. Favoured courtiers, or great officials, were occasionally allowed to keep a few pekes, but terrible punishments were inflicted on anyone else who removed a peke from the palace precincts. Only during the Ming period (1368–1644) was Imperial patronage largely withdrawn from the pekinese dog—for at this time it was temporarily transferred to the cat.

Portraits of these Imperial pekes were painted on scrolls, sculpted in bronze, modelled in porcelain, carved in ivory, jade and precious stones and embroidered in silk. It was not, however, until the eighteenth century (during the Manchu dynasty), that the pekinese was depicted in its completely natural guise, stripped of all the attributes it shared with the Buddhist lion. From this time onwards its image was multiplied in every conceivable form—portrayed on paper, silk, porcelain and lacquer; decorating fans, snuff-boxes and most objects of daily use.

At the end of the nineteenth century the Dowager Empress (whose reign coincided with that of Queen Victoria) was particularly keen to re-emphasize those features which the peke shared with the Buddhist lion, and she laid down the following instructions for its breeding: 'Let the Lion-dog be small; let its eyes be large and luminous; let its ears be set like the sails of a war-junk; let its nose be like that of the monkey-god of the Hindus; let its forelegs be bent so that it shall not desire to abandon close attendance on Her Imperial Highness; let its body be like that of a hunting lion; let its hair richly cover its feet that its footfall may be silent; let it be lively and entertain by its gambols; let it behave with the dignity of a duchess; let it learn to bite the white devil; let it venerate its ancestors and deposit offerings in the canine cemetery of the Forbidden City on each new moon.' She also laid down that the Imperial dog was to be fed on shark's fins, curlew's livers and the breasts of quails; that, for drink, it was to be given tea brewed from the spring buds of a bush that grew in the province of Hankow; the milk of an antelope pasturing in the Imperial parks; or broth made from the nests of sea-swallows, for thus, she said, 'shall it preserve its integrity and self-respect'. She encouraged comparison of her pekinese to the spirit-lions of Buddha and was specially interested in securing the white blaze on the forehead and the saddle mark on the back (Plate 5g). On the other hand, the Dowager Empress condemned and forbade all cruel practices by the eunuchs for developing abnormality or modifying the natural shape of the peke's body.

When, in 1908, this last great ruler of the Chinese Empire died, her favourite peke was led before her coffin by the chief eunuch accompanying her, as was the tradition, to her last resting-place.

In early dynastic China there were also cults of other ancient dogs. Emperor Ling-Ti of the Han dynasty bestowed some of the highest honours of the land on his dogs. He was particularly fond of one of unspecified breed—and gave it the official hat (which was nine inches high in front, four inches high behind and ten inches broad) of the Chien Hsien grade—the most important literary rank of the period—and an official belt. Most other dogs he reared were given the status of K'ai Fu (approximately that of a viceroy), while the bitches received ranks of the wives of corresponding officials. These dogs had their own bodyguard of soldiers, were fed on the best meat and rice, and slept on beautiful rugs.

In the seventh century a Turkish envoy brought two sacred dogs of the pekinese type to the Emperor which were said to be of great intelligence. They had been trained to lead their master's horses by the reins, and to light his path at night by torches carried in their mouths. A similar type of dog, known as the Lo Chiang, which was sent as a tribute from Korea to Japan in A.D. 732, was fashionable in the Imperial court for three centuries. During the Sung dynasty the Emperor was given a very small and intelligent Lo Chiang which followed him everywhere. When there was to be an audience it preceded him, announcing his arrival by its bark; when he was ill it refused to eat, and when he died it whined incessantly. The palace eunuchs failed in their efforts to train it to precede the new Emperor, and when it was carried, lying on a white cushion in an iron cage, to its master's tomb, it gave up the ghost. The new Emperor ordered the Lo Chiang to be wrapped in the cloth of an Imperial umbrella and buried alongside his predecessor.

Emperors of the Tang dynasty (seventh to tenth centuries) were specially famous for the care they bestowed on their dogs, and they bred them not only in palaces but in the Imperial ancestral temple. (This practice was prohibited five hundred years later, and when a eunuch was found keeping a small dog in this temple he escaped severe punishment only by the payment of a substantial bribe.) During this period much larger dogs—chow-chows—were members of the Imperial household, and they were awarded titles and decorations and were waited on by servants. One ruler was reported to have had two thousand five hundred chows, which were looked after by an army of servants, had a military escort, and slept on rich carpets. The ancient Chinese Book of Rites sets forth the procedure to be adopted in the presentation of dogs: 'When honouring by the gift of a dog', it says, '. . . it is to be led with the left hand . . . that the right may be ready to restrain the dog from biting.' If the gift is acceptable, the recipient's representative first takes the leading rope, then asks the dog's name. In the Middle Ages dogs' collars were often works of art: they were made of coloured leather or of silk, and were adorned with gold or silver lettering and hung with chiming bells.

Famous for his concern for dogs was a Japanese Emperor born in the seventeenth century in the zodiacal sign of the Dog. During his reign dogs were bred prolifically, and by special command every street had to keep, and provide with food, a specified number of dogs. Huts were built to which they were taken when they fell sick, and those that died were carried up to the tops of mountains, where they were decently interred. Severe penalties were imposed on those who insulted or abused dogs, and capital punishment was meted out to anyone who killed a dog.

3) *Fighting dogs* Dog-fights have provided entertainment in both Eastern and Western courts. Pekinese were good little fighters, and in the Imperial palaces the eunuchs often staged fights. In the late eighteenth century in Great Britain dog-fights were also popular among the aristocracy, and the Court regularly attended the dog-pit at Westminster.

It was in Japan, however, that there was a highly developed cult of the fighting dog. It is told how, at the beginning of the fourteenth century, the Emperor happened to see dogs biting each other in his garden, and he found it so fascinating that he ordered his subjects to furnish him with dogs instead of taxes. So all the principal families sent dogs, and the governors of provinces brought a dozen or so each as presents, until the numbers reached nearly five thousand and the palace was full of dogs. Imperial fighting dogs were fed on fish and fowl, dressed in brocade, and kept in elaborate and costly kennels. Twelve times a month there were 'great fight days' when several hundred dogs would be let loose from both sides of the arena, and a violent fight ensued in which they bit each other and rolled over and howled—the sky resounding with the noise. When champions of the fight were led through the streets or carried in sedan chairs by specially hired peasants, passers-by doffed their headgear or descended from their horses to kneel in reverence before them.

In addition to providing entertainment by fighting each other, dogs have also been extensively used by men for fighting human beings. In the first century mastiffs were employed as war-dogs in tribal wars against the Romans. They were heavily armoured and fought in packs. Three centuries later, in the days of Alexander the Great, mastiffs described as being 'Vaste, huge, ugly and stubborne, of a Hevy and Burthenous Body and therefore of but little Swiftnesse, terrible and frightful to Behold', were specially trained to be ferocious by being treated with great cruelty. In battle they wore heavy iron-spiked collars and spiked armour which tore and lacerated men and horses alike. In Madrid Museum there is a dog clad in finely wrought armour, wearing armorial bearings, plumed helmet, hauberk of chain armour, corselet and a surcoat of steel.

4) *Hunting dogs* Hunting dogs have often been treated with the respect normally reserved for highly bred human beings.

In the courts of medieval Europe huge packs of very powerful dogs (produced by crossing mastiffs with Irish wolf-hounds) were kept for hunting, and princes and knights vied with each other for possession of the finest specimens of them. They were fed on fat cattle and venison, and were given ranks. The most noble dogs were the 'dogs in waiting', which wore gilded collars; next came the silver-collared 'dogs of the bodyguard', while hunting dogs of the third rank were known as 'English dogs'.

(Another example of hunting dogs being similarly treated, comes from India. It is recorded how Sir Thomas Roe made a present of British mastiffs to the Great Mogul—the Emperor Jehanghir. *En route*, one of the dogs jumped overboard after porpoises diving near the ship, while another, on the way upcountry, seized an elephant.

This behaviour so enchanted the Emperor that he provided the dogs with servants; with carriages and palkis in which to take the air, and fed them with his own hands from silver dishes.)

In fifteenth-century England royal hounds were treated with the greatest consideration. According to a Bestiary, the Duke of York (who was killed at Agincourt) insisted that a 'dog-boy' should share the kennels with the hounds in order to keep them happy. The boy's duties were to exercise them twice daily and, after playing with them in sunny meadows, to comb each hound 'and wipe them with a great wisp of straw'. He then had to lead them to a place where tender grass grew and plants on which they fed as medicine. Since the boy's heart, it was explained, would be with the hounds, they would become 'goodly and kindly and clean, glad and joyful and playful, and goodly to all manner of folks save to wild beasts, to whom they should be fierce, eager and spiteful'. Dog-collars were sometimes worn by the attendants of royal dogs.

In the next two centuries greyhound packs were favoured by English monarchs, and they were often a thousand strong. A spectacle specially organized for Queen Elizabeth after a banquet was the tearing to bits by the royal pack of sixteen head of red deer.

DOG-HEALERS

According to the Oxford dictionary there is a word 'cynotherapy' which means 'the practice of healing by means of dogs'. There are four different ways in which the dog has been connected with healing : its image was common to the iconography of many divine physicians, some of whom it incarnated while acting as the agent of others; it appeared to heal many people by licking their injuries; parts of its body were used in folk medicine, and its blood was used to exorcise demons of disease.

1) *Divine physicians* In dynastic Egypt the apothecary and physician of the gods was Anubis, to whom dogs were sacred and who was himself dog-headed. The dog was the sacred emblem of Marduk, the Babylonian and Chaldean god of healing, who, as founder of the zodiac, bestowed health on mankind through the medium of the planets. The sacred animal of Gula, the Sumarian goddess known as the Great Physician, was a dog, and on boundary stones she was shown

seated on a throne with a dog squatting beside her. Gula, in addition to removing sickness and preserving the body in good health, also presided over the rebirth of man. Both she and Marduk were referred to as 'Restorer of the dead to life' in incantations in which they were appealed to for help against disease-demons whose grasp meant death; and they awoke individuals stricken with sickness to new life.

In ancient Greece, Apollo the sun-god was the supreme god of healing, and the dog was sacred to Apollo Maleatas (Apollo having taken over the sanctuary on Mount Kynortion of Maleatas, the earlier hunting god). Immediately below the Mountain of the Rising Dog was Epidaurus—the centre of the cult of Asklepios, Apollo's son, who was known as the Divine Physician and God of Medicine. In the middle of the sacred grove at Epidaurus there was a shrine containing an altar behind which stood the cult statue of Asklepios. This was an image carved in ivory and gold, of the enthroned god with a dog lying by his right side and a large golden snake rising up to his left hand. (A silver coin found in Epidaurus, and dated *circa* 350 B.C., shows Asklepios with a dog lying under his throne.) The sons of Asklepios were also sometimes depicted accompanied by dogs, as in the case of a votive relief from Epidaurus.

In view, therefore, of the repeated association of dogs with Divine Physicians, it may reasonably be assumed that the dog participated, at least symbolically, in their powers of healing.

2) *Dog-lick therapy* Some people believe that Asklepios inherited the symbol of the dog from Apollo Maleatas at Mt Kynortion, others that he came to be associated with dogs through the myth which told how, as an infant, his life was saved by a bitch which suckled and reared him (see p. 106). In one account of this myth, when a shepherd found the infant god lying in a dazzling light between goat and bitch, a voice was heard from the heavens proclaiming over land and sea that the new-born child would discover every cure for the sick. Mt Titthium (so named because Asklepios was suckled on it) was famed for the medicinal virtues of its plants, so it is possible that the god obtained his knowledge of them through having been reared there. On the other hand, other authorities maintain that he was brought up by Chiron, the centaur, who was famed throughout antiquity as the inventor of herbal medicine, and that Chiron gave

Asklepios drugs, and named him 'The guardian and protector of health, strength and of well-being'.

The temples of the Greek god of Medicine were not only places of worship but also health resorts. At Epidauros a wealth of buildings and monuments were crowded within the bounds of the sacred grove, including baths, a theatre, a stadium and the shrines of other gods and goddesses. The most important part of the sanctuary was the building where the incubations (healing sleeps in which patients received visions of the god) took place. This consisted of a great peristyle with double columns on the north side, and a west wing composed of two stories. One of its inner walls was adorned with innumerable votive tablets on which were engraved the official lists of cures that had taken place there. Dogs were kept in the temples of Asklepios at Epidauros, Athens, Rome, Piraeus, and at Lebene in Crete. They were believed to have a presentiment of epidemics, and they took part in the religious ritual.

Asklepios cured diseases of all kinds and his temples were always full of the sick. At night patients made their way to the sanctuary, where they performed rites of purification and placed a cock or ram on the altar as a sacrifice. After this they lay down on the floor of the incubation hall, and waited for the visitation of the god. Although Asklepios often helped the sick when approached by prayer, he was essentially a god of the dream oracle and was at his most effective when he appeared in their temple dreams. The candles that burned while patients were assembling were extinguished shortly before the god was expected to make his appearance. It was said that Asklepios revealed himself nightly to all who needed his help. Some incubants perceived him in a state half-way between sleep and waking; others in their dreams. Sometimes he came in the form in which his sacred statues portrayed him, and either touched the sick, bringing immediate healing, or else gave advice as to what treatment they should follow on awakening; at other times he appeared incarnated in the form of a dog or a snake. The sacred animals kept in the Asklepieion were trained to lick the patients' injured, or diseased, parts; and, in addition to visitations by the god incarnated as an animal, healing often came to patients by the lick of an actual dog or snake believed to be sent by the god as his agent.

Slabs found within the precincts of the temple at Epidauros, inscribed with the names of people cured by Asklepios and the malady from which each had suffered, included the following:

> Thuson of Hermione, a blind boy, had his eyes licked in the daytime by
> one of the dogs about the temple, and departed cured.

> A dog cured a boy from Aigina. He had a growth on his neck. When
> he had come to the god, one of the sacred dogs healed him while he was
> awake with its tongue and made him well.

After the healing, suppliants were submitted to blood-letting and
catharsis, and they made thanks offerings to Asklepios. Sometimes
these consisted of food such as honeycakes, cheese cakes and figs (and
in the Asklepieion at Athens patients also sacrificed cakes to the sacred
dogs); at others, of gold and silver models of the diseased parts of the
patients that had been cured or of the temple dogs.

A remarkable number of stone and brass figures of dogs were
found in and around a Romano-British temple excavated by Sir
Mortimer Wheeler in Gloucestershire. This temple, which was
dedicated to Nodens (an Irish god who was Lord of the Land of
Sleep), was not built in the usual Classical style, but in the form of a
great hall surrounded by alcoves or bays. It appears to have been a
centre of pilgrimage, and it is thought probable that there were
vestiges here of the Asklepion cult with people coming to take the
temple sleep and dogs playing an important part in the rites of healing.

The dog has an instinct to clean its wounds by licking, and it licks
those of others as if they were its own. It has been suggested that the
actual cleansing properties of the dog's tongue have been responsible
for its reputation as a healer, and this could afford another possible
reason for its association with Asklepios and other Divine Physicians.

The way in which the sacred dogs of Asklepios wandered among
the pilgrims licking the sick parts of their bodies brings to mind the
dog-lick therapy applied to the sores of Lazarus in the New Testament
parable of the wicked rich man (Plate 5e). It also seems probable that
the healing of the plague spots of St Roch (who is so frequently
depicted, as in Plate 4f, with his dog licking them) was effected in
the same way.

Belief in dog-lick therapy has been very widespread. The French
say:

> Langue de chien
> Sert de médecin,

and, in particular, they claim that ulcers can be cured by dog-lick. In

Scotland it is believed that a cure for suppurating wounds is to have them licked by a dog, and a 1921 edition of the medical journal, *Lancet*, recorded how a Durham family attributed their recovery from scabies to being licked by their pet dog.

In Venice people used to believe that dogs have balm in their tongues, and that it is this that heals wounds. In the Punjab wounds are treated by pouring curdled milk on them in order to attract a dog, and it was claimed that they were healed several days after the licking. Indians maintained that the curative property of the tongue was due to its containing ambrosia, and that the English killed dogs in order to extract this healing matter from their tongues.

(In ancient Assyrian literature there were mythical beings called '*Aralez*'—a word meaning 'licking continually or thoroughly'. They were supernatural creatures, born from a dog, whose function was to lick the wounds of warriors who fell on the battlefield and bring them back to life. In Armenia this belief survived up to the end of the fourth century.)

3) *The dog in folk medicine* In ancient China it was believed that disease came out of the earth and that a dog could be used as a weight to keep it in.

The Greek writer, Aelian, maintained that dogs can diagnose the healthfulness of air and of wells. He also explained: 'when dogs need to empty both stomachs (that is—stomach and intestines) they are said to eat some grass and as much of their food as remains undigested they vomit up, while the remainder is excreted. It is from this source that the Egyptians are said to have learnt the practice of taking purges and emetics'.

The flesh of puppies has often been used in folk-medicine: blind whelp was eaten for all sores in early summer; the flesh of a suckling puppy was taken with wine and myrrh as a cure for epilepsy; newly whelped puppy was considered excellent for weak stomachs, and was used as an ingredient in linaments for bruised limbs; and a salve was made of the tongues of puppies for wounded intestines.

Various parts of the body of adult dogs have also been used to heal the sick. A dog's head reduced to ashes was believed to cure diseases of the rectum, venereal disease, burns, sores, jaundice and chilblains; a dog's spleen was taken with food as treatment for diseases of the spleen or attached to the affected parts of the body. A cake of the heart of a white hound baked with meal was supposed to cure convulsions, while a dog's testicles cut in half provided treatment for an abscess. The right foot of a dead black dog hung on the arm, we are told, 'shaketh off the fever'; the brains of a dog, if spread on linen cloth and laid on broken bones, caused them to unite in four days; and toothache was treated with the canine teeth of a dog burnt to ashes and mixed with urine. The skin of a dog was said to cure rheumatism; if wrapped round a finger to relieve catarrh, and if passed three times round the back to cure quinsy.

The secretions and excretions of dogs have also been used. It is said that bitch's milk instantly cures a scalded mouth; if rubbed into the skin it prevents the growth of hair, and that it facilitates the delivery of women. A drink of dog's blood is supposed to relieve griping and poisoning; that of a white dog cures lunacy, and that of a black dog solves difficulties of parturition. Dog's excrement has been taken in mixtures by people suffering from syphilis. The ashes of the white part of a dog's dung mixed with oil of roses is said to remove warts, as is also dog's urine with the mud it has formed on the ground. Dog's gall is believed to cure gout if applied with a feather; dropsy, it is said, can be cured by the application of dog's vomit, for if applied to the stomach it drains off accumulated water.

The use of dog's blood to exorcise demons of disease will be dealt with in a later chapter.

OMINOUS DOGS

Another power attributed by many people to dogs was that of predicting the future.

Omens were drawn from the physical characteristics of dogs : animals with abnormal features such as three eyes, or more than eighteen visible claws, brought good luck; and the colour and markings of dogs were specially significant. In dynastic China omen-production was considered to be an important aspect of dog-breeding, for fortunate markings could bring honour to a family and its ancestors. According to an old geomantic book, if a man bred a white dog with tiger markings, he would shortly become an official entrusted with ten thousand piculs of rice from the government; if a black dog with two white forelegs, or a black or yellow-coated dog with a white head, he could also receive an official appointment; while if he bred a black dog with white ears, he would become rich and noble. If a man bred a white dog with a black tail, his family would ride in chariots through all generations; if a white dog with a yellow head, they would become prosperous; and if a black dog with white forelegs, many male children would be born to them. Assyrians and Babylonians derived omens from piebald, yellow, black and white dogs, and cuneiform tracts list disasters to be expected in accordance with the colour of a dog encountered. For example: 'If a brown dog enter the house it is disastrous to go forth; If a white dog enter a temple the foundations are unstable; If a spotted dog enter a temple the gods do not favour it.'

Various forms of canine behaviour have been considered ominous. When a dog ate grass, rolled on the ground, scratched, became drowsy, stretched its feet out, or curved its belly to the ground—it was a sign of rain. In southern India, if a dog scratched the wall of a house, it meant it would be broken into by thieves; if it made a hole in the ground in the cattle shed, the cattle would be stolen; if it scratched its body, a traveller would fall ill; if it lay down and wagged its tail disaster would follow. If, before travelling, a dog jumped on to you shaking its ears, the journey was likely to be unlucky; if one crossed your path from right to left, the time was auspicious for setting off. If a dog approached you with a meaty bone, it brought good luck; if with a dry bone, it brought death. A dog barking on the roof of a house during dry weather portended epidemic; if one climbed the roof, it presaged the death of several members of the family. If a dog broke into a long howl it portended sickness, calamity, or the arrival of the demon of death.

In Japanese palaces the birth of a puppy was an omen of royal birth. A typical Japanese legend tells how, before the Emperor Go Ichijo (1016–36) was born, a bitch brought forth young 'inside the Imperial curtains of the Empress'. A doctor was immediately consulted, and said that it meant a crown prince would be born and become Emperor. Since dogs litter easily and painlessly, if one is found sleeping in the sedan chair of a pregnant woman it is an excellent omen for her.

The Japanese also considered the excreting of dogs highly ominous.

In the Punjab, when people wanted to know the reactions of their ancestors to a proposed marriage, they strewed ashes on the floor, and if a dog's footmarks were seen it meant that the ancestors approved. In the Congo, divining dogs were (and probably still are) used. These are wooden instruments (Plate 5i) in the form of dogs which have wooden knobs attached to their backs. If a Congolese repeatedly fell ill, it was assumed that this must be caused by black magic, and it was customary to present a list of the names of possible sorcerers to a divining dog. The wooden knob was then briskly rubbed up and down the dog's back until it stuck: the name at which the knob stuck indicating the identity of the sorcerer.

There is little consistency in the omens drawn from dogs: such as there is arises from the context (in terms of nationality, epoch, culture, beliefs, myths, etc.) in which they are found.

DOG-CHARMS AND TALISMANS

Charms and talismans are objects imbued with the power either to attract good fortune or to repel evil influences. Since the dog has been believed by so many people to possess supernatural power, its image has been widely used in the formation of such objects.

Although the words 'charm', 'amulet' and 'talisman' are used somewhat loosely and interchangeably, there is a difference in the emphasis of their powers, and a charm is primarily something that brings its owner good fortune.

1) *Attraction* In dynastic China many precious substances, such as ivory, jade and amber, became charms (that is—imbued with occult power) when the image of the lion-dog was carved on them, and such pieces were carried about, or worn, by people to bring them good luck.

A temple in Tokio held a special service twice a month for pregnant women, and when this coincided with a dog-day, dog-charms could be bought there which were believed to ensure easy birth. (The dog-day seems itself to have been considered a charmed day, for when, during the fifth month of pregnancy, Japanese women put on special girdles, a dog-day was always chosen for the rite.)

The most popular of Japanese dog-charms was the *inu-hariko*—a papier mâché dog-box. These objects varied in size, but they always had the body of a sleeping dog and the face of a child, and were white with black dots scattered over them. They often wore, in front, a gold and red garment with blue and red ornaments representing the sun; and, at the back, the '*tomoe*'—a circle containing three comma-shaped figures, symbolizing the male and female principle of the universe.

In olden times the *inu-hariko* was used as a wedding gift. The parents of an aristocratic bride had it placed by the young couple's bed. The next day a go-between brought it back to the parents, and they preserved it as a guarantee of the luck and harmony of the young couple's children. The *inu-hariko* was used extensively in lying-in rooms. According to a seventeenth-century work, it contained brushes, powder, napkins, cotton wool and navel bandages. It was dressed beforehand in the baby's first clothes, which were transferred to the child when it was born. It was kept by the baby's side and was believed to be in such close magical contact with it that when the child had a cold and its nose was blocked this could be cured by the piercing of the nose of the dog-charm! These charms were made and sold by nuns, who believed that in so doing they wiped out their sins. Later there were male and female dog-boxes: the male ones looked to the left and contained the baby's charms; the female ones looked to the right and had toys and the mother's toilet requisites in them.

2) *Protection*   Dog-talismans and amulets—objects imbued with magical power used primarily to ward off evil influences—protect their owners as real dogs do. Sometimes they have been real dogs. In ancient Rome, for instance, fierce watchdogs were chained to the thresholds of houses to keep off intruders, and their images were painted on the walls, or depicted in mosaic, with the warning: 'Cave canem', to give protection against supernatural evil (Plate 51). Similarly, in China chow-chows were used as watchdogs, and their images were painted on the doors of jails. The halls of geisha girls were often guarded by fierce dogs whose powers of protection were believed to be supernatural. Men who were not regular customers were not allowed to enter unceremoniously, and if they forced their way in the dogs bit them to death.

Usually, however, the presence of a three-dimensional dog was not considered necessary to ward off supernatural evil, its image alone being quite sufficient for the purpose. These dog-figures varied greatly in size, form, solidity and in their placement.

The largest talismanic dogs were probably the lion-dogs used to protect the Imperial Palaces in China from evil spirits. A twelfth-century work describes how two of these figures, which would guard a new Empress throughout her life, were placed before the Imperial curtains facing one another. At the death of the Empress the lion-dogs would be put aside against the wall of an empty room. (When, in 1074, the consort of Emperor Ichijo died, a temple was erected in her honour and at its dedication lion-dog dances were performed with the dancers wearing dog-masks to drive away evil spirits.) The Emperor himself was guarded by four lion-dogs—two copper ones placed within the Imperial curtains and two shadow-dogs painted on a door of the room. Lion-dogs also guarded the throne room during Imperial audiences, and they were placed on both sides of the palace gates when a new Emperor succeeded to the throne. Later both lion-dogs and shadow-dogs were used in front of, and within, Shinto temples. Some say these talismanic creatures are really lions, but that they have the dog's power of driving away evil spirits. As the dog protected the houses of ordinary people, so the lion-dog protected the palaces of Emperors and the temples of gods.

Next in size among talismanic dogs are probably those described in a Rabbinical legend. This tells how the Egyptians, to prevent Joseph's body being taken from them, had two golden dogs made and endowed by witchcraft with the power of frightening away intruders, and placed them on his tomb. When Moses came to take Joseph's bones away the dogs barked, but he rebuked them: 'You are the work of deceit and you would not move your tongues if you were real dogs.'

The Hittites used apotropaic magic, and in a rite to expel evil spirits from the royal palace they placed a small dog made of tallow on its threshold, saying: 'You are the little dog of the table of the royal pair. Just as by day you do not allow other men to enter into the court-yard so do not let in the evil thing during the night.' Assyrians buried clay models of coloured dogs under the threshold of their houses so that dog-spirits would repel the attacks of any demons that might try to enter. Ten were the usual number of dogs to be buried—five on each side of the doorway. Among early Chinese tomb furniture many pottery dogs were found—smooth-haired watchdogs protecting their dead masters from supernatural evil.

In Japan the dog-box was used as a talisman as well as a charm, for in addition to bestowing easy birth and good luck, it also had the power of protecting a child from bad demons including fever spirits and wer-animals. The *inu-hariko* placed by the side of a baby during day-time would at night often be hung above it to banish evil spirits from its dreams. When a Japanese baby cried at night people would murmur: 'Puppy, puppy', calling on the dog to protect it. (A Chinese book written in A.D. 752 described a different use of canine protection. It states: 'If a baby cries at night one must immediately take the hair beneath the throat of a dog, put this into a red bag, and bind it on the hands of the baby, then the child stops crying at once.')

A month after a Japanese child was born it was taken to a temple and given its name. A dog-day was usually chosen for this rite (as it also was for the mother's first day out after deliverance), so that it was performed under a protective influence. On leaving the temple the parents called on relatives, and the child was given numerous dog-boxes; the more visits they paid the more *inu-hariko* it received, and mother and child could be seen returning home in a rickshaw heavily hung with papier mâché dogs.

Even the Chinese character for 'dog' was considered sufficient to give protection, and was often written on babies' foreheads to protect them against an evil bird to which they were specially vulnerable. (This bird entered peoples' houses at night and robbed them of their souls. It had ten heads and, since one had been devoured by a dog, it feared the canine race. When parents heard it flying in the night they extinguished all lamps, and twitched the ears of their dogs to rouse them, and even made barking noises themselves. When older Chinese and Japanese children were taken out at night the 'dog' ideograph would be written in red ink on their foreheads to guard them against evil influences and particularly against fox, cat, and badger-demons.)

Fox-possession was a special fear of the Japanese, and when some-one was afflicted with this complaint members of their family would go to the temple of a mountain god called Mitsumine to obtain an amulet. Sacred dogs known as the 'servants of Mitsumine' were kept in the temple, and the amulets which were sold at the entrance con-tained pictures and characters of these animals. Such a pilgrimage was known as 'going to borrow a dog', and it was believed that the amulet was accompanied by a supernatural dog which was invisible and would drive the wer-fox away. When the pilgrims arrived home they stuck the pictures on the walls of their houses to prevent the entrance of any more fox-spirits.

The name of a dog was used as a talisman by Mohammedans. The dog that guarded the Seven Sleepers of Ephesus (see p. 90), was called 'Katmir', and they wrote this word on letters to be sent far away for protection.

In ancient Rome the Lares, which were household genii and

guardians of the home, frequently took the form of dogs, and in art the figure of a barking dog is often found at the feet of these household deities.

In addition to all the talismanic dogs that warded off demons, there were others that had the power to exorcise evil spirits that had already infiltrated. Among those were the dogs of the Parsi funeral rites, whose gaze dispelled invading corpse-demons (see p. 126), and a later chapter will give an account of the many dogs whose lives were sacrificed as a result of belief in the exorcising power of their blood.

DIRTY DOGS

Among the many beliefs perpetuated about dogs is the one that they are unclean. This reputation derives mostly from the behaviour of pariah dogs and there are various different aspects of it.

1) *Uncleanliness* The pariahs of Eastern streets were scavengers feeding on such refuse and offal as they could find, and in the New Testament it is claimed that 'dogs return to their own vomit'. But their reputation for uncleanliness probably arose more directly from their carrion-eating habits. 'Where carcases are dogs will gather'—and pariahs not only ate the putrefying flesh of dead animals, but, like jackals, they haunted burial-grounds and dug up human bodies from shallow graves. (As we know—p. 126—people of several races and religions ritually exposed corpses to be devoured by dogs.)

Moses decreed that the dog should be treated as an unclean animal, and the Jews regarded it with abhorrence. In the New Testament this attitude does not appear to have been contradicted, and an artist has interpreted it in a painting of the Magdalen now at Turin. This shows, on one side, Mary washing Christ's feet and, on the other, a dog emerging from under a table where it has been eating crumbs. In crawling out it touched the robe of a Pharisee, thus rendering it unclean, and the Pharisee gathers up his garment in indignation, showing the hem to a bystander and pointing accusingly at the dog.

Both Mohammedans and Hindus believed the dog to be unclean, and if they accidentally came in contact with it they had to submit to purification rites. If Mohammedans believed a dog had drunk from a vessel, it had to be ritually washed seven times and scrubbed with earth. If, during Hindu lessons, a dog passed between the teacher and his pupil, it was assumed that the work would be poisoned, and tuition was suspended for at least a day and night.

Sometimes the birth or death of a dog rendered the place unclean. In northern India if a dog was born or died in the house of a family of Gonds they had to undergo ritual purification. In ancient Japanese writings there are frequent references to the postponement of religious ceremonies because the birth or death of a dog in the palace had rendered it unclean. When in A.D. 927 a dog bit a child on the leg, there was much discussion at court as to whether or not this caused uncleanliness. Finally it was decided that it did not, so the religious ceremonies planned were able to be celebrated.

2) *Contemptibleness* When people speak of 'dirty dogs' the expression implies contempt, and the fact that dogs eat carrion is only one of several reasons for this attitude. (It is interesting to note that members of a sect who follow Bhairava, the 'untouchable' Hindu god whose vehicle was a dog, deliberately eat filth and do their utmost to acquire ritual impurity. This is said to be due to their belief that all is Brahman.) The pariah, like the jackal, is a treacherous coward; and is considered a worthless outcaste. The Hindus outcasted it in formal terms, not only because it conferred pollution, but also because it was incestuous (incest being the one taboo that is never broken), and they spoke of the pariah as a 'cur'. (The word 'cur' tends to be overloaded with contempt. It is of Celtic origin and derives from an ancient law which prevented the dogs of common people joining in hunts with the hounds of chiefs and noblemen unless their tails had been shortened. Such dogs were described as *'courtault'*, and later as *'curtal'*, and, finally, dogs generally came to be spoken of as 'curs'.)

In the Old Testament, and in the sacred writings of Mohammedans and Hindus, 'dog' is a byword of loathing and contempt. According to Mohammed, the angels of the Lord would not cross the threshold of a house where so much as the hair of a dog was to be found. The Hindus believed dogs were animated by malignant spirits condemned to do penance for crimes committed in previous lives. (The dog of Yudhisthira, and that of the seven sleepers of Ephesus, found in Hindu and Mohammedan mythologies, were famous exceptions to this attitude.)

'Dog' was the most scurrilous epithet that Hindus, Moslems and Jews could bestow on Christians; and Christians, in their turn, referred to heathens in the same reproachful way—the Samaritans being called 'dogs' because they were 'as adhesive to idolatrous customs as the dog is to the flesh of carcasses'. False teachers, persecutors, and those 'sunk in vileness and sin', were all referred to as 'dogs'; and the term was used as a form of self-derogation as in the case of someone who, in addressing his superior, signed himself 'thy servant a dog'.

The prefix 'dog' has come to denote spuriousness, as in dog-Latin, dog's logic, and dog-cheap; or inferior quality, as in dog-rose, dog-violet, dog-wheat, etc.

The word 'cynopic' means not only dog-faced but shameless, and the dog's salacity provided the ancients with a further reason for regarding it with disgust and contempt. (According to legend the dog was the only animal that would not abstain from copulation in the Ark!) In Homeric works the dog is used as a symbol of shamelessness —apparently because it 'couples openly'—and it was not allowed to enter the Acropolis at Athens or to appear on the sacred island of Delos.

In medieval Europe contempt for the dog was expressed by forcing it to participate in the punishment of criminals or specially despised people. In Germany an ignominious punishment inflicted on aristocratic criminals before they were executed was known as 'carrying the dog'; while in France, up to the fourteenth century, Jews were hanged head downwards between two dogs. (It is recorded that when, later, Napoleon arrived in Germany he ordered the removal of notices stuck on public buildings in Frankfurt which read: 'Jews and dogs are not allowed here.')

3) *Contamination* To return to the pariah dog—another reason for its being considered dirty was that, as scavenger and carrion-eater, it was a carrier of disease. Dogs were often regarded as creators of illness, or as actual demons of disease—especially of the plague.

According to Chaldean belief, at the beginning of the world there were seven malevolent demons that continually waged war against the moon. It was they who produced disease, and one of them (the fifth) was a dog.

Gula, the Babylonian goddess known as 'The Great Physician', was, like Greek Apollo, a death-dealer as well as a life-saver. She would strike the enemy with blindness, and she kept a pack of hounds which were the 'hounds of plague'. In the same country the pest-demon,

Labartu, often depicted with snakes in her hands, suckled a pig at one breast and a dog at the other. Terracotta figures of Labartu were commonly used for attracting demons out of the sick. Three to five days' ritual was performed during which the figure was fed, dressed and received sacrifices. When the transference of the disease-demon from the sick person to the effigy was complete, the figure of Labartu was put into a boat with four live dogs—two white and two black— and propelled out to sea never to return.

When Apollonius of Tyana arrived at Ephesus he found it smitten with the plague. He ordered a beggar, whose form he believed the plague-demon had taken, to be stoned to death, and when, at the last moment, the demon left him, it manifested itself as a mad dog. When, in sixteenth-century Switzerland, witch-hunting was at its height, witches who worshipped a black dog and suckled dog-familiars were believed to have been responsible for spreading the plague. Since epidemic diseases were commonly personified as women who travelled from place to place, it seems probable that these witch-dogs were taken to be disease-demons.

In the Lower Congo members of the Bakongo tribe used the nail fetish dogs (see p. 79) to cause disease among their enemies.

MAD DOGS

One of the main forms of contamination to which men were exposed by dogs was, of course, rabies; and in the folk mind there seems to have been some confusion between canine madness and the plague, as was demonstrated in the story of the plague-demon cast out by Apollonius. The origin of rabies (or 'hydrophobia' as it was popularly named) was unknown, and the terror it spread gave rise to many superstitious beliefs and practices.

1) *Rabies* The most common belief as to the cause of canine madness was that it was due to possession by evil spirits. The ancient Egyptians, Greeks and Romans came to this conclusion because they would see a docile and friendly dog suddenly become vicious without any apparent cause and, after a period of maniacal behaviour including violent cramps and spasms, develop paralysis and die. Sometimes the spirits that possessed rabid dogs were thought by the Greeks to be unquiet ghosts that had returned from the land of the dead to terrify the living;

at others the fire of rabies was believed to have been injected into dogs by Hecate. (In Christian mythology Satan has been known to take the form of a mad dog as when, according to an apocryphal gospel, he was forced by the presence of the Christ Child to quit the soul of the boy Judas.)

Another widely held belief was that rabies was produced by the heat of the dog-star, Sirius. Dogs were supposed to be specially liable to madness during dog-days, and in the British Isles they were forbidden by the Dog's Act to be at large during this period under the threat of dire penalties.

According to Slavonic folk-lore rabies was due to the presence of minute insane whelps in the dog's blood. There were those who claimed it was caused by the dog's excessive bile, or by it having tasted the blood of a woman; while others maintained that it was the result of the dog's having been born with a worm in its tail, in its tongue or its brain.

The use of the word 'hydrophobia' for canine rabies is both curious and significant. It was thought that, not only did rabid dogs dread water, but that if a dog appeared to dislike water this was itself a sign of madness. (In fact, rabid dogs do not fear water—on the contrary, since the disease brings great thirst, they often appear avid for it, and will plunge their whole heads into it.)

In classical literature we find references to the belief that, if a man's body was touched by the saliva of a mad dog, he went raving mad, and that if a stone that had been touched by a rabid dog was put into wine at a banquet, all who drank it went mad.

The Slavs who believed in the presence of insane whelps in the rabid dog's blood, maintained that, when a human being is smitten, he is infected by the transmission of embryonic mad dogs which incubate in the blood under his tongue. Only those who happen to have been born on the same day as the dog that bit them will prove to be immune. Central Indian tribes still believe that when a man is bitten by a rabid dog the union of the animal saliva and human blood causes puppies to be born in his belly. These make a nest and multiply rapidly, then gradually creep along his veins until they overrun the whole of his body. Within four or five weeks the scores of puppies begin to quarrel and their barking can clearly be heard. Eventually the noise forces its way into the man's throat, and he himself barks like a dog.

Although rabid dogs do not, in fact, suffer from hydrophobia, infected human beings do; for any attempt to drink brings painful spasms of the throat muscles, and it is not long before the patient refuses all liquids and the very sight of water elicits the symptoms. Some people believe that when a man is about to develop 'hydrophobia' he will see the image of the dog that bit him in the water he drinks.

2) *Physical treatment*   The treatment of rabies has always varied according to the beliefs in its cause, and in the means by which it is transmitted to man.

Those who believed dogs were liable to be driven mad by the presence of a worm in their tongues or tails did their best to prevent the development of rabies by docking their tails, and by 'worming their tongues' (that is, surgically removing the fibrous cords by which the tongues were controlled).

When rabies occurred in human beings, the Slavs, who accepted the theory that minute rabid whelps were incubated in the blood under the tongue, extracted them by cutting the vein so that they flowed out with the thick blood. Alternatively, they took off all their clothes and left them under a stone in the open for forty days, during which time the whelps, so they claimed, worked their way out and thus could be killed and removed from the clothes.

Indians who believed in the birth, in the victim's belly, of proliferating puppies which took possession of him until he barked like a dog, treated him by binding him head and foot and then forcing emetics down his throat in the hope that the invading puppies would be expelled. Members of these tribes tell stories of a medicine-man who collected longicorn beetles and picked leaves of a certain shrub, ground them together and made them into pills. Within two or three days the patients who took these pills began to suffer from 'labour pains' (men suffering more acutely from them than women), and before long the tiny puppies appeared, consisting mostly of black heads and tails. Only if the puppies were expelled was the infected person believed to stand a chance of survival.

Belief in the suffering of rabid dogs from hydrophobia brought its own remedies. Many Hungarians claimed that, if dogs were given the names of rivers, they were never likely to go mad. When a mad dog bit another, Celts believed in swilling water over its teeth and then using it to wash the victim's wound. Philostratus claimed that a drink of water would cure a mad dog if it could be induced to take it.

Emphasis on the hydrophobia experienced by men who had been infected by rabid dogs, gave rise to various 'water-cures'. A man bitten by a dog suspected to be mad would be tied to a tree and submitted to having two hundred buckets of cold water dashed over him. At a ferry on the River Severn, just below Gloucester, such men were totally immersed and held under until they nearly drowned.

The most usual treatment for the bite of a rabid dog has, however, always been homoeopathic, and the placing of the 'hair of the dog that bit you' on the wound is still a remedy employed in many parts of the world. A gipsy version of this is to fry in oil the hairs taken from the rabid dog, and mix them with rosemary before applying them to the wound. In Sicily, instead of applying the hair of the dog to the wound, a tuft is plucked, plunged into wine with a burning cinder and then drunk by the patient. When the southern Slavs used hair of the rabid dog they believed that it cured rabies by attracting to itself, and so draining out from the blood, the minute, insane whelps that were doing the damage.

Sometimes the liver of a mad dog was extracted instead of its hair, and used as treatment. (In 1866 when, in Scotland, an inquest was held on a child that had been bitten by a rabid dog, it was divulged that a relative had fished the dog's body out of a river so that its liver could be cooked and eaten by the child.) At other times the ashes of the dog's burnt head were used for it, and it was said that they 'casteth out all the venom and the foulness, and healeth the maddening bites'. In Scotland the remedy was 'to extract the heart of a mad dog, dry it over the fire, grind it to powder and administer it with a draught to the patient'.

3) *Healing rites* The most highly developed religious ritual used for the healing of rabies was that which formed the body of the cult of St Hubert, the French patron saint of dogs.

Early books on the lives of the saints tell how, when St Hubert was celebrating the Mass of his consecration, he received from an angel sent by the Virgin a miraculous stole (Plate 5j). He also received a golden key from St Peter and was thus endowed with special power for use against evil spirits, particularly against their effects on animals. St Hubert acquired a reputation as a great healer, for he performed many miracles in which men and dogs were cured of rabies.

The body of this saint was buried, in A.D. 825, in the abbey founded by him in the Ardennes. Near by there was a hospital for people suffering from rabies, but when this building was eventually destroyed the cult became concentrated in the ancient abbey church, and it was here that the recorded cures took place. The holy stole (not the body of St Hubert) was regarded as the principal relic in this church. It has been described as a band of silk, mingled with gold thread of about a yard long and two inches wide. It is alleged to have been taken out of the saint's coffin, and its miraculous virtue has arisen more from the fact that St Hubert wore it than from the claim that it was brought by an angel from the Virgin. People who had been bitten by dogs or wolves came to St Hubert from far and wide, and it was to the miraculous stole that they believed they owed their preservation. Holy stoles have always been used in rites of exorcism, and the choice of this particular relic for the cure of rabies implied a belief that canine (like human) madness was due to demonic possession.

There were two different healing rites available to people who made the pilgrimage to the abbey church of St Hubert: one was known as 'The Incision', and the other as 'The Respite'.

The Incision—a ritual operation—was a favour not granted to all who desired it, for only those who had reached an age of discretion, and those whose wounds had bled, were eligible. Once this rite had been decided upon the sick person had first to hear Mass and take communion. Having achieved a state of grace, he was introduced into the treasury where the relics were kept, and here he knelt before a priest repeating special prayers to St Hubert. Only then was he ready to sit in an arm-chair with his head bent backwards, while the priest used a little knife to make a perpendicular incision (of about an inch long) in his forehead. A tiny portion of golden thread from the holy stole was introduced into the incision, which was then covered with a black bandage bound round his head to prevent the relic being lost. The priest entered the patient's name and address in a register, and told him which rites he should perform over the next nine days, during which period the bandage had to be kept on. These included confession and the taking of holy communion; and it was essential that he should sleep alone in white sheets, eat only specified foods, and drink only wine or pure water. (If the pilgrim had been bitten by several mad animals, a fast of three days was also imposed.) On the tenth day the bandage was removed by the priest and burnt, and, provided the patient had carried out all the instructions and that he continued every year to keep the feast of St Hubert, he could assume that his cure of rabies would be permanent. It is recorded that, in 1661, Calvin sent his son, who had been bitten by a mad dog, to St Hubert and, as a result of the ritual Incision having effected a complete cure, he abjured his father's principles. (A further proof of the miraculous quality of the sacred stole lay in the fact that, in spite of the frequent detachment of its threads over hundreds of years, it never diminished in size. Many people and churches have portions in their possession.)

The Respite was not a surgical operation. Those eligible for it were children, or adults whose flesh had not been sufficiently penetrated by the bite to draw blood, or who had been bitten by an animal not known to be mad. It was also used on people who had only been scratched by dogs, and in such cases their fear of rabies was treated as an illness.

The patient taking the Respite knelt before a priest who touched his brow with the reliquary covered with a fragment of the holy stole. He then had to make a *novena* of prayers to St Hubert, unless he was a child, in which case this would be done by his parents on his behalf and renewed by him when he grew up. When people with superficial wounds received treatment for their fear of rabies, the Respite was aimed at restoring their 'moral tranquility' as well as their bodily health. Between 1806 and 1835 the register of the abbey church of St Hubert showed more than 4,800 patients.

On feast days a huge trade grew up in objects such as crosses, beads and rosaries, which had been blessed and touched by the stole of St Hubert. No pilgrims left without a supply of them, for they were worn as talismans. Some pedlars carried around an image of the saint in a little box, and rings and rosaries touched with this were believed to acquire great preservative virtues. Anyone who carried such a talisman, and knew by heart the prayer of St Hubert, was safe wherever he went among wild animals. (The prayer started: 'Great St Hubert, may God keep us from the aspic and the serpent, the mad dog and the evil wolf.')

Membership of the brotherhood of St Hubert was another means of gaining protection from rabies. Whole families would join this society, making annual payments to the saint. The brotherhood was very old, and had been enriched by the many privileges and indulgences which had been granted by different popes.

So much for the ritual treatment of human beings who had been, or were suspected to have been, infected by rabies.

When an animal was bitten by a mad dog it was treated by 'sacred cauterization'. So-called 'hunting horns' (pieces of cone-shaped iron fixed on to long wooden handles), and the 'keys' of St Hubert, sanctified by being blessed and touched with the holy stole, were heated in a fire and used to brand bitten animals, either on their wounds or on their brows. They would then be kept shut up for nine days during which time the priests fed them with pieces of blessed bread, and their owners each recited five *paters* and five *aves* a day in honour of God, the Virgin Mary and St Hubert.

At some local chaplets dedicated to St Hubert, red-hot irons or keys to the church were applied to the heads of mad dogs, while at the same time the gospels were recited over them. At others, such dogs were plunged into holy wells or fountains. (In Luxembourg there was once a 'pond of St Hubert' into which rabid or bitten animals were driven, and from which, it is said, they emerged cured.)

In the hunting rites of St Hubert, and at the 'Mass of the dogs' annually celebrated until recently at Chantilly and Sillé-le-Guillaume (see p. 124), prayers were offered for the protection of all hunting dogs against rabies. In Brittany, on St Hubert's Day, huntsmen brought bread to be blessed by the priest after Mass, and used it to preserve their kennels against canine madness. In Flanders it was a common practice, on St Hubert's Day, for people either to take pieces of bread to be blessed after Mass or else to buy little rolls of black bread, called 'rolls of St Hubert', from the beadle at the church door. When they returned home they would all eat a piece and give the remainder to their animals to protect them.

In addition to St Hubert, there were several other saints whose power was specially invoked (though far less often) against rabies.

St Dominic (who had a miraculous power over wolves) could cure cases of rabies and of snake bite. Every year, on the first Thursday in May (his feast day) a figure of the saint, draped with live snakes, is still carried in procession through the Italian mountain village of Cocullo. This festival constitutes a propitiatory rite designed to protect the entire village from rabies and the bites of snakes.

In Sicily, St Vitus, who was a great expeller of demons, was the patron saint of rabies, as well as of the nervous affliction named after him, of insanity, epilepsy and snake bite—all illnesses which manifested themselves in spasms and contortions of the nerves. (St Vitus's Dance was apparently believed by Sicilians to be produced by dogs, for they prayed to the saint to 'keep the dogs chained'. In India, Hindus believed epilepsy to be caused by dog-demons, and when an epileptic boy was having a fit his father would pray: 'Doggy, let him loose; reverence be to thee, barker and bender.') In the native village of St Vitus the saint was usually depicted as accompanied by two dogs, and in the sixteenth century the church of Capa S Vito was a centre of pilgrimage by people who had been bitten and sought miraculous cures. In Regalbuto, in western Sicily, the waters of a 'spring of S Vito' were reputed to be effective in driving out the evil demons from those smitten by rabies. In an Apulian town a rite performed to cure someone of rabies consisted of a ninefold procession made round the town while a special prayer was chanted to St Vitus. This referred to the saint as he 'who guards the Apulian shore . . . who relieves the rabid bite and calms the madness of dogs'. Then, addressing him as 'holy one', it beseeched him to 'ward off cruel rabies and the dog's dreadful snarls', and ended, 'go far from here, rabies, let all frenzy be far from here'.

Eastern saints have also been invoked against rabies. Dr Margaret Murray, in her book *My First Hundred Years*, has given a graphic description of the rite of *Tarabo*, a Coptic saint, in which she participated for the avoidance of rabies after a dog-bite.

When, in 1920, Dr Murray was visiting Egypt to study the archaeology of the Copts, she stayed in the small Coptic town of Naqada. During a stroll one evening a large black dog charged through the crowd and bit her on the leg. Since it was the height of summer and rabies was common, she was told she must undergo '*Anba Tarabo*'—a certain cure for the bite of a mad dog.

So, the next day, Dr Murray went to the living-room of a Moslem house which was filled to capacity by her party, her host's family, the servants and villagers. A space was left in the centre of the floor, and here she sat with the Omdeh (the head of the townlet). In front of them a tray was placed on a low wooden stool, and on it were seven dates, seven loaves and a coffee-cup containing a little olive oil. Vessels of water were placed at his right side and her left. Two Coptic priests took up their position facing Dr Murray and the Omdeh. The senior priest asked her name and both started murmuring prayers. Her hands were then tapped five times with an iron and ebony staff, and the water was blessed and sprinkled over them both three times.

When the prayers ended and the junior priest had withdrawn, the elder priest then called up seven small boys who were called 'the dogs of *Anba Tarabo*'. They linked their fingers and formed a circle round Dr Murray and the Omdeh, and, chanting all the time, moved round them three times in a clockwise direction, then stopped and made three anti-clockwise circles round them. Eventually, at a signal from the priest, the seven boys flung themselves on Dr Murray, barking, snarling, growling and pretending to bite. At the sight of her startled face, the onlookers all roared with laughter, and she soon joined in the joke. When the hilarity had subsided the priests moved back into position, and one anointed the Omdeh on his forehead, throat and the inside of each wrist with the sign of the cross. Dr Murray was anointed on her forehead and each of her wrists, but not on her throat. The other priest then cut pieces out of each date and barley loaf, tied them up in a rag and gave them to an attendant to throw out in the desert. (It was believed that if any animal found and ate them it would go mad, while if a human being ate them he would go mad and bark and bite like a dog.) The Omdeh and Dr Murray each ate one of the seven dates and a piece of barley loaf, and drank a mouthful of blessed water. This appeared to complete the rite, but later, it seems, a dog was executed and buried in the Coptic cemetery. Dr Murray, in her book, aptly quotes Goldsmith's poem:

> The man recovered of the bite,
> The dog it was that died.

DOG-SACRIFICE

The supernatural power with which man has endowed dogs has resulted in many of them losing their lives. Dog-sacrifice has been practised in many parts of the world, the reasons for it varying according to the prevailing dog-beliefs.

1) *The messenger* One reason for the ritual killing of a dog was the belief that it could be used as a messenger to the gods. And the annual sacrifice by the Iroquois of a messenger dog was the most highly developed of all sacrificial dog-rites.

This tribal festival, celebrated over many centuries, has been kept up with all the pomp and ceremony of ancient times. Every year the Iroquois sent to the Great Spirit that ruled their lives the spirit of a white dog, with a petition. The sacrifice was preceded by four days of preparation and religious observances, during which priests went from home to home exhorting people to clean out their houses and to leave all their sorrows behind. When the time came for them to meet, they appeared dressed in brilliantly coloured clothes. The dog chosen for the rite had to be entirely white (free from blemishes), and it was first daubed with red paint and tied up with red, blue, green and purple ribbons. The message for the Great Spirit was written out and tied on to a bunch of feathers which were attached to the dog's neck. When the animal was finally placed on a funeral pyre, parcels of tobacco, used as incense, were burnt with it. (In practice, it is said, the dog was killed by strangling before the pyre was set alight.) After the sacrifice there was great rejoicing, and the ashes of the sacrificial dog were sprinkled at the door of every house.

2) *The guide* People of many tribes have killed dogs on graves, and buried them with their owners, in the belief that they would act as guides through the Underworld. Skeletons of dogs have often been found in Peruvian tombs. When a Greenland child died the head of a dog was buried with it, while in other places dogs were tethered to the right hands of corpses to facilitate their guide work.

In ancient Mexico one of the chief Aztec funeral rites consisted of the killing of a little red dog by thrusting an arrow down its throat. A cotton string was tied round its neck; its body was placed by the side of the deceased, and then burnt, or buried, in order to accompany him in his journey to the land of the dead. According to Aztec beliefs, when the dead reached the Underworld they had to overcome numerous hazards and ordeals before taking up life there. One of the greatest was the crossing of the rushing torrents of the River Chiconahuapan (nine waters) and this could only be achieved on the back of a little red dog. (The dog thus took the part of the ferryman who, in Greek mythology, bore souls across the River Styx, which was the ninth head of Oceanus.) A slightly different version of this belief was that the little red dog actually preceded its master, so that when he arrived at the river he saw it awaiting him with other dogs, on the opposite bank. As soon as it recognized its master it swam over and bore him safely across the broad waters. The string on the dog's neck is thought to have served, either as a means of identification, or as a passport.

People of the East also sacrificed dogs to ensure their finding their way through the Underworld. The ancient Persians slew them at tombs; and the Garos of Assam burnt them with human corpses. In China the live dogs slain at funerals were gradually replaced by clay models of them, many of which have been found in early tombs, complete with well-defined leading harnesses to facilitate the guide work expected of them (Plate 5k).

3) *The exorcist* Many dogs have been sacrificed as a result of the widespread belief in their power to expel evil spirits. We have already seen how live dogs have been used as talismans to give protection against threatening evil, and in ancient China such dogs, first placed at the four gates of the capital to keep out thieves, were later believed to ward off supernatural forces such as demons of disease. Unfortunately for the dogs, however, their blood was thought to possess specially strong powers of exorcism, and from A.D. 676 onwards four were annually crucified to expel fever spirits and keep out calamity; and, more recently a single white dog has been ritually slaughtered in the first month of each year, and its blood spilled over the city gates to prevent misfortune.

The blood of a dog poured out in sacrifice both revealed and dispelled spectres and demons. It was believed to break all spells, disarm magicians and avert sorcery.

According to Pliny, nothing was more potent against poison than a dog's blood. Its exorcising power was used in folk medicine wherever sickness was believed to be caused by demonic possession (thus accounting for the sacrifice of many dogs for healing purposes in addition to those the parts of whose bodies were used more generally in treatment of the sick). A Chinese witch-doctor, wishing to expel a specially malignant spirit, would slay a black dog, gather its blood into a bowl and sprinkle it before the demon, a sacrifice which supported by prayers, spells and charms. A pint of hot blood extracted from a white dog cured patients alleged to be suffering from spectre blows, and also those suffering from fever and from insanity. A reliable remedy against evils affecting the whole body was to fumigate the house, smearing its walls and posts with either a dog's blood or a black dog's gall. In north-eastern India disease was averted from villages by the annual sacrifice of dogs at the gates, and the setting up of their heads on poles.

A Taoist ceremony performed for the expulsion of evil spirits believed to induce suicide necessitated the sacrifice of a dog's tail. When the officiating priest had made many symbolic signs and performed the kow-tow, he received a small black dog from the family, together with a chopper and a block. With one sharp blow he severed the dog's tail from its body, and it was dragged, howling, by the head of the family into every nook and corner of the house. Finally, it was taken to the front door and kicked into the street, for it was believed that a bleeding, yelping dog put evil spirits to flight. The priest then purified the house, sprinkling it with various ingredients taken from a mixture he carried around in a brass pan.

4) *The purifier* In Greece the dog was the sacrificial animal of Hecate, goddess of death. Hecate was a wayside goddess, and black dogs were ritually sacrificed to her at cross-roads for purposes of purification. Such rites were performed to purify houses after childbirth, and to free households from restless ghosts. In Boeotia a method of public purification was to walk between the parts of a dog's body cut in half.

5) *The propitiator* Dogs were commonly sacrificed to gods in propitiatory rites. In Central America dogs were sacrificed whenever rain and food were badly needed. In Mexico, when the rains failed and the land was parched by drought, great processions were made in which a number of hairless dogs were carried on decorated litters to a place devoted to the rain-god. Here they were sacrificed by cutting out their hearts, and their carcasses were eaten amidst great festivities. In Maya festivals dogs with peculiar markings were sacrificed, and people performed dances carrying little clay images of the dogs. In India, also, puppies were burnt in rain-making rites.

On 25th July every year the ancient Greeks held a ceremony known as the *Kunophontes*—or 'massacre of the dogs' to disperse violent storms and drought, and it was on the same date that the Romans sacrifice red suckling whelps to propitiate Sirius, the dog-star, whose rising, they believed, was responsible for the destructive summer heat.

Dogs were sacrificed to household deities, the Lars, at the Roman festival, *Laribus*; at the spring festival they were sacrificed to Mars, the god of Latvium; some lost their lives to the fertility god whenever crops failed, and red suckling whelps were annually offered to Robigus—the spirit of the red mildew that attacked corn and was a terrible scourge in ancient Rome.

Dogs were often sacrificed to propitiate goddesses of childbirth. Lapp women offered dogs to the goddesses of childbirth just before their delivery. In north-east India the Minyongs sacrificed a dog whenever a woman's delivery was delayed, killing it above her head so that the blood fell over her body. In ancient Rome bitches were killed in honour of Geneta Mana, the goddess whose name meant 'flowing birth'.

In Greece, Spartan lads sacrificed puppies to their war-god before fighting, believing the most valiant of animals must be acceptable to the most valiant of gods. Sometimes dogs were replaced by clay images of them, and many such figures were found in a cave dedicated to the nature god, Pan.

In Assam dogs were often sacrificed to gods invoked to witness the swearing of oaths, the making of peace, the cementing of friendship and the marking of boundaries. The shedding of their blood sanctified the agreements.

6) *Spiritual food* In addition to the killing of dogs, and the eating of various parts of their anatomy for medicinal purposes, dogs have been ritually eaten by man for other reasons. One is the belief that in so doing the bravery and sagacity of the dog is acquired.

In eastern Dakota there were people known as 'dog-liver eaters' who, on special occasions, would, for this purpose, eat the raw liver of a dog. When they had all assembled to perform the dog-rite, a dog with its legs pinioned was thrown into the middle of a group of dancers. It was immediately dispatched by the medicine-man, its liver extracted, cut into strips and hung on a pole. The performers danced round it, grimacing and smacking their lips, and one by one each grabbed at it. After dispensing with the first dog, they sat round in a circle and smoked until another dog was thrown in, whereupon the ceremony was repeated. It was necessary that they should eat the warm, raw liver of every dog presented to them; and while eating it no one but the medicine-man was allowed to touch it with his hands.

Dog was also ritually eaten by dog-worshippers. The people of Huanca, who annually selected a dog as the living representation of their god, prayed to it, offered it sacrifices and, when it was well fattened, served it up at a feast with solemn ceremonies, believing that in so doing they were eating the body of their god.

7) *The scapegoat* The lives of many dogs have been sacrificed in order that human beings might live and be freed of their sicknesses and sins.

People have often used dogs to relieve themselves of fever. In Oldenburg a man sick with fever would set a bowl of sweet milk before a dog, with the words: 'Good luck, you hound. May you be sick and I be sound.' If he drank three times alternately with the dog, the latter, so it was said, took over the fever. It was believed that if a 'spaniel gentle' was held close to the abdomen of a feverish person the fever passed into the dog; and in Jamaica hairless dogs known as 'fever dogs', were stretched across the body to neutralize fever.

Dogs took over other illnesses, too. Blind puppies applied to the chest and stomach are said to have cured 'concealed maladies incident to the intestines'. When the illness had passed into them and they died it was important that they should be buried in the earth. In the Carpathians, when cattle belonging to a pastoral tribe fell sick the farmer threw glowing coals into a vessel of water, then poured the water over a black dog. The cattle were immediately cured, their sickness passing into the dog.

In central Brittany rites were performed in which black dogs took over the wickedness of dead men. In order to lay a ghost which was troubling people because it was too wicked to be allowed in the next world, a black dog had to be found and also a priest courageous enough to touch the ghost. When the priest used the edge of his stole for this purpose, the ghost immediately passed into the body of the dog. The priest then dragged it to the Youdik (a huge unfathomable crevasse in a mountain range believed to be an entrance to the Underworld) and, crossing himself three times, threw it in, turning his head away as he did so.

Finally we come to a widely practised ritual in which dogs were sacrificed—the uprooting of mandrakes. The mandrake is a narcotic plant the roots of which are forked and commonly considered to resemble human limbs. (The word 'mandrake' means 'dragon resembling man', and Pythagoras called it an anthropomorphic plant.)

Hildegarde claimed the mandrake was fashioned from the same earth as Adam, and that its likeness to man was due to the wile of the Devil. Greek and Roman writers referred to male and female forms of the plant, and a seventeenth-century botanical work states that in England there were mandrakes and womandrakes. The resemblance of its roots to human form has resulted in the growth of many superstitions and legends about it.

The mandrake was indigenous to countries bordering on the Mediterranean. It was also found in Syria, Palestine, Crete, Sicily, Spain, north Africa and China, and was introduced to India in the tenth century. It has been venerated for over three thousand years, and the ancients generally regarded it as the abode, if not the embodiment, of a demon or evil spirit, due probably to its poisonous properties. Some people called it the 'Devil's Candle' because of its shining appearance at night; some said it had at its roots a human heart which was watched over by Satan. In Iceland the mandrake was called the 'Thieves' Root' because it was believed to spring from the froth of hanged men's mouths; while, in Germany, it was commonly known as the 'Little Gallows Man', for it was alleged to grow beneath gallows, drawing its life from the semen or urine voided by criminals just before death.

Although the mandrake was believed to be devil-possessed, once dislodged from the ground it became the good genius of its possessor. The uprooting of this plant was, however, fraught with danger, for it incurred the wrath of its resident demon, which was liable to take its revenge on whoever tried to drag it out of the earth. As the roots of the mandrake broke, it shrieked, and anyone who heard it died. Consequently many mysterious rites became associated with the gathering of this much-prized plant, and most of them included the use of a dog as a scapegoat for the human mandrake-gatherer.

The Jewish historian, Josephus, who wrote in A.D. 93, appears to have been the first to record the practice of using a dog for uprooting the plant, and its death when the mandrake shrieked was considered to atone for the outrage perpetrated on the plant-demon. Several centuries later the Greek poet, Aelian, in giving directions for such a rite, described how a dog must be kept for several days without food, then tied with a stout cord to the plant. When pieces of meat are thrown at it, as it springs forward it pulls up the plant (which came to be known to the Greeks as 'kynos pastos'— 'dog-dragged', and, to the

Persians, by a word meaning 'dog-dug'); it will die at sunrise and must be buried with secret rites.

An Anglo-Saxon Bestiary describing the rite emphasizes that the mandrake-gatherer must 'fly round about' the plant, taking care not to touch it. The dog must have fasted for three days, and when it is shown bread must be called from afar. The man must stop his ears to avoid hearing the shriek, but, once the demon has passed into the dog and killed it, the plant can safely be handled. (Sometimes the gatherer draws a circle on the ground to protect him from the fury of the mandrake-demon.) According to a Chinese version, a trench should be dug round the root and the leg of a large dog tied to it. 'Now flog the dog,' it says, and 'he will, striving to avoid the danger, pluck the substance from the ground but he will die instantly'. Medieval herbals show roots of this plant in male form, often with bunches of leaves growing out of its head and with a dog either chained to the mandrake's waist (Plate 5m), or dying in agony in the background.

Additions to the mandrake legends were constantly being made, and the rites were elaborated, as in the case of the following sixteenth-century German tradition. The digger goes forth on a Friday before sunrise (having first stopped his ears with wax), taking with him a black dog without a white blemish on it. When he finds the plant he makes the sign of the cross three times over it; then digs around it until only one thread of the root remains in the earth. He then ties a cord round this root and the dog's foot or tail, and quickly withdraws as he throws food to the dog. After prayers have been said over the sacrificed animal, the mandrake is taken home, washed in red wine, wrapped in white and red silk and laid in a casket. It is subsequently bathed every Friday, and given a clean white shirt every new moon.

Later variations insist that mandrakes must only be gathered on moonless nights; that the dog must be whipped at the stroke of midnight; and that a trumpet must be blown to drown the shrieks.

In Kent, where mandrake superstitions lingered until recently, pieces of the root of the plant were carried by women as charms to promote fertility.

MAN'S RELATIONSHIP WITH CULT DOGS

Man's relationship with dogs he has endowed with supernatural power appears to have been a complex one.

His treatment of divine dogs—that is, dogs believed to be incarnations of gods—has varied according to their form and nature. To benevolent dog-gods man responded with worship and gratitude, while less 'spiritual' members of the canine tribe, enjoying the protection of the dog-deity, were treated by men as if they participated in the sanctity of their god. To malign dog-gods man reacted with propitiatory sacrifice, with protective ritual, and often with the persecution, and even sacrifice, of the earthly dogs he kept as pets.

Man's attitude to sacred dogs seems to have varied with his reasons for regarding them as sacred. On the whole he treated them as precious objects to be guarded, venerated, cherished and ritually used.

Dogs endowed with 'secular' power were enthroned by man, and treated with all the pomp and ceremony due to kings, emperors and high officials. Men paid homage to successful fighting dogs, and court hunting dogs were treated as aristocratic human beings.

Many sick people were treated by the licking of dogs, and, after successful cures, thank-offerings were made to them. Men appear to have been healed by medicine made from various parts of dogs' bodies; to have learnt certain medical treatments from them, and to have used them for diagnostic purposes.

People have been provided by dogs with foreknowledge—both good and bad—of the future; they have used the magical power of dogs, and their images, to manipulate the future and to protect them from both physical and supernatural evil.

Man has not, however, only venerated dogs, he has also despised them and, as objects of his disgust and contempt, they suffered at best purification rites and at worst, death. He regarded mad dogs with the terror, not only of rabies, but also of human insanity (and the plague with which he often confused it). And he did all he could by means of both religious and magical rites to protect himself and dogs from rabies and to effect a cure once the disease had been contracted.

Finally, man has ritually sacrificed dogs—in many different ways and for a variety of reasons arising from the beliefs he held about them.

In his relationship with dogs man appears, therefore, to have run the whole gamut of emotions, and the dogs themselves must have suffered as much as they have gained from man's cult of them.

PART V

'Dogmanity'

Having investigated the many aspects of the dog-man relationship, there only remains unexamined the curious phenomenon in which dog and man are not separate entities but merge. In addition to the records of men transforming themselves into dogs—many descriptions have been given of various types of dog-men—some of whom have been respected as heroes, priests or saints, and we will now try to discover what is meant by (to use a word coined by Horace Walpole) 'dogmanity'.

CYNANTHROPY

'Cynanthropy' is a word with two meanings. It is, on the one hand, man's practice of transforming himself into a dog by magical means (or a dog's practice of transforming itself into a man); and, on the other, a form of insanity in which the patient imagines himself to be a dog and exhibits the tastes, voice and habits of one.

During the Middle Ages belief in the power of shape-shifting was very widespread; and behind the accounts of the metamorphosis of man into dog and dog into man lay a strong tradition of the interchange of form between man and other canids—in particular the wolf and the fox.

Lycanthropy was perhaps the most common type of shape-shifting, and men who voluntarily changed themselves into wolves (with all their characteristics and appetites) were known as 'werwolves'. The rites by which such transformations were effected included the drinking of magical draughts while spells were being uttered; the donning of a wolf-girdle, or a whole wolf-skin, obtained from the Devil; the application of magical ointments; or the bathing in, and drinking, lycanthropous water. The following was a common form of incantation:

Make me a werwolf! Make me a man-eater!
Make me a werwolf! Make me a woman-eater!
Make me a werwolf! Make me a child-eater!
I pine for blood! Human blood!
Great Wolf spirit! Give it me and
Heart, body and soul, I am yours!

(It was said that, although their heads, fur and claws were those of animals, werwolves had no tails and retained their human eyes and voices.) It was assumed that such people were sorcerers, for a pact with the Devil was an essential condition of shape-shifting, and they were all branded with the Devil's mark. Of all Satan's servants, werwolves were considered to be the most depraved. They roamed at night, seeking to assuage their ravening hunger for raw flesh. They attacked their human victims with unbridled ferocity, tearing their bodies apart with teeth and claws, and drinking their blood. In particular they devoured infants and exhumed corpses.

A typical account taken from one of the sixteenth-century werwolf trials reads as follows: A man went out one moonlit night with a soldier companion. When they were on high ground surrounded by gravestones the soldier turned aside among the monuments. After a while, the man followed his footsteps to see what he was doing and found him stripped naked with his clothes in a heap by the roadside. As the soldier pissed in a circle round his clothes, he changed into a wolf, gave vent to a long howl and rushed off into the woods. When he later broke into a farm and was playing havoc among the sheep and cattle, he was jabbed by the farmer, across the neck with a pike. When the man eventually returned home, it was to find his soldier friend in bed, being attended by a doctor for a deep gash in his neck which was profusely bleeding. It was by such discoveries that werwolves were brought to trial.

From the first century B.C. onwards Chinese literature contained stories of the transformation of dogs into men and men into dogs.

When wer-dogs took human form it was often in order to gratify their sexual lust through women. Typical is the story of a woman whose husband was in mourning for his mother, and was sleeping in the mourning shed. (In China, sexual intercourse was forbidden during mourning.) One night a man entered her room and, although she queried: 'Sir, may you visit me in this place of abstinence?' he ignored her question and made love to her. A few days later, when she saw her husband, she reprimanded him for what he had done, and he became suspicious that some supernatural power was at play. Then, when he was unable to sleep one night, he saw a large white dog scratch at the shed, take his mourning clothes in its jaws, change into them, and in human form enter his wife's room. Hurrying after him, the husband found the dog-man about to get into his wife's bed. He beat him to death—and his wife, we are told, died of shame!

The victim, as in the above case, often cannot tell which is her husband and which the wer-dog. In another story where a white wer-dog had competed with a woman's spouse the magistrate settled the problem of who had joined her first by having her stripped naked. Since jaw-prints were found on her breasts it had obviously been the dog-man, and he received the usual punishment of being beaten to death. Dog-lover tales are also prevalent among American Indians and Eskimos. Typically these tell of a girl with an unknown lover who is dog by day, man by night.

Dogs did not, however, only assume human form for sexual purposes. There is the famous Tang dynasty story of a Mr Ham who, every morning, found his horses sweating and panting as if exhausted by a long ride. He punished the groom, but this made no difference. So one night the groom decided to watch through a crevice in the stable door and see what was happening. He saw Mr Ham's black dog enter the stable, change into a man with a black hat and cloak, saddle and mount one of the horses, and gallop off. When the man returned he reassumed dog form. Next day the groom resolved to follow the wer-dog, and after the man had dressed in black and had galloped ten miles, he dismounted, tied the horse to a tree and entered an old grave where he conversed with confederates. When Mr Ham heard what had happened he had the black dog whipped to death. Later he sent ten strong men armed with bars, spears and clubs to the old grave which, on opening, they found occupied by a number of dog-men whom they promptly destroyed.

Sometimes card players turned out to be wer-dogs. One group was recognized by the smell of singeing hair emitted when their clothes were accidentally touched by a torch. When one of them was stabbed with a knife, it uttered a human cry, and, on dying, turned back into a dog.

Human beings sometimes assumed canine form in order to obtain power. According to a Roumanian story, a man transformed himself every night into a dog and roamed over heaths, pastures and through villages, killing horses, cows, sheep, swine and goats and appropriating to himself their vital forces. As the result of this practice he appeared to be in continual rude health and vigour. The witches who regularly transformed themselves into dogs did so in order to exercise the power of revenge they had acquired from the Devil. Plate 6b shows four old sorcerers confecting charms in a hovel and transforming themselves into dogs.

Cynanthropy also occurs in fairy tales, where it is used by women as a means of procuring husbands. A fairy tale of the Arawaks of Guiana tells of a lovesick maiden who begged her father, who was a sorcerer, to transform her into a dog so she could follow the man she loved, who was indifferent to her charms. Her father gave her a dog-skin, and told her to wear it over her shoulders. The object of the maiden's love was a huntsman who took four dogs with him every morning into the woods. In the evening, however, only three dogs returned with him, and when he reached the cottage he found it swept and clean, the fire burning and bread freshly baked. He assumed a neighbour must have done it for him. Then one day, noticing he had only three dogs out of the four again, the huntsman tied them to a tree and went in search of the missing animal. Peeping through a crack in his cottage door, he saw a lovely maiden, and a dog-skin lying over a chair near by. He darted into the room, threw the dog-skin into the fire, and claimed her immediately as his bride.

A rather different folk-tale from Russia tells of a young man who transformed himself into a dog and allowed his father to sell him to a great lord (who was, in fact, the Devil in disguise), warning him that he must on no account give up the collar. The lord bought the dog for two hundred roubles, but insisted on having the collar, too. When the old man refused to part with it he was called a thief and, in his distraction, he eventually let it go. As a result the dog-son found himself to be completely in the power of the Devil. So much for the form of cynanthropy in which the transformation is voluntarily made.

In the second category cases are to be found of people who were turned into dogs as a form of punishment. A popular Japanese tale tells of two servants, who, because they had killed and eaten their master's favourite pet, became dogs, taking meals in the garden, sleeping under the furnace and barking at passers-by. It is also told how a couple, who had refused to give food and lodging to a Buddhist priest, were deprived of their voices and were only able to express themselves by barking.

In the realms of folk-lore, the symptoms of people infected by rabies were very similar to those of the form of insanity known as cynanthropy. In both diseases patients behave as if they had been transformed into dogs—a boy bitten by a mad dog, it was said, barked, howled, tried to bite people and walked on all fours. (The belief that a man who contracted rabies barked like a dog was undoubtedly due to the fact, that in the last stages of the illness his throat was so constricted that he could only make unnatural sounds.) Furthermore, the ancients believed that St Vitus's dance and epilepsy (see p. 154) were also due to possession by dog-demons.

In the sphere of Greek mythology it will be recalled that, when Pandareus stole Zeus's golden mastiff (see p. 93), the king of the gods, in an almighty rage, slew Pandareus and his wife, delivered their daughters to the Furies to be their slaves and inflicted them with an illness called 'dog-disease'. It has been suggested by classicists that the punishment for the theft of the sacred dog was cynanthropy.

According to the Oxford dictionary, the word 'cynanche' ('dog + to strangle, throttle') is a generic term for 'diseases of the throat characterized by inflammatory swelling and difficulties in breathing, swallowing, especially quinsy'. Reference to such a disease appears in Greek mythology, for, according to a Homeric hymn, when Hermes wanted to steal the cattle of Apollo, he gave the guard dogs 'cynanche' to prevent them performing their duty.

In Indian folk-lore, whooping-cough was believed to be caused by the displeasure of Bhairava, the dog-god, and the whoop was regarded as a sort of bark emitted by a child who was Bhairava-possessed. A charm commonly used against this dog-disease, and suspended from a sick child's waist, was an old coin hammered into a flat round disc with the figure of a dog engraved on it.

DOG-MEN

Many people have believed themselves to be descended from a dog, and there is an Italian legend which explains that woman was not originally born of a man but of a dog. It tells how, when Adam was asleep, a dog carried off one of his ribs. Adam ran after the dog to recover it, but retained only the dog's tail, which came away in his hand.

American Indian tribes, such as the Koniagas, trace their origin back to a dog. The Aleuts, of the Aleutian Archipelago, believe that their 'First Father' fell from heaven in canine form; and that, in the beginning, there was a bitch on one of their islands to whom the Great Dog swam from the land of the Koniagas—and it was from this union that the human race sprang. The Chepewyans of Alaska derive their origin from a dog; and at one time their respect for their canine ancestry was so great that they stopped employing dogs to draw sledges and replaced them with women!

The account of the ancestry of Dog-rib Indians varies. According to one—at the beginning of the world an Indian possessed a bitch heavy in whelp. When her puppies had been littered he returned from fishing one day to hear the sound of children talking and playing together, but on entering his house only puppies were to be seen. After this had happened several times, the Indian pretended to go fishing, but, in fact, stayed hidden at home. He saw a group of beautiful children at play, with dog-skins lying beside them. Picking up the skins he threw them into the fire, and it was these dog-children (who grew up in human form) that were the ancestors of the Dog-rib Indian tribe. Another account tells of an Indian woman who took a strange man as her husband, and, although he was human by day, he took the form of a dog at night. In due course she gave birth to six puppies—three of which remained dogs, and three turned into children who were the ancestors of the Dog-rib tribe.

The Eskimos say Indians and Europeans are descended from a dog. According to them, at the beginning of the world a woman had ten children by a dog, five of which became inlanders, and five which she set afloat on a raft became Europeans!

A Chinese legend tells of the ancestry of the 'Dog-headed Jung tribe'. A Chinese chief promised his daughter to anyone who brought him the head of the chief of every other tribe. A large white dog, belonging to one of the generals, overheard this statement, and, at midnight, stole into the tent of each chief, gnawed through his neck and carried off his head in its mouth to place it at the feet of the Chinese chief. Greeted with the question: 'How can I possibly marry off my daughter to a dog?' it asked whether the marriage would be allowed if it changed itself into a man. Receiving the chief's reply in the affirmative, the dog gave instructions that it should be placed under a large bell and not looked at for two-hundred-and-eighty days. For two-hundred-and-seventy-nine days the bell remained unmoved, but on the last day the Chinese chief could restrain his curiosity no longer, and, tilting the bell, peeped underneath—to find the dog transformed into a man all except for its head. The spell having been broken, the dog's head remained, but the chief kept his promise, and the children born of his daughter and her dog-husband were the ancestors of the dog-headed (and dog-worshipping) Jung tribe. (At the time of the old Chinese New Year members of this tribe painted a large figure of a dog on a screen, and worshipped it, saying it was their ancestor and that he had been victorious over the Western invader.)

The early Chinese imagined themselves superior to all foreigners, and claimed human ancestry for themselves alone. They assigned canine origin to all their neighbours, expressing this in writing by the character 'I'. (Only in 1858 was Lord Elgin able to obtain the promise, as a stipulation of the Tientsin Treaty agreement, 'that henceforward the character "I" shall not be applied to the Government or Subjects of Great Britain".)

Among the highly imaginative writings of early travellers there are a number of references to people who are partly human, partly canine. One of the earliest references to 'dog-heads' is to be found in the works on the 'Marvels' of India, by Ctésias, a Greek doctor who frequented the Persian court in the fifth century B.C. Ctésias describes beings dressed in animal skins, with the heads and tails of dogs, who, although they could only howl, understood the language of Indians. They walked upright, were very swift of foot, and ate wild beasts which they cooked by the heat of the sun. They drank only the milk of goats and sheep which they bred for the purpose.

Strabo, the geographer of c. 50 B.C., wrote of an Ethiopian tribe consisting of 120,000 dog-headed men known as the Cynamolgi. These people conversed in yelps and barks, lived on bitches' milk, and bred hounds which they used to hunt cattle straying in from neighbouring territory.

Among north-eastern Indian tribes, there was a belief in a 'Land of Dogs' which lay 'beyond the great Ocean'. While the men had dog-heads and could only bark, the women were fully human. Consequently, whenever a man from another country arrived, the women (who were very beautiful) quarrelled over possession of him; but as soon as their dog-men heard, they attacked the invader and tore him to pieces, and they killed any male children born with human faces. (It was said that any woman who called her husband a 'dog' went to the 'Land of Dogs' as a form of punishment after death.)

It has been recorded by early travellers such as Marco Polo that the Nicobar, or the Andaman, Islands in the Bay of Bengal were inhabited by a race of dog-heads. One says these beings live 'in an island near India and worship the ox', and that 'they always wear upon the forehead an ox made of gold and silver in token that he is their god'. The dog-heads were said to be good warriors and to eat any man taken in battle. A fifteenth-century edition of the travels of Sir John Mandeville has drawings of cynocephali. They are shown naked except for loincloths, of large stature, bearing great shields which cover the whole of their bodies and carrying long spears, and they are depicted with little images of oxen on their heads. (Traditionally cynocephali were identified with giants: the thirteenth-century Hereford map of the world, with its pictures of fabulous races and monsters, shows two dog-headed men facing each other, barking, and underneath is the inscription *'gigantes'*.)

A sixth-century Chinese work tells of an island in the China sea which was inhabited by a tribe of men with human bodies and dog-heads. They had round houses, wore cotton clothes, ate beans, and they barked. Again, the women of this tribe were fully human, and when they married they cooked food only for themselves, since their dog-husbands continued to eat raw vegetables.

According to Estonian and Latvian folk-belief, dog-men lived on the edge of the world. They either had human bodies and dog-heads (with one large central eye), or were vertically divided into dog and man. They ran on all fours, and their reasoning was a mixture of human- and dog-sense. They frequently attacked human beings, robbing, murdering and eating them: they would take women and children captive, fatten them up, then kill them, feasting their families on human flesh.

The twelfth-century writer, Hadasi, who lived in Constantinople, described dog-men whose top parts were canine but who were human from the waist downwards. They had three eyes (two in front and one at the back of the head), webbed feet, human bodies, but barked like dogs. They were cannibals, who lived and traded in 'a land where pepper grows'. When they caught a man they made him drunk, then threw him in a pit to be fatted up. Later, they impaled him on a spit, roasted and ate him; but if he was not fat enough they cut up his flesh, salted it and ate it in slices.

Celtic legends tell of an ancient race of dog-heads—the Concheannaich, who inhabited Moygonihy in Kerry, and the 'Book of the Dean of Lismore' contains a reference to a dog-headed battalion. In Celtic, the prefix *'cu'* meant 'dog', and Celtic mythology is full of dog-places and dog-men. In County Monaghan, *'Coinsi'* or *'Cu-innis'* meant 'Dog of the Island' or 'Dog-Island', while *'Cu-mara'* (which became Macnamara) meant 'Dog of the Sea'. The inhabitants of Connaught were said to be descendants of dog-tribes. There were kings called *'Cunobelinn'* (Dog of Mars), and *'Cunoglasus'* (Grey Dog); while *'Cugeal'* (White Hound) was the chief of the Gilkelly family, *'Cucalma'* (Brave Hound) was a chief of the MacGeorghagan family, and *'Cumeala'* (Honey Hound) was a chief of the O'Mealas. A man who always spoke boastfully and bitingly was known as *'Conan'* (Little Dog).

In the third century B.C. the Greek philosopher, Diogenes, was popularly known as 'The Dog'. He was a pupil of Antisthenes who held his school in the Cynosarges gymnasium (see p. 96), members of which were known as 'cynics'. These philosophers were contemptuous of luxury and ease; they were misanthropic, and believed human conduct to be directed wholly by self-interest. Later the word 'cynical' came to mean surly, snarling and 'currish'.

We still sometimes refer to men as 'dogs'. The word 'dog' is often used for 'chap' or 'fellow', as in the expression 'gay dog', 'surly dog', 'sad dog', or 'dirty dog'. We have already noted (p. 145) the word 'dog' used as a form of contempt, and, according to Rabbinical literature, a time of general degeneracy is a time when 'the generation will have the face of the dog'.

DOG-HEROES

Some dog-men have been thought of as heroes (or heroes as dog-men).

Among the Celts the term 'dog' (*'cu'*) was a designation of honour: *'Cu-chulainn'* was the 'Hero of the Feats' (see p. 93); *'Cu-Luachra'*—the 'Hero of Luachur'; *'Cu-Munnir'*—the 'Hero of Munster'; *'Cu-Connaught'*—the 'Hero of Connaught', and *'Cu-Uladh'* the 'Hero of Ulster'.

There is a popular Japanese legend (similar to that of the Chinese Jung tribe) which tells of the birth and escapades of eight dog-heroes.

There was once a beautiful girl, called Fuse-Hime, whose father's province was being besieged, and he promised to give her in marriage to whoever brought him the head of his enemy. His words were unfortunately overheard by his big dog, which promptly ambushed the enemy chief, killed the latter and presented his head to its master. The promise was kept, but, as the result of prayers and exorcisms, Fuse-Hime (it was claimed) was never touched by the dog. Nevertheless, she miraculously became pregnant, and when she realized this killed herself. From her death-wounds there rolled forth eight gems, which disappeared, but were later found in the hands of eight newly born babies—the eight 'dogs'. These children grew up to be heroic warriors, and were regarded as personifications of the eight cardinal virtues attributed to the big dog, namely filial piety, goodness, politeness, faithfulness, justice, goodwill, courage and wisdom.

DOG-GUARDSMEN

In early times Japanese emperors were guarded by dog-men known as *hayabito*. An eighty-century work tells how, originally, a man who fought and was conquered by his younger brother, who used supernatural forces, said: 'from now on during eighty generations, my descendants will be your dog-men'; and it is for this reason, explains the author, that 'up till now the *hayabito*, all of whom are descendants of the older brother, never leave the enclosure of the Imperial Palace and serve the Emperor as barking dogs'. These men wore dog-masks when discharging their special duties, which were to guard the Emperor and bark during certain court ceremonies. When the Emperor set out on a journey, the *hayabito* would bark like dogs at all curves on the road, river crossings and at frontiers.

A tenth-century work describes how, on New Year's Day, at an emperor's accession to the throne, or when foreigners visited the court, the dog-guardsmen sat in rows outside the palace gates. When the officials entered for the first time they barked thrice, or in the case of foreigners visiting the court, any number of times. Not only did the *hayabito* protect the living Emperor from all evil influences, but at his death their stone images appear to have guarded his tomb. At Nahoyama there are three 'dog-stones' standing by the tomb of an eighth-century emperor, on which are carved in relief figures of naked men with dog-heads.

In France today the word for 'dog' is often used for human guards: *'Chien d'eglise'*, for instance, is a sexton; *'Chien du cour'* is a supervisor of schoolchildren; and *'Chien du commissaire'* is the secretary of the Commission of Police.

DOG-PRIESTS

We have already noted that the priests of Hermanubis wore dog-masks when in their college, when performing rites in the Anoubeion, and when participating in the procession of Isis, the mother-goddess. The 'canine phantoms' of the Greek Mysteries, alluded to by Virgil, are thought to have been dog-headed priests.

The Roman household gods—the Lares—had dog-attendants. Sometimes these gods were depicted with a dog sitting between them, but Plutarch maintained that their priests were men wearing dog-skins. (The Lares were also divine guardians of Roman boundaries, and, like dogs, they were 'dreadful to strangers but gentle to housemates', and 'skillful in following the scent of evil-doers'.)

At the temple of Malhari in Dharwar (northern India), the priests of a Dravidian sect who worship a dog-god dress in blue woollen coats, tie bells and skins round their waists, and meet pilgrims, barking and howling like dogs. Each priest has a bowl in which pilgrims put milk and plantains. They quarrel like dogs over the bowls, and pick up in their mouths food spilt on the ground.

Many priests have been called 'dogs'. The Celtic word for parson was *'Cucrichi'*—'Dog of the Boundary', and his manse was *'Conbhair'*—the word for 'kennel'. In parts of ancient Peru, where people worshipped a canine god, a priest was called *'allco'*—'dog', and he summoned his attendants by blowing through instruments made from dog's skulls.

The temple priests of the Phoenician mother-goddess, Astarte, who practised sodomy and wore womens' clothing, were popularly known as *'Kelabim'* or *'Kedeshim'*—'dogs'. It was the custom in Phoenician cults for persons of both sexes to prostitute themselves in the service of deity to whom their wages were dedicated. Moses, preaching against the pagan practice of religious prostitution by both sexes, warned: 'There shall be no harlot of the daughters of Israel neither shall there be a sodomite (*kedeshim*) of the sons of Israel', and 'Thou shalt not bring the hire of a whore, or the wages of a dog (*kedeshim*) into the house of the Lord thy God' (Deut. 23: 17–18). It is considered probable that it was the 'shamelessness' of dogs in sexual matters (see p. 146) that gave rise to the custom of referring to the sodomites officially attached to temples as 'dogs'.

Priests have often been spoken of as 'watch-dogs of the flock', and in an old religious tale from the fifteenth century, *Gesta Romanorum*, priests are exhorted to emulate the following four excellent qualities of a dog:

(i) The healing lick: as the dog heals mens' bodies with its tongue, so the priest should heal the sick in heart, probing their wounds of sin.

(ii) The distinguishing nose: as the dog, by keenness of scent, distinguishes between fox and hare, so should the priest, by quickness of perception, be able to distinguish between the various causes of sins disclosed to him in confession.

(iii) Unshakeable love: as the dog is faithful to its master 'unto death', so should the priest be to the catholic faith, if necessary laying down his life for the salvation of his brethren.

(iv) Unremitting watchfulness: as the dog, by barking and biting at the approach of thieves, prevents invasion of its master's property, so the faithful priest is a watchdog of Christ who, by barking (preaching) and vigilance defeats the Devil's schemes against souls.

A twelfth-century Bestiary refers to priests as guards of the 'Treasury of God'—that is, of Christian souls. It likens the cleansing of physical wounds by dog-lick to the cleansing of the wounds of sinners by confession and penance; and states that, as the tongues of puppies cure diseases of the intestines, so may the inner secrets of men's hearts be purified by the preaching of priests.

DOG-SAINTS

Dog-saints are of two types, for like the ancient Egyptian god, Anubis, they sometimes take the form of an animal and sometimes that of a human being with an animal head. In the first category we find St Dominic and St Bernard, who are themselves represented as dogs; and, in the second, the Byzantine St Christopher who was depicted as a young man with a dog's head. (St Roch could be considered a third type of dog-saint, but although, in this case, dog and man were very closely associated, they were never identified.)

According to the Golden Legend, before St Dominic was born his mother dreamt that she 'bore a little whelp in her belly which bore a burning brand in his mouth'. A less-known account tells how, before his mother became pregnant, she made a pilgrimage to the tomb of St Dominic of Silas to beg for a son. The saint appeared to her, promising that her wish should be granted, and she looked down to see at her feet a white dog with a flaming torch in its mouth. It has also been told how, when St Dominic's godmother was holding the infant by the font, she saw on his forehead a clearly marked star which was so bright it appeared to illuminate the whole world.

St Dominic realized his mother's dream, for, as the Golden Legend says, 'when he was issued out of her womb, he burnt all the world'. He was consumed by a burning desire for the salvation of souls, and he and members of his order (the Dominican friars) travelled far and wide spreading their gospel. St Dominic waged continuous war on heretics, and he was the founder of the terrible Inquisition where many hundreds of them were burnt to death. He was specially famous for fighting the Albigensians (a sect who believed everything material was evil), to whom he was 'a veritable firebrand'. (It is further said that, in a disputation ordained against the heretics, the judges ordered that books of both the heretics' and St Dominic's teaching should be cast into a great fire. The books of heresies were burnt, but that of St Dominic's teaching was saved, leaping out of the flames without having been damaged by them.)

St Dominic is commonly represented with a dog carrying a flaming torch in its mouth near a globe. In the saint's right hand he holds a palm branch as a symbol of the peace he made with those who declared themselves good Catholics. In his left hand is a sword, denoting the war he waged on heretics (Plate 6a). In Florence there is a statue of St Dominic with a dog at his side over the portal of the convent of St Mark.

In 1232 the Pope appointed the Dominicans as papal inquisitors, and they performed their dreadful duties so efficiently that they earned the title, *Domini canes*—the 'Sleuth-hounds of the Lord'. Their habit is white (denoting purity) and black (denoting mortification and penance). When they are represented as dogs they have white coats with black patches. A famous fresco in a chapel in Florence shows five or six 'dogs of the Lord' chasing off wolves (the heretics) from a sheepfold. The sheep—the flock of the faithful—peacefully feeding at the foot of the papal throne, are guarded by other members of the pack of hounds. A further duty of these 'dogs' was to guard the gates of hell, preventing souls from entering, for the Dominicans believed that the burning of heretics saved their souls.

St Bernard was another saint whose mother dreamt of a dog during her pregnancy. According to the Golden Legend, she dreamt she had 'a whelp all white and red upon the back, barking in her belly'. When she told her dream to a holy man, he prophesied: 'Thou art mother of a right noble whelp, which shall be a warden of the house of God, and shall give great barkings against the enemies. For he shall be a noble preacher, and shall guerish much people by the grace of his tongue.'

This child grew up to become the Augustine monk who founded (c. 1050) the famous hospice of St Bernard. Here pilgrims and travellers of all kinds were provided with a refuge, and many lives were saved by the great white dogs with red patches on their backs employed by the monks.

Members of their Order have compared the white markings above the St Bernard dog's nose, which continue in a streak up its forehead extending in a narrow line down to where it meets the white collar round the neck, to the Augustine badge—a white band, single behind, slit to pass over the neck, with the two ends tucked into the black dress in front at the waist. Icons of St Bernard usually depict him with a white, or red and white, dog at his feet, and often with a devil (the 'demon of heresy') on a chain. St Bernard was said to have likened the love of the angels for man to man's feeling for his dog.

In the Hospice the monks still say Mass on 15th June each year— St Bernard's feast day—in a room which used to be his chapel, and the dogs, once known as the 'Holy Bread', are sprinkled with holy water and given blessed bread before going out on rescue work.

The legend of St Christopher of Western Christianity is well known. It tells of a Canaanite, of gigantic stature and terrible appearance, who lived in a hut on the banks of a fast-flowing river, in which many people were drowned each year. He took travellers on his back and, with the help of a stout stick, bore them across the rushing torrent. One day the ferryman, hearing a child calling him, came out, hoisted it upon his shoulder, and struck out across the river bed. Before he had taken a few steps the water rose and a gale blew up. The more the waters mounted, the heavier the child became, until the giant was bent nearly double and only just managed to hold his footing against the elements and to stagger across to the other bank. On arrival, he asked the little boy who he was, and received the reply that he was the Divine Child, and that the giant had sustained on his back the weight of the entire world as well as of its Creator. The truth of Christ's words was proved by a miracle, for when the giant stuck his staff in the sand it immediately sprouted leaves and flowers. The Child then took the mighty head of the giant and, dipping it into the water, baptized him naming him 'Christopher' or 'Christ-bearer'.

When Christopher was in Samos preaching the gospel to pagans, and the king of the infidels asked who he was, he replied: 'Before my baptism I was called "Reprobate", now they call me "Christopher", the one who carries Christ.' The saint was tortured by fire when he refused to sacrifice to heathen gods, and he was shot at by arrows. He miraculously reversed the direction of one arrow so that it blinded the king, but he told him, however, that he would himself be killed next day and that the king should then mix his blood with clay and rub it upon his eye. The following day, after St Christopher had been beheaded, the king's blindness was in fact cured by the martyr's blood.

In the late Middle Ages, St Christopher was a very popular saint. To gaze at him meant protection from sudden death, so his image was depicted on the gates of Western cities and on bridges, and statues of him (some of which had serpents sculpted at his feet) were placed at the entrances to churches. He also gave protection against the plague. (Most saints martyred by arrows were thus invoked, for in antiquity the plague was believed to be preceded, or accompanied, by 'arrows of God').

All the most ancient representations of St Christopher are, however, dog-headed, for in the Greek Orthodox Church he has never been connected with Christ-bearing. According to oral tradition, St Christopher was once an outstandingly handsome Roman soldier who, on account of his good looks, was constantly in trouble with both women and men. So one day he prayed that he might be made ugly and thus delivered from temptation, and immediately he grew a dog's head.

There is, however, one legend that links the two images of St Christopher, and this is to be found in an Irish version of the sixth-century Passion of the saint. It tells of a holy man who, in the time of the Emperor Decius, was tortured for refusing to sacrifice to the pagan gods. It includes the miracle of the staff sprouting flowers and leaves, and tells how the pagans failed to kill him by burning, but succeeded in executing him. When questioned by Decius, the saint replied: 'I am a Christian. "Reprobus" was my name before I believed, but "Christopher" has been my name since my baptism. *My face shows that I am of the race of dog-heads.*' He had apparently only been able to speak the language of the cannibalistic cynocephali, and had prayed thus for the gift of speech: 'Open my mouth, and make plain thy might that those who persecute thy people may be converted.' Then an angel of the Lord came to St Christopher, raised him from the ground 'and struck and blew upon his mouth and the grace of eloquence was given him as he had desired'. He began preaching, but one of the heathen reported to the Emperor: 'I have seen a man with a dog's head on him, and long hair and eyes glittering like the morning star in his head and his teeth were like the tusks of a wild boar.' It was then that the persecution of the new Christian began. (In a ninth-century record of correspondence between two monks, one asked whether a cynocephalus could be redeemed. The other replied that there was no doubt it could be, since it shared human reason; and added that St Christopher, the valiant martyr of Christ, was a cynocephalus.) The dog-headed St Christopher probably came to Ireland, by way of the Greek colonies of Provence, with other traditions of the Byzantine Church. It was not until much later that he carried the Christ-child.

There is also a painting on a window in the Cathedral of Angers which links the Greek and the Western image of St Christopher. This shows the giant, with the head of a dog and dressed (like the Greek) in a tunic and a cloak, ploughing through torrential waters carrying the Christ-child on his shoulders.

The earliest reference to the dog-headed saint occurs in the Gnostic 'Acts of St Bartholomew', a document which originated in fourth-century Egypt. This apocryphal work tells how St Bartholomew and St Andrew found, in several towns they visited, a cynocephalic man who was causing terror among the inhabitants by indulging in orgies of slaughter and cannibalism. The Apostles converted and baptized this creature, as a result of which he gave up his former habits and lived like a civilized man. Many people who saw the change which had come about the cynocephalus, were converted, and he accompanied the Apostles wherever they went, helping them with their missionary work. It was felt that he ought to be given the benefits of his new religion, and so after his death his image was placed upon altars, and the Copts annually honoured him at the festival of St Cynocephalus.

In the fifth century, during the reign of Justinian, there was an icon of the dog-headed St Christopher in a monastery on Mt Sinai. During the sixth century his cult, which had an immense appeal, spread throughout Egypt, Syria, Palestine and Sicily. In the Middle Ages it was widely diffused, spreading through Roumania and Russia and occasionally into Germany. The dog-headed St Christopher can still be seen, for his image was depicted on sixteenth- and seventeenth-century frescoes on the walls of monasteries on Mt Athos, and was faithfully preserved in the Greek Church until the end of the eighteenth century. The frontispiece shows an icon of the Byzantine St Christopher with a hymn to the saint written down the right hand side of it. This is translated as:

> St. Christopher,
> Dog-headed,
> Valiant in faith,
> Fervent in prayer.
> Thou soldier of Christ
> Raised to sanctification,
> O victorious Christopher
> Feared by the king of idols
> And glorified by the songs of Angels,
> Thou paragon of martyrs.

He was sometimes represented carrying a cross, sword, spear, or a palm sprouting leaves and flowers. (The latter, and also the reference in the hymn to the king of idols and martyrdom, indicate contamination of Eastern by Western beliefs.) The St Christopher of the Eastern Church is thought to have inherited the power and character of the Alexandrian Hermanubis, with whom he has much in common. Both were dog-headed, wore military costume and carried palm—the symbol of triumph and martyrdom. The Western St Christopher and the Greek Hermes were both carriers of the Divine Child, and conductors of souls across rivers of death. All three of them were believed to protect travellers.

It has been suggested that the story of St Bartholomew's cynocephalus was an attempt by the converted Copts to Christianize their beloved dog-headed god so that they would not be deprived of him. The image of the dog-headed St Christopher seems to be a consummation of the dog-man, dog-hero, dog-guard, dog-priest sequence, and to form part of an iconographical stream which flowed from Anubis to Christ.

SUMMARY

The purpose of shape-shifting between men and canine animals appears to have been mostly to satisfy a lust—which was for blood, sex, power, or a combination of these. In the case of men or women changing into canids, their capacity to shape-shift was the result of a pact with the Devil. The fairy-tale girls who chanted into dogs in order to win husbands, could only do so if they were given dog-skins.

When human beings were involuntarily transformed into dogs, it was usually considered to be due to possession by dog-demons, and it was the latter's attacks on their throats that produced barking men.

The same two forms of cynanthropy can be traced through the descriptions of the various types of dog-men. The element of choice is obviously missing among, for instance, those specimens of 'dogmanity' discovered by early travellers. On the other hand, certain of the dog-guards, dog-heroes, and dog-priests, deliberately imitated the behaviour of dogs.

The tribes of cynocephali were submen, and in so far as they were dogs they were less than human. But in dog-heroes, dog-guards and to some extent dog-priests, the addition to humanity of some of the highly developed instincts of dogs resulted in superhuman beings.

In the image of St Christopher dogmanity was consummated, for in him the savagery of the dog was redeemed through Christianity, its instincts having reached a peak of refinement. Whereas, in other forms of dog-men they had been humanized, in St Christopher they were transformed into spirit.

PART VI

The Dog in Depth

We discovered a great deal about the nature of the dog of daylight reality, and of what it has meant, and still means, to human beings.

We have seen how the hunting dog serves man by both supplying him with food and ridding him of vermin, and how he relies on its ability to run down, sight, point, smell out, unearth, and retrieve game.

We have seen how man is served by working dogs: by those that protect his person and guard his treasures; that control and organize his herds and flocks; that save his life when he is lost, drowning, snow-bound or frost-bitten; hold criminals and missing persons; that haul merchandise, medicine, food and men over frozen steppes, through snowdrifts and dense forests; and, also, how he is amused, delighted and comforted by dogs that provide responsive, loyal and affectionate companionship.

We know that, in training dogs, man dominates them with his will, controlling them by methods of reward, example and compulsion, but that he is met half-way by the dog's natural impulses (for originally the dog took the initiative in entering men's camps in order to share their food, fire and shelter; and voluntarily co-operated with them in hunting expeditions). We have observed that the dog shows every sign of needing, desiring and enjoying the services it renders to man, and is unique in treating man as a friend and behaving protectively towards him.

There is no doubt, therefore, about the reality of the solid, three-dimensional dog of everyday experience (although at night there does seem to be something uncanny in the way its eyes beam out through the darkness and it howls at the moon).

We may, however, feel less certain of the existence, and know little about, the nature of the two-dimensional dog of inner reality—the 'dog in man'—to which it has been maintained the outer dog responds.

The dogs referred to as 'psychic phenomena' are half-seen in the half-light; and they are half-'true', since man's experience of them is of half-outer and half-inner reality. The revelation that outer dogs are not the only ones that exist has sometimes come to man when, for the first time, he tries to stroke a family dog and his hand passes straight through its body; or when he watches such an animal fade through a wall. It is proved that there is no solid dog in his room, yet he did, in fact, experience 'dog', so it must have been with his mind's eye that he saw it—a two-dimensional creature whose reality was, to a large extent, an inner one.

The twilight dogs such as these are personal to the percipient. Such phenomena are sufficiently like solid dogs easily to be confused with them, and behave in much the same way as dogs of daylight reality, acting as guards, guides, providers of food and medicine, and as companions. Less personal are the images of the black dogs that give warning of death. Confronted by a supernatural animal man is frightened, for with the foretold death of consciousness comes the end of his control and domination over the dog. The more threatened he feels, the larger and more demonic the dog becomes, until, having swelled to the height of trees and developed eyes like balls of fire, it is obvious that it has no outer reality at all, and his experience is of a collective image—the dog-archetype. (Archetypes are pictorial forms of the instincts which normally inhabit the depths of the unconscious mind. They are pure beings, with absolute power and freedom, and their lives are unlimited and indestructible.)

Numerous examples have been given of transition from outer into inner experience, and indeed the solid dog, or man's personal image of it, can, and often does, activate the dog-archetype. Thus, when the glint in the poodle's eye becomes a ball of fire, the terrier's barks and yaps become bloodcurdling shrieks, the speed of the courser becomes that of the spectral pack; and when man sees the black retriever grow larger than life, and, watching a hunt, sees huntsmen, horses and pack rise to the clouds—he is undergoing a lowering of consciousness.

Sometimes the personal image is linked, or even confused, with the collective (archetypal) one: the black dog phantom of Blythburgh is sometimes described as the ghost of a dog killed in a local shipwreck, sometimes as Black Shuck (the Devil). The wild huntsman is sometimes a wicked man, sometimes the King of the Underworld; the spectral pack is believed to be the souls of the damned, or hell-hounds. And behind man's fear of the innocuous dog-ghost lies his terror of the Devil and of devouring Death.

The many rites practised by those pursuing a cult of the dog show the confusion that has arisen between the outer and inner animal. It is not the solid dog but the dog-archetype that is pampered, served, honoured or worshipped; and in folk-medicine the dog's body can only heal in so far as it activates the dog-archetype. (In Epidauros no one was allowed to be born or to die in the temple, so that there could be no doubt that the birth, and death, experience was a spiritual one.)

The dog-archetype may be heard (howling or padding along behind), felt (as cold air or a weight), or seen (as a phantom with fiery eyes). Often, however, it cannot, or must not, be seen, for as an inner power its image is perceptible only by *in*sight, and closing the outer eyes opens the inner ones.

The nature of the dog-archetype is revealed by examining the part played by dogs in myth, legend, folk-lore, fairy-tale and primitive beliefs, for it is into these that the archetypal images are externalized from the deepest layers of human psyche. Such dogs are found emerging from, and returning to, the earth, the waters, and the sky, for the strange territory of the Unconscious has been projected into all three spheres. The elements inhabited by the archetypal dog are psychic ones: the contours and pathways are those of the mind.

In the individual, and the group, psyche the image of the dog is a power point. (It seems natural that men should have endowed the dog with power, for in many cases they owe their livelihood, if not their lives, to it; while encounters with the dog's lupine ancestors have resulted in loss of human life.) The energy of the dog-archetype can be used equally well for destructive or creative purposes—appearing both as the Hound of Hell and the Hound of Heaven.

THE HOUND OF HELL

In the realm of the unconscious mind many normal conditions are reversed (as exemplified in Welsh myth, where the baying of the spectral pack increases in volume as it becomes more distant). And, far from dominating the dog as in daylight reality, man here becomes its prey, for he is tracked down like game, chased like a fox, obstructed like a wolf, encircled like a buffalo, paralysed like a rabbit, thrown over hedges like a rat, shocked and agonizingly killed like any other animal. He is, in fact, hounded by the dog-archetype. In outer life the wolf, alone among canids, dominates man. At dusk—*in canem et lupum* —dog and wolf are scarcely distinguishable, and it is therefore in its lupine aspect that the dog-archetype hounds man's ego.

We have seen the different circumstances under which man is hounded—in places such as churchyards, ancient burial sites and spots where violent death has taken place; on occasions such as before the death of a relative—and the souls of the wicked are hounded by the Devil as they die. Man's pursuer, a single dog-phantom, varies, therefore, between being an omen of death, an inflicter of death, a hell-hound, or the Devil himself.

To see the spectral pack is an omen of death. These creatures usually hound the souls of the dying; and wicked men are doomed to perpetual toil in which they are hounded through eternity by the Devil and his pack, who seize their souls if they pause in their labours. Sometimes, however, these hounds are themselves the souls of the wicked, driven to hunt for ever by the Devil, or they are the souls of unbaptized children pursuing their negligent parents. (To be condemned for ever to hunt and never catch the prey is very like being eternally hounded, and in myth, huntsman and hound often merge—as in the case of the Danish king of the Wild Hunt who spent nights in the form of a black dog.)

In addition to the single phantom dogs and the spectral pack with their warnings of death, there are the two four-eyed dogs of the Hindu god of hell that come up to earth to claim their victims.

The living are also hounded by the Devil. In Christian tradition the Devil has been portrayed as a wolf: 'darkly prowling around the sheep-fold of the faithful so he may afflict and ruin their souls'; and the dog, in so far as it is the Devil, is living out its lupine inheritance.

Whereas, to redeemed souls, the Devil is a hounding attacker whose power constantly threatens and overwhelms them; to the degenerate the Devil is a dog-god in whose power his servants participate. Nevertheless, they still suffer some degree of hounding, for the Devil constantly pursues them with his demands on their bodies, the pleasure of which he considers to be 'his due'.

Treasure-lifters are liable to be hounded by the Devil-dog (and it is typical of the way in which situations are reversed in the Unconscious that the dog which, when solid or a personal image, leads man to treasure, when encountered in the deepest layers of the mind, acts as a barrier to treasure).

The Greek Hell-hound, Cerberus, is tethered to Hades, and the souls of dead men are propelled towards it on their way to the Underworld. So, Death is here portrayed primarily as a devourer and consumer rather than as a relentless pursuer. In this fiery, bloody-mouthed, serpent-maned monster we find the source of all that is most deadly and diabolical: of the insatiable lust, savagery and venom of the demonic dogs, the death-hounds and the dog-Devil. Here the bisexual dog, in its lupine form, is no longer split up into a pack of numerous hounds or into two hounds with numerous eyes, but is horrific in its singularity—focused and stationary at the entrance to hell. Cerberus is, at the same time, the Guardian of hell, the King of hell, and Hell itself: it dwells in the deepest layers of the unconscious mind, devouring everything that comes its way with any number from three to fifty heads.

In the outer world, whereas live men are devoured by wolves, dead men are devoured by jackals; and, in Egyptian myth, the god of death —who was first Anubis the jackal and later Hermanubis the dog—was associated more with the decay and putrefaction than with the devouring of men (the difference being only one of emphasis). In so far as man is hounded to death by disease, he is hounded by the dog in its jackal aspect.

So, man seems to be hounded by two dark powers, or, rather, by one dark power in two aspects—namely the Devil and Death. (It is significant that in pagan myths everyone is pursued by death-hounds, and it is only in the Christianized versions that the moral element appears, limiting the hounding to the wicked and unbaptized.) The prey of both these hounds is the human soul.

(One wonders why Death and the Devil should be imaged out as dogs. The archetypes always take suitable forms, and the choice of the dog to represent Death is no doubt due to the hounding aspect of dog-nature; while there is little difficulty in imagining the savage, lupine dog to be diabolical. The Devil, however, takes several different animal forms, including those of cats and asses, and it probably varies according to whom he appears. He presumably uses a form meaningful to his victims, and to people who are dog-conscious—keeping dogs, loving or hating dogs, dreaming of dogs—he naturally assumes canine form.)

Many people say they feel hounded by Work—and this experience is well expressed by the legend of the Cornishman who is pursued day and night by demonic dogs that will seize his soul if he pauses in his labours. His tasks are both unfulfillable and unending, he always feels about to be overtaken, and is only able to keep 'just ahead of the pack'. This merges with the feeling of being hounded by Time, and the hound in both cases is Death, for ultimately it is death alone that prevents man completing his work, or fulfilling his ambitions 'in time'.

The pursual of man by Death is the hounding of the ego by the Unconscious, for only by continual effort can man retain his hard-won consciousness. If instincts are too harshly repressed, they turn against the ego, hounding it, and man is in danger of his consciousness being 'carried away' by the pack. Some people feel they are hounded by the demands and attacks of others; by laws; by life—but since paranoid feelings only arise where life is proving to be 'too much', the pursuer is still the projected Hound of Death.

It is the Devil that hounds man with temptations to sin, and the avenging hounds are the product of feelings of guilt. Man is hounded by conscience, and by what Freud called 'superego'—conscience being a sense of ethics which rises from the centre of the total personality; superego—a spurious faculty, springing from an area of infantility, whose judgements tend to be moralistic. Similarly, when man is ridden by the Devil, the weight on his shoulders may be the normal burden of life such as sin, responsibility and grief; or the spurious load of false guilt, resentment and morbid fantasy which are instead of the real feelings and cause 'depression'.

The hounding (whether by Death or the Devil) appears to be produced, to a large extent, by running away. Man is not pursued by Death (or Time or Work) if he stands still in acceptance of the limitations of life: only when he tries to evade or escape from reality does he start to feel pursued. He feels hounded by life only in so far as he refuses the pain of it, and by guilt only if he omits to take responsibility for his sins and their consequences. In addition, however, to man's unnecessary activation of the Hound there is some movement from the other side: the two forces in the psyche are the will towards Life (towards self-fulfilment and greater consciousness), and the will towards Death (towards self-destruction, a return to the womb, and total unconsciousness); and in so far as the ego identifies with the former drive, it is pursued by the Hound of Hell.

We have observed how, in the outer world, the dog renders great service to man, including that of saving his life. The legendary dog that leapt the gap and took its place by the side of man, disidentified with its wolf, and jackal, ancestors and co-operated with humans in hunting its kith and kin. (The rabid dog may be described as one that has been drawn back by its shadowy ancestors, and is wolf- or jackal-possessed.) In the individual psyche the dog represents the power of the wolf reduced to manageable proportions, and voluntarily placed at the disposal of the ego. Among the instincts symbolized by various animals, those represented by the dog (in its creative aspect) are specially valuable in that it alone is basically committed to carry out the will of the conscious ego and protect it against the more destructive psychic drives.

Man cannot safely confront a wolf alone, and nor can the ego safely deal alone with the dog-archetype in its lupine aspect (for, as we have seen, man is liable in such an encounter to be struck dumb or un-conscious, paralysed, torn to shreds or burnt to ashes). But the dog that jumped the gap knows all about wolves, since it is one of them, and the ego can safely leave communication with, and protection from, impinging unconscious forces to this archetype.

It is also the work of the psychic dog to subdue and organize those more innocuous instincts symbolized by cattle and sheep, so that they may be of service to the ego. And, as the solid hunting dog kills not only dangerous animals but also vermin, and continually provides its owner with meals, so the archetypal dog destroys elements likely to contaminate the ego and provides it with food to increase its strength.

Whereas in the realms of the Unconscious many conditions of the outer world are reversed, others are (as we have seen) merely extended. In the deepest layers of the mind from which myth springs the dog-archetype is to be found with the powers and virtues of three-dimensional dogs magnified to the ultimate degree: its protection is absolute; its sense of direction infallible; its loyalty unsurpassable, unbreakable and unending. As the primary concern of the Devil-dog is with the souls of the wicked and it renders valuable service to sorcerers and witches, the dogs that are on the side of man are mainly concerned with the souls of the good, and it is heroes and saints who receive their most valuable services. (Sorcerers, heroes and saints have in common the fact that their souls belong to a supernatural power: the souls of sorcerers were Devil-possessed, those of Christian saints had been given to God, while the pagan hero had one divine parent. All three had an innate power on which to draw—that of the dog-archetype in its dark or light aspect.) Celtic heroes were protected by dogs with magical qualities such as foreknowledge of evil, irresistibility in battle, and a death-dealing claw. Their dogs hunted with unlimited strength and speed, never failing to catch their quarry, and they provided the heroes with riches. Christian saints were fed and healed by extraordinarily perceptive and gifted dogs to whom they often owed their lives. (Only men with the power of heroes and saints could hope to overcome the Hell-hound.)

Behind the image of the watchdog that guards man's possessions, lies that of the personal dog-ghost that protects him on lonely roads; and, deeper still, lies the image of the divine dog that protects man's soul on its way to paradise. Behind the image of the guide dog that leads the blind is that of the personal dog-ghost that guides its master to treasure, and ultimately the divine dog that guides souls through the darkness of the Underworld. (Harnesses moulded on the clay images of dogs found buried with their masters in Chinese tombs are similar to those used by the blind.) Behind the image of the dog that hauls medicine and food to outposts is that of the personal dog-ghost that brings these commodities to the bereaved, and—on the deepest level —that of the divine dog-physician and the suckling bitch-goddess. Dogs on all three levels guard treasure, hound criminals and provide faithful companionship: all three take the initiative in approaching man.

Dog-deities provided the light of the sun, moon and stars, and the waters that fertilized the earth. They were responsible for the potency of man and fertility of women, and they gave protection against all evil influences.

The dog received the souls of dying men. It also judged souls after death, and maintained equilibrium between the light and dark elements. As an incarnation of the Buddha, the dog brought man enlightenment.

Finally, we come to the Hound of Heaven—Christ—the Guide, the Protector, the Healer, the Light of the world, the Judge—who everlastingly pursues man's soul, and operates in the individual psyche as the will towards 'Life more abundant'; as the drive towards greater consciousness.

THE TRANSFORMER

There have been many references to transformation: that of dog into dog-ghost, hunt into Wild Hunt, man into dog, dog into man, hero into dog-star, star into dog, dog into coal, coal into gold, and others. In addition, the dog seems to have been closely associated with the greatest of all transformations—the rebirth of man.

We have seen how, in its dark aspect, the dog-archetype not only foretold death but inflicted it; how, as a single ghost, it haunted graves and sites of death; as a pack of hounds it tore men to pieces; as a dog-god it brought violent death, and infected men with fatal disease; as the Hell-hound it eclipsed the light in mens' lives and devoured their souls.

We have also seen how, in its light aspect, the dog- or bitch-archetype not only foretold birth, bestowed easy birth, gave protection to women during pregnancy and parturition, but how, as the Great Mother-goddess, it brought fertility and was reputed to have given birth to, or assisted in the creation of, the first human beings.

Certain dog-deities such as Marduk and Gula presided over the rebirth of man. In addition to awaking people stricken with sickness to a new life, they were capable of resurrection of the dead. As god of embalmment, Anubis gave back to the deceased the powers of the living body. The Eleusinian Mysteries in which dogs took part were concerned with rebirth of the soul, as were also the healing rites performed (partly by dogs) in the temples of Asklepios. In these shrines of the Divine Physician the death principle was transmuted into the principle of healing; and the epiphany of the dog, as the incarnation or agent of the god, was the moment of the 'change for the better', the 'turn of the tide', of *metanoia* and renewal. (It is interesting to note that it was as a dog-man that St Christopher caused arrows to stand still in mid-air and change their direction.)

The goal of all initiation ceremonies (whether the puberty rites of primitive societies or the religious Mysteries of ancient civilizations) is transformation. In primitive rites there are dangers to be faced, tasks to be performed and suffering to be endured, in order that, having gained independence of the body, a birth of higher consciousness may take place in the initiate. The treasure-seeking dog-legends contained many of the elements of primitive initiation rites. In the Dobb Park Lodge tale the hero made the typical descent into the dungeon (into the labyrinth—a symbol of the unconscious mind), with its tortuous paths full of snares and frustrations, where he was confronted with the terror of the demonic dog, performed difficult tasks, and was rewarded (if only temporarily) with the vision of the chest of gold (the gold being a symbol of new consciousness). The healing rites of Asklepios and of St Hubert, with their purifications, abstentions and sacrifices—the one culminating in the transforming vision, the other in the insertion of a gold thread in the forehead (the seat of creative realization)—reiterated the same pattern.

The dog is a threshold animal. In its phantom form it haunted boundaries, cross-roads and bridges; in myth, it guarded bridges and gateways into the Underworld. Sometimes the archetypal dog is a barrier, sometimes a link; as a doorkeeper it is a controller of exits and entrances. The boundary kept by the dog-archetype is that between life and death, outer and inner, day and night; between the conscious and unconscious mind. Its image appears not only at the brink of death, but in transitional stages and at turning-points in life: the points at which arrows change their direction; where despair changes into hope; poisoning into healing, and death into new life. From this position the dog-archetype controls the balance of life, for it stands at the centre, weighing sin against truth, evening up until there is equilibrium.

In these examples of the process of transformation the psychic dog takes a varying degree of responsibility. But it is in the pre-Christian Gnostic system of alchemy that the dog-archetype comes into its own as the Transformer. (Although the manifest aim of the ancient alchemists was to produce a substance capable of transmuting base metals into gold, the hidden goal of the more enlightened ones—many of whom were physicians and mystics—was to transmute instinct into spirit, thus bringing about rebirth. Such men projected their own images into the materials with which they worked, and made no distinction between the chemical transformations and those taking place in their own psyches.)

The transforming substance with which the alchemical process culminated was thought of as 'treasure' and often referred to as the 'Philosopher's Stone'. It will be recalled that mythical dogs not only guided men to treasure and guarded it, but actually produced jewels from their paws and silver and gold from their mouths; and, in some ancient alchemical works the dog was designated the 'Transformer'— the 'Puppy (*filius-canis*) of celestial hue'. (Analogy has been established between the Transformer and Christ, and there were alchemists who maintained 'the Logos is a dog who guards and protects the sheep against the wiles of wolves, and chases the wild beasts from creation and slays them and begets all things'. The dog, they said, 'being a certain divining Logos, has been established judge of the quick and the dead'). And thus, as a dog had assisted in the creation of the first human beings, the hermaphroditic 'Puppy' played its part in the re-creation (or rebirth) of alchemists, bringing illumination— enlightenment—such as was symbolized by the star depicted on the forehead of St Dominic, the 'Sleuth-hound of the Lord'.

Central to the whole mythology of the dog is the image of the Hound on the Hearth. One little hound, we are told, separated out from the Wild Hunt pack, and settled on the hearth of someone's house, where its nature could be examined at close quarters.

The hearth was the place where, in prehistoric times, the dead were buried—where heat brought about transformation. The dog has appeared on the hearth before: Mephistopheles in poodle form, took up his position behind Faust's stove; the Mauthe dog lay in front of the fire at Peel Castle, and the temple dogs at Etna guarded the sacred volcanic fire. The hound has also been likened before to coal: the black bitches of Hecate emerged breathing flames from the bowels of the earth, and the black ghostly dogs of East Anglia had red-hot tongues and eyes 'like glowing coals'.

In so far as these creatures were Death-hounds, their indwelling fire was the fire of hell. Hellfire is believed permanently to hound, torture and consume the souls of wicked men. There are, however, other aspects of fire. The indwelling fire of the heavenly dog was that of the sun, moon and the star: the light of the Hound of Heaven was that which illumined men's lives; the heat was man's inner flame of consciousness.

The head of the cult statue of Hermanubis was, however, half black and half gold; and the image of the dead black dog thrown on the hearth whose skin burst open and poured out gold coins, further suggests that what appears to be two hounds is really one ambivalent hound divided into the two aspects of its nature.

The problem, therefore, of the woman on whose hearth the Hound landed (since it was impossible either to kill it, appease it or drive it away) was how to transform the hellfire into the fire of heaven; the wind that devours and tears everything to pieces into the 'rushing mighty wind' (the Holy Ghost); the Death-hound into the Hound that gives new life.

She was virtually in the position of the alchemist, for it was at the centre of her psyche that the transformation of the archetypal hound took place. It was often said that hounds of the Wild Hunt were only visible when they appeared singly on the ground, and 'coming down to earth' meant 'coming up to consciousness'. It was revealed to her that, as a lump of black coal contained fire, so the dead body of the black hound contained gold. It is in the depths of darkness and degradation that the treasure of new consciousness is found, and it was from the body of the savage devourer, of the evil contaminator, of the despicable carrion-eating cur, that substance of the greatest possible value poured forth. The dog's body is, however, a barrier to those seeking treasure, and it was only when the dog had died, when the Devil-dog had been overcome, when dark resistant matter had been dissolved, that the power was diverted from the Hellhound to the Hound of Heaven, and the alchemist became aware of his, or her, enrichment.

PART VII

Man and the Dog

The main forms, therefore, in which man experiences the archetypal dog is as the Hound of Hell, the Hound of Heaven and the Transformer; and the relationship between his ego and this psychic power should be recognized as a crucial one in his life.

To take, first, examples of bad relationships: the cynocephalus was a man in whom dog-nature and human-nature were unconsciously merged, resulting in a false amalgam. The egos of cynocephali were possessed by the dog-archetype (they were often giants—the archetype, which is larger than life, being expressed on a physical level), so their instincts were uncontrolled and unrefined, and, as submen, they were mere geiger-counters of sensation.

In cases of human rabies, and of the form of insanity known as cynanthropy, man's ego is possessed by the archetypal dog. Rabies is a dog-disease, and man develops it in so far as he is a dog. It was said to be caused by Hecate, Satan, Sirius, The Furies, evil spirits or unquiet ghosts—all of which took dog-form, and when contamination was caused by transmission of 'minute whelps in the blood', it was the archetype that was passed over. When a rabid man looked into water and saw the reflection of a dog he was seeing the image of his dog-possessed self, and in cases of cynanthropy it was the archetypal dog in man that barked. (It is typical of the confused state referred to as 'dogmanity' that men should bark and dogs speak, also that 'hydrophobia', a symptom of human rabies, should be attributed to rabid dogs.)

In *cynanche*, it is by the archetypal dog that man is throttled (as the Devil in dog-form tried to throttle St Stanislaus Kosta). The throat is a tunnel which links the inner and outer worlds, and swallowing is the last conscious act in the process of assimilation, for once food is swallowed the unconscious reflexes take over. As we know, it is precisely in the tunnel, on the border, by the gateway, and on the bridge of the two worlds, that the archetypal dogs hold sway. And in those suffering from quinsy the psychic dog is insisting on closing the gate to the great distress of the ego whose life is threatened. (It is this 'dog-throttling' that causes man to 'bark'.) The kind of situation liable to activate the throttling dog is when life is offering something which man feels he cannot 'swallow', cannot 'stomach', or cannot 'take in'. Then he unconsciously calls up the demonic dog to prevent an experience which could enrich his life if allowed to be transformed and become part of him. On the other hand, the throat-dog can render him a good service by preventing the assimilation of unpleasant facts which he longs to repress, but which would poison him if relegated to the Unconscious.

Not only are epilepsy and St Vitus's dance 'dog-diseases', but all diseases curable by the use of part of a dog's body are presumably due to possession by the archetypal dog. Since the cure of dog-disease is always homoeopathic, it is necessary to find out by what aspect of canine nature the patient is possessed that he produces symptoms which only dog can cure.

Sometimes dog-possession was deliberately brought about by the ill-will of Chinese sorcerers who used their familiar spirits for this purpose. They maintained, however, that only people 'in whom light was diminished' were open to such possession. The sexual possession of women by dogs that had taken human form was an example of an archetype using the ego to feed and renew its power. In the practice of cynanthropy, when man chose to transform himself into a dog, he consciously identified with, and allowed his ego to be taken over by, the archetypal dog in its savage lupine aspect. The witch's black dog-familiar represented the shadow side of her personality—her 'bitchiness'—and when she transformed herself into a black dog she was totally identified with this. (The relationship of the witch to the Devil was of the personal, to the collective evil: of the personal dog-ghost to the dog-archetype in one of its darkest aspects.)

The degree of possession by the dog-archetype varied greatly. In the *kelabim*—the male temple prostitutes, known as 'dogs', who were enslaved by the Bitch-Mother-goddess and drained by her of their masculinity—there was partial unconscious identification with the archetypal dog, as was also the case in men known as 'cynics', and still obtains in people whose faces resemble those of, for instance, bulldogs, pekes or poodles. The gangs of delinquent youths by which society is beset today are dominated by the pack instinct: many men continue to be ruled by the territorial instinct, whether expressed in terms of national boundaries or of those of their back gardens; others are driven by the instinct to hunt—their prey being lions, fame, money or women. Then there are the reliable characters with highly developed intuition and a strong sense of loyalty; the surly, gruff, snarling men who are overprotective, and hound their fellows; the 'dirty dogs' and the 'gay dogs'; the yapping, whining, snapping 'bitches'; the fawning cringing shame-faced people who exhibit dog-like devotion and whose primary aim in life is to be approved by others. All these could justifiably be designated dog-men, and their need is to learn to dis-identify their egos with the dog-archetype operating within their psyches.

One other form of dog-men is to be found among those who consciously identify with certain instincts of dogs in their light aspect. The good huntsman, for instance, while avoiding possession by the dog-archetype, so empathizes with his hounds that he virtually becomes one of them. The good doctor deliberately allows the psychic dog to 'sniff out' disease, to guide him through the labyrinthine pattern of illnesses, to reveal the remedies required to combat sickness and regain equilibrium. Japanese guards and Egyptian priests placed dog-masks on their heads, or dog-skins over their shoulders, when they intended to live out certain aspects of their dog-nature: and the priest still puts on a 'dog-collar' before taking up his position at the boundary between inner and outer life, and embarking on his duties as 'guardian of the flock'.

(Dogmanity seems mostly to have been expressed as dog-headedness, but the dog-head did not always symbolize the same thing. If, for instance, it belonged to members of a race of cynocephalic submen, it stood for the confused unconscious state in which they lacked human intelligence and the capacity for thought and speech. If, on the other hand, it was an attribute of dog-saints or dog-gods, it stood for the capacity of the superhuman being in whom the highly developed instincts of the dog were added to the gifts of humanity and consciously exercised. Transformation of the one type of dog-head into the other was described in the only Western version of the legend of St Christopher, for, according to this, when the dog-head of the submman 'Reprobus' was baptized it became that of the Christian saint, and this sufferer from canine inarticulacy was transformed into a symbol of Logos—the divine, creative Word.)

In addition to the men that appear to be dogs, there are examples of dogs appearing to be men. (Indeed, the world of art is full of the images of creatures, portrayed both in words and paint, which are not dogs so much as canine burlesques of men.) In the case, for instance, of Roman war-dogs, although man disidentified with the savagery of the dog-archetype and was thus free to behave like a rational human being, the confusion between dog and man was not properly resolved, for the ferocious dogs he set against the enemy were dressed and honoured as men.

So much for the unrelatedness of man's ego to the dog-archetype, which was due to possession, identification, fusion and confusion.

When ego and archetype are separate, whether the archetypal dog appears as the Devil or a god depends on whether the power concentrated in its image is used against, or on behalf of, the ego. The psychic dog may be a devourer or creator, a wounder or healer, a contaminator or purifier, an inflictor of unconsciousness or bestower of consciousness. It may represent the dark and evil, or the light and redemptive, elements in man's life. In the burglar, the watchdog will activate the image of the Hell-hound; in its owner, that of the Heavenly Protector. Many examples have already been given of the best way of dealing with demonic dogs of all kinds, and also of taking best advantage of the services rendered by the Hound of Heaven.

The 'roots' of man's psyche have power which can be used by the ego if contact can be made with them. An example of the use of a solid dog to pull up into consciousness its psychic counterpart was to be found in the rite of raising the mandrake. The demon which inhabited the mandrake appears to have been a canine one, for many of the powers attributed to it were those of the dog-archetype. The dog is virtually a wolf whose energy is used for, instead of against, man; the good genius was the mandrake-demon that had been pulled up into consciousness and placed at the disposal of the ego. But new power and consciousness can only be obtained by sacrifice, and man had to lose the outer, three-dimensional, dog in order to receive the grace of the inner one. (In the Christianized version of this rite the uprooted mandrake was treated by its owner as a symbol of the Body of Christ, and was, at regular intervals, ritually bathed, entombed and brought back to life.) A similar sacrifice was made in the anti-rabies rite undergone by Dr Margaret Murray. Although the rabid dog-spirit was cast out of her into food which was thrown into the desert, nevertheless an actual dog had to die—as if it were necessary for the archetype to be incarnated.

The dog-man relationship needs (like the Hound itself) to undergo alchemical transformation. The false amalgam of dog-man as an unconscious subhuman entity must be placed on the Hearth and heat applied. If the various processes are accomplished, an image will finally be produced of a dog-man in which there is no confusion, but a creative merging of separate beings such as exists in the deep *rapport* achieved between a blind man and his canine guide.

In the relationship of man and solid dog there is a natural boundary where instinct ends and reasoning begins. This boundary is crossed, from one direction, by the man who allows his psychic dog to play the part that comes so naturally to it of bridge or ferry, for it is to the 'dog in man' that outer dogs respond. Something, the nature of which is uncertain, comes back from the other side, and the 'deep *rapport*' would seem to exist where inner and outer dogs have united.

In guide work with the blind, the dog's harness is the bridge—the instrument of communication. Dog-collars have their own symbolism: according to legend they are the seat of the dog's magical power, and the means by which their owners can make contact with, and control, it. Once, therefore, man has discovered the creative dog in his depths —the 'seeing eye' and the 'guiding star' in the darkness—his best attitude is to keep close contact, through the collar or harness, with its power, and, like the blind person he is in this sphere, allow himself to be guarded and guided in the knowledge that the dog can be relied on to know the Way.

References

PART I

COLBERT, E. H., 'The Origin of the Dog.' Guide leaflet series of the American Museum of Nat. Hist., no. 102. Reprinted *Nat. Hist.,* vol. XLIII, no. 12, Feb. 1939.

DARWIN, C., *The Expression of the Emotions in Man and Animals.* New York, 1873.

HARTING, J. E. (ed.), *The Zoologist,* 3rd series, vol XII. London, 1888.

HILZHEIMER, M., 'Dogs,' *Antiquity,* vol. VI, no. 24, Dec. 1932.

JOHNSTON, H., *British Mammals.* London, 1903.

LONDON, J., *White Fang.* New York, 1906.

LORENZ, K., *Man Meets Dog* (trans. M. Kerr Wilson). Boston, 1955.

—— *King Solomon's Ring.* New York, 1952.

MIVART, G., *A Monograph of the Canidae.* London, 1890.

SANDERSON, I. T., *Living Mammals of the World.* New York, 1955.

SMYTHE, R. H., *The Mind of the Dog.* London, 1958.

VESEY-FITZGERALD, B. (ed.), *The Book of the Dog,* Los Angeles, 1948.

YOUNG, S. P., *The Wolves of North America,* pt. 1. Washington, D.C., 1944.

ZEUNER, F. E., *A History of Domesticated Animals.* New York, 1964.

PART II

ASH, EDW. AND C., *Dogs: Their History and Development.* London, 1927.

BARAZETTI, W. F., *The St Bernard Book.*

BROKE, W. DE., *Hunting the Fox.* London, 1921.

BUDGETT, H. M., *Hunting by Scent.* New York, 1933.

CARRIGHAR, S., *Husky in the House.* London, 1960.

CARTER, R. G., *White Harnesses.* Altrincham, 1961.

CASHMORE, L. G., *Dogs that Serve.* London, 1960.

CHERN, M. B., *The Complete Newfoundland.* New York, 1955.

DALZIEL, H., *Mad Dogs and Hydrophobia*. London, 1888.

DENLINGER, M. G., *The Complete St Bernard*. Richmond, Va., 1952.

FISHER, C., *The Dog*. London, 1960.

FREE, R., *Beagle and Terrier*. London, 1946.

GOODGER, W. E., *The Pug Handbook*. London, 1959.

HAFEZ, E. S. E., *The Behaviour of Domestic Animals*. Baltimore, 1962.

HERBERT, W., 'Huskies from Greenland.' B.B.C. script, 13 March 1963.

H. M. STATIONERY OFFICE, *Police Dogs*. London, 1963.

HUBBARD, C. L. B., *Working Dogs of the World*. London, 1947.

KNAUR, K. and R., *Dogs of Character* (trans. K. Kettle). London, 1957.

LEIGHTON, R., *The Complete Book of the Dog*. London, 1922.

LLOYD, J. IVESTER, *Beagling*. London, 1954.

LONDON, J., *Call of the Wild*. New York, 1903.

LYTTON, J. A. D., *Toy Dogs*. London, 1911.

MACINNES, J. W., *Guard Dogs*. London, 1949.

MOORE, C. B., *Ways of Mammals*. New York, 1953.

MOST, K., *Training Dogs* (trans. J. Cleugh). London, 1954.

PRICE, P. HOWARD, *The Miniature Poodle Handbook*. London, 1960.

STETSON, J. (ed.), *This is the Newfoundland*. Orange, Conn., 1956.

STONEHENGE (ed.), *The Dogs of the British Islands*. London, 1867.

TRACY, T. H., *The Book of the Poodle*. New York, 1951.

VORREN, J., and MARKER, E., *Lapp Life and Customs*. New York, 1962.

WIMHURST, C. G. E., *The Book of the Greyhound*. London, 1961.

PART III

ANDERSEN, HANS C., *Fairy Tales*. New York, 1899.

Anglo-Saxon Chronicle (trans. G. N. Garmonsway). London, 1953.

APOLLODORUS, *The Library*

BARING-GOULD, S., *Iceland: its Scenes and Sagas*. London, 1850.

——— *A Book of the West*. London, 1899.

——— *Curious Myths of the Middle Ages*. London, 1869.

BLOOM, J. HARVEY (ed.), *English Tracts*, 1473–1650, vols. I and II.

BLOOMFIELD, M., *Ceberus, the Dog of Hades*. London, 1905.

BREWER, J. MASON, *Dog Ghosts*. Austin, Texas, 1958.

Brewer's Dictionary of Miracles. London, 1884.

BRINTON, D. G., *The Myths of the New World*. New York, 1876.

BROWN, THEO., 'The Black Dog.' *Folk-lore,* vol. 69, Sept. London, 1958.

BUDGE, E. A. W., *The Gods of the Egyptians.* New York, 1967.

BUTLER, *Lives of the Saints.* London, 1812.

CAHIER, C., *Charactéristiques des Saints dans L'art Populaire.* Paris, 1867.

CAMPBELL, J. G., *Superstitions of the Scottish Highlands.* Glasgow, 1900.

CAMPBELL, J. G., *The Fians.* London, 1890.

CAVELL, E. B. (ed.), *The Jataka & Stories of the Buddha's Former Births,* vol. IV. Cambridge, 1901.

CAXTON, W., *The Golden Legend.* London, 1483.

Celtic Magazine, vol. XIII, 'The Three Green Dogs'. Inverness, 1888.

Chambers' Book of Days. London, 1888.

CONWAY, M. D., *Demonology and Devil-lore,* vols. I and II. London, 1880.

DAVIES (ed.), *The Mythology and Rites of the British Druids.* London, 1869.

DAVIES, R. TREVOR, *Four Centuries of Witch-Beliefs.* London, 1947.

DAY, J. WENTWORTH, *Here are Ghosts and Witches.* London, 1954.

FLEMING, A., *A Straunge Wunder in Bongay.* London, 1577.

Folk-lore and Legends. Scandinavian. W. W. Gibbings, London, 1890.

FONTAINE, J. DE LA, *Tales and Novels,* vol. I. Paris, 1884.

FORBES, A. R., *Gaelic Names of Beasts, Birds and Fishes.* Edinburgh, 1905.

GOETHE, *Faust* (trans. A. Swannick). Bohn's Library, London, 1914.

GRAVES, R., *The Greek Myths.* New York, 1955.

———— *The White Goddess.* New York, 1966.

GRIFFITHS, R. T. H., *The Hymns of the Rigveda.* Benares, 1892.

GRIMM, J., *Teutonic Mythology* (trans. J. S. Stallybrasse). London, 1883.

GUBERNATIS, A. DE, *Zoological Mythology.* London, 1872.

GUEST, LADY C. (trans.), *The Mabinogion.* London, 1906.

GUNTHER, A. VON, *Tales and Legends of the Tyrol.* London, 1874.

HARDWICK, C., *Traditions, Superstitions and Folk-lore,* London, 1872.

HARTLAND, E. S., *English Folk and Fairy Tales.* London.

HENDERSON, W., *Folk-lore of the Northern Countries.* London, 1879.

HESIOD, *Theogeny.*

———— *Shield of Heracles.*

HEWETT, S., *Nummits and Crummits*. London, 1900.

HOLE, C., *Witchcraft in England*. New York, 1966.

────── *Haunted England*. London, 1940.

HOMER, *Iliad*.

HOPKINS, MATTHEW, *The Discovery of Witches*. London, 1647.

HUNT, R., *Popular Romances of the West of England*. London, 1881.

HUTTON, LUKE, *The Black Dogg of Newgate*. London, 1638.

INGRAM, J. H., *The Haunted Homes and Family Traditions of Great Britain*. London, 1905.

JOHNSON, W. BRANCH, *Folk-lore of Normandy*. London, 1929.

JOYCE, P. W., *Old Celtic Romances*. New York, 1962.

KELLY, W. K., *Indo-European Tradition and Folk-lore*. London, 1863.

KEREYNYI, C., *The Gods of the Greeks*. New York, 1951.

LEATHER, E. M., *The Folk-lore of Herefordshire*. London,. 1912.

LETHBRIDGE, T. C., *Witches*. New York, 1962.

LUM, P., *The Stars in our Heaven*. London.

MACGREGOR, A. A., *The Ghost Book*. London, 1955.

MITRA, R., 'The Origin of the Myth about Kerberos.' *Proceedings, Asiatic Society of Bengal*, May 1881.

O'GRADY, S., *The Coming of Cuculain*. London, 1894.

────── *Finn and his Companions*. London, 1921.

OVID, *Metamorphoses*.

RAY, P. C. (trans.), *The Mahabharata*. Calcutta, 1894.

RHYS, J., *Studies in the Arthurian Legend*. Oxford, 1891.

RIEU, E. V. (trans.), *Homer: The Odyssey*. Baltimore, 1946.

RUDKIN, E. H., 'The Black Dog.' *Folk-lore*, vol. XLIX. London, 1938.

SALE, G. (trans.), *The Koran*. New York, 1877.

SCHOEPPERLE, G., *Tristan and Isolt*. London, 1913.

SCHOLFIELD, A. F. (trans.), *Aelian on the Characteristics of Animals*. London, 1959.

SERGEANT, P. W., *Witches and Warlocks*. London, 1936.

STAAL, J. D. W., *Patterns in the Sky*. London, 1961.

STEWART, W. G., *Popular Superstitions of the Highlanders*. Edinburgh, 1823.

SUMMERS, MONTAGUE, *The History of Witchcraft and Demonology*. New York, 1926.

SWAN, C. (trans.), *Gesta Romanorum*. London, 1904.

SYKES, WIRT, *British Goblins*. London, 1880.

THORPE, B., *Northern Mythology*, vol. III. London, 1852.

VISSER, M. W. DE, 'The Dog and the Cat in Japanese Superstition.' *Transactions*, Asiatic Society of Japan, vol. XXXVII, pt. 1. 1909.

WILDE, LADY, *Ancient Legends, Mystic Charms and Superstitions of Ireland*. London, 1899.

WILKINSON, J. G., *The Manners and Customs of the Ancient Egyptians*. London, 1878.

WOODS, B. A., 'The Devil in Dog Form.' *Folk-lore Studies II*. Univ. of California Publications, 1959.

———— 'Goethe and the Poodle Motif.' *Fabula Journal of Folklore Studies*, vols. I and II. Berlin, 1958.

British Museum: Collection of pamphlets. B.M. No. E.3. No. 17. *A Dog's Elegy*. London, 1644.

———— No. 23. *A Dialogue*. London, 1642–3.

PART IV

ANDREWS, W., *Curiosities of the Church*. London, 1890.

American Antiquarian. 'Iroquois Sacrifice of the White Dog,' vol. VII. New York, 1885.

APULEIUS, *The Golden Ass*.

ARGENTI, P., and ROSE, H. H., *The Folk-lore of Chios*. Cambridge, Mass., 1954.

BALL, K. M., *Decorative Motives of Oriental Art*. London, 1927.

BANCROFT, H. H., *The Native Races*. San Francisco, 1883.

BELL, H. INDRIS, *Cults and Creeds in Graeco-Roman Egypt*. Liverpool, 1953.

BLACK, W. G., *Folk-Medicine*. London, 1883.

BONNER, C., *Studies in Magical Amulets*. Ann Arbor, Mich., 1950.

Brewer's Dictionary of Miracles. London, 1884.

BRINTON, D. G., *The Myths of the New World*. New York, 1876.

BROWN, THEO, 'The Dartmoor Entrance to the Underworld.' *Notes and Queries*, XXIX. Devon and Cornwall, 1926.

BUDGE, E.A.W., *Amulets and Superstitions*. New York, 1961.

———— *From Fetish to God in Ancient Egypt*. London, 1934.

———— *The Gods of the Egyptians*. New York, 1967.

CARUS, PAUL, *The History of the Devil*. London, 1895.

CATON, R., *The Temples and Ritual of Asklepios*. London, 1960.

Chambers' Book of Days. London, 1888.

CIACERI, E., *Culti e Miti*. Catania, 1911.

CIRLOT, J. E., *A Dictionary of Symbols*. New York, 1962.

COLLIER, V. W. F., *Dogs of China and Japan in Nature and Art*. London, 1921.

CONWAY, M. D., *Demonology and Devil-lore*. London, 1880.

CROOKE, W., *The Popular Religion and Folk-lore of Northern India*. London, 1896.

DALE-GREEN, P., *Cult of the Cat*. Boston, 1963.

DALZIEL, H., *Mad Dogs and Hydrophobia*. London, 1886.

DAVIES, E., *The Mythology and Rites of the British Druids*. London, 1869.

DIXEY, A. D., *The Lion Dog of Peking*. London, 1934.

DRAKE, M. and W., *Saints and Their Emblems*. London, 1916.

ECKENSTEIN, L., *A Spell of Words*. London, 1932.

EDELSTEIN, E. J., Asclepius: *A Collection and Interpretation of the Testimonies*. Baltimore, 1945.

EDMUNDS, W. H., *Pointers and Clues to the Subjects of Chinese and Japanese Art*. London, 1934.

ELWIN, VERRIER, *Myths of the N.E. Frontier of India*. India, 1958.

―――― *The Tribal World of Verrier Elwin*. New York, 1964.

FARNELL, L. R., *The Cults of the Greek States*, vol. IV. Oxford, 1907.

FERGUSON, G., *Signs and Symbols in Christian Art*. New York, 1959.

FOLKARD, R., *Plant Lore, Legends and Lyrics*. London, 1884.

FORBES, A. R., *Gaelic Names of Beasts (Mammalia), Birds, Fishes, Etc.* Edinburgh, 1905.

FOWLER, W., *The Roman Festivals*. London, 1899.

FRAZER, J. G., *The Fear of the Dead in Primitive Religion*. New York, 1933.

―――― (trans.). *Pausanias's Description of Greece*. London, 1913.

―――― *The Golden Bough*. New York, 1930.

GAIDOZ, H., 'A propos des Chiens d'Epidaure.' *Revue Archéologique*. Paris, 1884.

―――― *La Rage et St Hubert*. Paris, 1887.

GANNEAU, CLERMONT, 'Esculape et le Chien.' *Revue Critique*. Paris, 1884.

GASTER, M., *Studies and Texts in Folk-lore*. London, 1929.

GASTER, T. H., 'Some Ancient Oriental Folk-lore.' *Folk-lore,* vol. XLIX. London, 1938.

The Golden Legend or Lives of the Saints. Wm. Caxton. London, 1900.

GREGORY, LADY, *Cuchulain of Muirthemne*. London, 1902.

GUBERNATIS, A. DE, *Zoological Mythology,* vol. II. London, 1872.

Hastings' Encyclopaedia of Religion and Ethics, 'Dog', vol. III. Edinburgh, 1910.

HULME, F. E., *Natural History, Lore and Legend.* London, 1895.

JAMESON, A. M., *Legends of the Monastic Orders.* London, 1863.

JASTROW, M., *The Religion of Babylonia and Assyria.* Boston, 1898.

Jewish Encyclopaedia. Funk and Wagnall. New York, 1903.

JOLY, H. L., *Legend in Japanese Art.* London, 1908.

KEMP, P., *Healing Ritual:* studies in the technique and tradition of the Southern Slavs. London, 1935.

KERÉYNYI, C., *Asklepios* (trans. R. Manheim). New York, 1959.

KING, C. W., *The Gnostics and Their Remains.* London, 1887.

KIPLING, J. L., *Beast and Man in India.* London, 1891.

KNIGHT, R. P., *The Symbolic Language of Ancient Art and Mythology.* New York, 1892.

LEHNER, E. T. J., *Folk-lore and Symbolism of Flowers, Plants and Trees.* New York, 1960.

MACCULLOCH, J. A., *The Childhood of Fiction.* London, 1905.

MACKENZIE, D. A., *Myths of Pre-Columbian America.* London.

MEISSNER, B., *Babylonien und Assyrien.* Heidelberg, 1925.

MERRIAM, A. C., 'The Dogs of Aesculapius.' *American Antiquarian,* vol. VII, no. 5. Chicago, 1885.

—— *Marvellous Cures at Epidaurus,* vol. VI, no. 5. 1885.

MORET, A., *Kings and Gods of Egypt.* London, 1912.

MURRAY, MARGARET, *My First Hundred Years.* Toronto, 1963.

O'GRADY, STANDISH, *The Coming of Cuculain.* London, 1894.

—— *Finn and his Companions.* London, 1921.

PAUSANIAS, *Mythology and Monuments of Ancient Athens* (trans. M. de G. Verrall). London, 1890.

—— *Description of Greece* (trans. J. G. Fraser). London, 1913.

PEET, T. E., *The Cemeteries of Abydos:* 34th Memoir of Egypt Exploration Fund. London, 1913.

PERDRIZET, P., 'Anubis Greco-Roman Imagery.' *Revue Egyptologique.* N.S.I. 1919.

—— Les Terres cuites Grecques d'Egypte de la Collection Fonquet. Paris, 1921.

PHILOSTRATUS, *Life of Apollonius of Tyana,* bk. VIII.

PICART, M. B., *The Ceremonies and Religious Customs of the Various Nations of the Known World.* London, 1734.

PLINY., *Natural History*.

PLUTARCH, *Moralia*. Loeb Classical Library (trans. F. C. Babbitt). Cambridge, Mass., 1957

RAY, P. C. (trans.), *The Mahabharata*. Calcutta, 1894.

REAU, L., *Iconographie de L'Art Chrétien*. Paris, 1958.

REINACH, S., *Les Chiens dans le Culte d'Esculape*. Rv. Arch. Paris, 1884.

ROSE, H. J. (trans.), *The Roman Questions of Plutarch*. New York, 1924.

SALE, G. (trans.), *The Koran*. London, 1877.

SASTRI, H. K., *S. Indian Images of Gods and Goddesses*. Madras, 1916.

SCHOLFIELD, A. F. (trans.), *Aelian on the Characteristics of Animals*. London, 1959.

SCHOLZ, H., *Der Hund in der Greich-rom. Magie und Religion*. Diss. Berlin, 1932.

SHORTER, A. W., *The Egyptian Gods*. London, 1937.

SMITH, W. ROBERTSON, *Religion of the Semites*. Edinburgh, 1889.

STURLSON, SNORRI, *Heimskringla: Sagas of the Norse Kings* (trans. A. Laing). New York, 1930.

SWAN, C. (ed.), *Gesta Romanorum*. London, 1904.

Tales and Novels of J. de la Fontaine. Paris, 1884.

THOMPSON, C. J. S., *The Mystic Mandrake*. London, 1934.

THORNDIKE, L., *A History of Magic and Experimental Service*. New York, 1929.

THURSTON, E., *Omens and Superstitions of S. India*. New York, 1912.

TWENTYMAN, L. R., 'The Changing Face of Medicine'. *British Homoeopathic Journal*, vol. LI, no. 4, London.

TYACK, G. S., *Lore and Legend of the English Church*. London, 1899.

VAILLANT, G. C., *The Aztecs of Mexico*. New York, 1944.

VAUX, J. E., *Church Folk-lore*. London, 1902.

VOLKER, T., *The Animal in Far Eastern Art*. Leyden, 1950.

WALTON, A., 'The Cult of Asklepios.' *Cornell Studies in Classical Philology*, no. III. New York, 1894.

WERNER, E. T. C., *A Dictionary of Chinese Mythology*. Mystic, Conn., 1958.

WHEELER, SIR MORTIMER, 'Excavations in Lydney Park.' *Reports of the Research Committee of the Society of Antiquaries of London*, no. IX. London, 1932.

WHITE, T. H., *The Book of Beasts*. London, 1956.

WILKINSON, J. G., *The Manners and Customs of the Ancient Egyptians.* London, 1878.

WILLOUGHBY-MEADE, G., *Chinese Ghouls and Goblins.* London, 1928.

WITTMAN, W., *Das Isis-buch des Apuleius.* Stuttgart, 1938.

The Zend Avesta, pt. I, 'The Venidad' (trans. J. Darmesteter). Oxford, 1880.

PART V

AMEISENAVA, Z., 'Animal-headed Gods, Evangelists, Saints and Righteous Men.' *Journal of the Warburg and Courtauld Institutes,* vol. 12. London, 1946.

BUTLER, *Lives of the Saints.* London, 1812.

CLARKE, H. F., 'The Mandrake Fiend.' *Folk-lore,* vol. 73. London, 1962.

FRASER, J., 'The Passion of St. Christopher.' *Revue Critique.* Paris, 1913.

GAIDOZ, H., 'St Christophe à Tête de Chien en Ireland et en Russie,' *Memoires de la Societé Nationale des Antiquaires,* tom. 76. Paris, 1924.

GROOT, J. H. DE, *The Religious System of China,* vol. IV. Leyden, 1901.

JAMESON, A. M., *Legends of the Monastic Orders.* London, 1850.

O'DONNELL, ELLIOTT, *Werwolves,* London, 1912.

SAINTYVES, P., 'St Christophe Successeur d'Anubis, d'Hermès, et d'Heraclès.' *Revue Anthropologique,* année 45. Paris, 1935.

SMITH, R. V. (ed.), *Letters Addressed to the Countess of Ossory from the year 1769–1797.* London, 1848.

SUMMERS, MONTAGUE, *The Werewolf.* London, 1932.

WITTKOWER, R., 'Marvels of the East: A Study in the History of Monsters.' *Journal of the Warburg and Courtauld Institutes,* vol. V.

PART VI

JUNG, C. G., *Psychology and Alchemy.* New York, 1953.
——— *Mysterium Coniunctionis.* New York, 1933.

HEYDT, V. VON DER., 'Alchemy.' *The Guild of Pastoral Psychology,* Lecture no. 105. London, 1959.

Index